Arthritis:
A Patient's Guide

Arthritis:
A Patient's Guide

SHARON E. HOHLER

McFarland & Company, Inc., Publishers
Jefferson, North Carolina, and London

Disclaimer: The information presented in this book is for educational purposes and should not be taken as medical advice. Readers are encouraged to seek competent medical care, learn about the resources available and work with their doctors to improve their health status. Advances in medical knowledge and care will render the information in this book (at present accurate and timely) out-of-date. Individuals are encouraged to use the reputable resources listed to access the latest and best information.

LIBRARY OF CONGRESS CATALOGUING-IN-PUBLICATION DATA

Hohler, Sharon E., 1953–
    Arthritis : a patient's guide / Sharon E. Hohler.
      p.   cm.
    Includes bibliographical references and index.

    ISBN 978-0-7864-3450-3
    softcover : 50# alkaline paper ∞

    1. Arthritis—Popular works.   I. Title.
RC933.H57   2008
616.7'22—dc22   2008013216

British Library cataloguing data are available

Cover photograph ©2007 Comstock Images

Manufactured in the United States of America

McFarland & Company, Inc., Publishers
  Box 611, Jefferson, North Carolina 28640
   www.mcfarlandpub.com

To David who believes in me.
To Edna and Earl who taught me to love books.

Acknowledgments

Where does one begin to thank the people who have contributed to the life and knowledge of a middle-aged working nurse?

To family (Walkers and Hohlers) who've loved me and cheered me on throughout my life, thank you for your love and encouragement.

To Dr. Robert and Jana Gile, Dr. R. August and Laura Ritter who took valuable time to proofread my manuscript and answer questions. Thank you for your help.

To special friends who've enriched my life, thank you.

To physician and nursing colleagues who have contributed much to the knowledge that made this book possible, thank you.

To Heartland Writers Guild friends who've taught me how to write and inspired me, thank you.

Thank you to John and Carol Fisher, Peggy Gabriel, and Dr. Jon Robison for granting an interview and permission to include information in this book.

Thank you to the following companies and organizations who provided images, documents, and the permission to include them in this book: American Chronic Pain Association, Depuy Orthopaedics, Elsevier Publishers, National Sleep Foundation, Smith & Nephew Co., Inc., Wright Medical Technologies, Zimmer, Inc.

Table of Contents

Preface

The Bone and Joint Decade, 2002–2011, emphasizes health for joints and bones through research and education. Over 750 organizations in 50 countries join in supporting this initiative. The goals involve educating people about musculoskeletal diseases and injuries while providing increased funding for prevention strategies and research into treatments.

The Arthritis Foundation, one member of the Bone and Joint Decade team, serves as the source of information and research for people dealing with arthritis and valuable information can be accessed at www.arthritis.org.

This book deals with two common types of arthritis, osteoarthritis and rheumatoid arthritis. Overall, arthritis affects one in three adults (70 million) and 300,000 children in America while ranking second after heart disease as a cause of work disability. It costs the U.S. economy more than $86.2 billion annually in medical care and loss of productivity.

According to the Arthritis Foundation, half of people who suffer from arthritis pain think nothing can be done. This lack of knowledge limits their choices and dooms them to suffering, often needlessly. Many conservative treatment options provide partial or total relief of symptoms and improve the lives of individuals dealing with arthritis. Conservative treatments include pain control, exercise, diet and nutrition, and alternative treatments.

For patients who require further intervention, knowing the best surgical options will provide comfort and good outcomes. After reading information about joint replacements, a person will better understand why an infected toenail might cause his surgery to be postponed for antibiotic treatment. As a registered nurse working in an operating room for many years, this writer has seen the improvements in surgical techniques which provide quality outcomes to many.

Many children, teenagers and adults injure their joints during sports activities. The American Academy of Orthopaedic Surgeons provides recommendations for preventing injuries during specific sports at http://orthoinfo.aaos.org/menus/safety.cfm. Research into causes of rheumatoid arthritis may provide prevention strategies and better treatments. The Bone and Joint Decade team advocates public education, research into prevention, causes and better treatments for both osteoarthritis and rheumatoid arthritis.

Reputable resources such as the Arthritis Foundation, National Sleep Foundation, American College of Rheumatology, American Pain Foundation and Academy of Orthopaedic Surgeons provide up-to-date guidance. Using these and other reputable resources, individuals can obtain the latest, most accurate information about their health. Books such as the GOOD LIVING with Rheumatoid Arthritis, Alternative Treatments for Arthritis, and All you Need to Know About Joint Surgery from the Arthritis Foundation provide valuable and reliable information in printed form. Patients are urged to consult their doctors, become proactive with their treatment plan, and improve their quality of life by limiting the effects of arthritis.

1

Understanding Osteoarthritis

Osteoarthritis (OA), the most common type of arthritis, affects almost 27 million Americans.[1] Researchers estimate OA costs each person living with it approximately $5,700 annually.[2] Called "degenerative joint disease" by doctors, OA occurs when the smooth articular cartilage covering the end of the bone wears thin. Articular cartilage is the covering on both ends of a chicken leg bone. Pain results when the joint moves and raw bones rub against each other.[3] Over time the joint may lose its normal shape and bone spurs may form. These bone spurs, called "osteophytes," can break off and float inside the joint, causing pain. Osteoarthritis affects joints, not internal organs as rheumatoid arthritis does.

Physical Symptoms of Osteoarthritis?

Pain, called the "cardinal symptom" by the Arthritis Foundation,[4] sends people to the doctor. This pain can occur in just one joint or multiple joints. Pain begins gradually and becomes worse with repetitive movement; consequently, rest in the affected joint often relieves the pain. Early pain symptoms may be relieved by analgesics and nonsteroidal anti-inflammatory drugs (NSAIDs). The most common locations for OA are hip, knee, and hand. Other joints affected include lower spine, neck, and feet. In advanced OA, pain occurs at rest and even at night.

Morning stiffness occurs with OA but usually for 30 minutes or less. "Gel phenomenon" describes stiffness after periods of inactivity and rest and resolves within minutes.[5]

Cool, rainy weather worsens pain and stiffness in OA joints.

Swelling and tenderness in joints, a crunching feeling doctors call crepitus, or the sounds of bone rubbing on bone indicates possible osteoarthritis.

Causes of Osteoarthritis?

Researchers suspect genetics, or inherited genes, play a role in 25 to 30 percent of all osteoarthritis cases and as many as 40 to 65 percent of cases of hand

and knee osteoarthritis.[6] A 2004 study conducted in Nottingham, England, agrees. Researchers found that 737 siblings of 490 patients who needed total knee replacement were "more than twice as likely to have knee osteoarthritis" when compared with the 1,729 people on the family-doctor patient lists.[7] They recognize that women whose mothers have OA find themselves dealing with cartilage breakdown also.[8] However, genetics alone cannot explain osteoarthritis because identical twins do not experience osteoarthritis in the huge percentages expected.

Scientists recognize one inherited form of osteoarthritis that starts early in life. They've identified a mutant gene that affects the cartilage component called collagen. This gene defect "weakens collagen protein which may break or tear more easily under stress."[9]

According to the Arthritis Foundation, obese women are "four to five times more likely" to develop OA in their knees than women of average weight.[10] Being overweight or obese creates increased stress on hips, knees and feet and contributes to OA development. The good news is weight loss helps prevent osteoarthritis and has benefits even for the OA patient because of decreased pressure on knees and hips.

Injuries cause post-traumatic osteoarthritis. Acute injuries including fractures, torn ligaments and meniscus tears contribute to OA development. Menisci are two crescent-shaped cartilage found inside the knee joint. Many surgeons believe that menisci (one located medially or on the inside portion of knee and one located on the lateral or outside portion of knee) act as cushions in the knee. Efforts to preserve this cushion, menisci, have fueled the technology of knee arthroscopy. Researchers in Sweden followed up on 170 patients who had meniscus repair surgery approximately 20 years ago. "Researchers found that 34% of patients did have osteoarthritis in their hands; most (84%) had it in both hands."[11] Researchers wonder if a meniscus tear indicates early development of inherited OA or whether the meniscus tear contributes to development of OA. Doctors recommend prevention of sports injuries to protect the joints. Chapter 5 contains prevention strategies.

Some occupations increase the risk of developing OA. Farmers face the risk of developing OA in their hips. Jackhammer operators put stress on their elbows. Miners' knees and spines are candidates for developing OA while cotton mill workers' hands get abused at work.[12]

A study conducted at University of Virginia raised an interesting question. Can a woman's shoes contribute to OA of knees? This study documented that women "wearing high heels increase the pressure on their knees over 23% compared to wearing flat shoes." The researchers recommend that women wear shoes with no more than 1½ inch heel.[13]

Osteoarthritis affects men more than women before age 50. After age 50, more women deal with OA than men.[14] Scientists and doctors wonder, "Does estrogen prevent development of osteoarthritis?" A study conducted at University of California San Francisco and published in 1996 found that 5,000 post-menopausal women who took estrogen supplements had 38 percent decreased incidence of hip OA. After ten years of estrogen replacement therapy, their risk decreased to 25 percent. However, this study found the protection disappeared when the estrogen replacement was discontinued. "The risk of osteoarthritis of the hip in past users of estrogen was not different from that of those women who never used estrogen."[15] A Danish study published in February 2004 compared the knees of two groups of female rats, those whose ovaries were surgically removed vs. those female rats who did not have surgery.

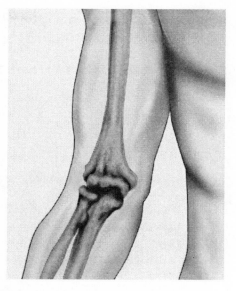

Healthy non-arthritic elbow joints move easily and pain free (courtesy Zimmer, Inc.).

This study found that "estrogen deficiency accelerates cartilage turnover and increases cartilage surface erosion."[16] This means the cartilage breakdown occurred faster than the body could repair or replace it. Some scientists believe a combination of hormones, including estrogen and progesterone, help shield females from OA development. Recent research regarding estrogen replacement therapy and its effects on women's heart health make this issue complex. Each woman should talk to her physician about overall health and risks when considering estrogen replacement.

People with bow-legs (genu varum) and knock-knees (genu valgum) have increased risk of abnormal stresses on their knees, which may contribute to OA development. Many children born with those conditions grow out of it as their legs grow and muscles strengthen.

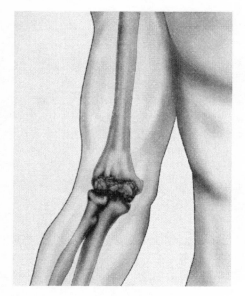

This illustration shows arthritic elbows as raw, painful bony surfaces (courtesy Zimmer, Inc.).

Uncorrected deformity can cause dislocation of the kneecaps with resulting damage.[17]

Researchers searching for the causes of OA suspect that genetics plus a "combination of factors, including being overweight, the aging process, joint injury, and stresses on the joints from certain jobs and sports activities" explain the development of OA.[18] While osteoarthritis occurs more in older people and age is considered a risk factor, the Arthritis Foundation wants the public to know that "osteoarthritis is not inevitable."[19]

How the Body Is Affected

Bones, the hard structure that makes up the human skeleton, are living tissue with an internal blood supply. The body constantly breaks down old bone and rebuilds that bone as new. The human body comprises 206 bones.[20]

Articular cartilage covers the end of bones inside joints and functions as a shock absorber and friction reducer. Articular cartilage consists of 65 to 80 percent water, chondrocytes, and two special proteins, collagen and proteoglycans. Chondrocytes are body cells, *cytes*, which build cartilage, *chondro*.[21] Collagen, one of the body's building blocks for skin, bone and connective tissue, is a colorless, fibrous protein. Collagen is woven together with proteoglycans, a sugar-protein compound. The collagen-proteoglycans compound gives articular cartilage the ability to absorb physical shocks.

Joints are the area where two or more bones meet and move against each other. Synovial tissue lines the inside of joints and makes lubricating fluid (synovial fluid). This fluid contains hyaluronan, which has the consistency of uncooked egg white. The theory behind the hyaluronan injections is to inject more lubricant into the joint.

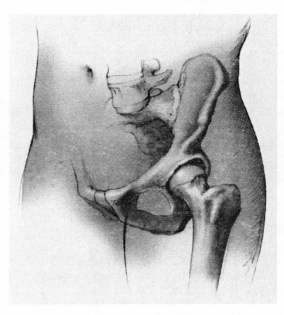

Notice the smooth, shiny surface of a hip joint. Healthy, smooth cartilage covers the femoral head and acetabulum (socket) of the hip (courtesy Zimmer, Inc.).

Muscles, tendons, and ligaments allow stable movement of the bones. Muscles cause movement when they contract after receiving the stimulation from the nerve. Many joints in the human body contain muscles that flex and extend, resulting in opposite movements. For example, when palm and fingers muscles flex, the fingers close and make a fist. Extending the fingers opens the fingers and exposes the palm. Ligaments connect bones to bones and stabilize movements in the body. Tendons connect muscles to bones.

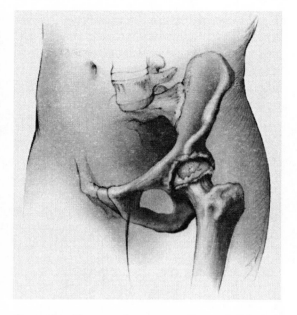

What Happens During Osteoarthritis?

Compare the rough, raw surface of this arthritic hip to the healthy hip shown on the opposite page (courtesy Zimmer, Inc.).

Osteoarthritis results from "failure of chondrocytes within the joint."[22] What happens to change a healthy normal knee into a painful knee? An unknown trigger starts the breakdown of articular cartilage. One study being conducted involves the unknown trigger. Do genetic, inherited factors or injuries cause the development of OA? Is this failure of chondrocytes an inherited time bomb waiting to cause OA? Has the cartilage been damaged due to excess stress? Researchers hope to have answers soon. Often the individual is unaware that osteoarthritis damage has occurred until pain starts. Occasionally, a traumatic event like a fracture or torn ligament or meniscus occurs that contributes to osteoarthritis.

Translucent, white and smooth describe the surface of healthy articular cartilage, which covers moveable joints in the body. The finish of healthy cartilage compares to a slick, shiny billiard ball of a different shape. What happens to change the appearance of that cartilage? Sick cartilage appears dull white with tiny hair-like projections called fibrillations. Normally, a constant cycle of building, or synthesis, of new cartilage and breakdown, or degradation, of aging cartilage occur in the joints. After osteoarthritis begins, the ability of chondrocytes to make good quality cartilage decreases while these cells produce increased enzymes that break down cartilage. The cartilage becomes soft. Surgeons call this "chondromalacia" or softening of cartilage. As damage continues, the cartilage wears thin, and craters, cracks or holes expose raw bone. It's no wonder people suffer pain from these developments.

Osteophytes, called bone spurs, form during osteoarthritis. These bone spurs impinge, get caught on soft tissue, and can cause pain.

Cartilage functions normally by absorbing the shocks and aiding smooth movement of bones inside a joint. The fluids and proteins called synovial fluid provide additional lubrication. During walking or other weight-bearing activities, the person's weight exerts pressure on the cartilage, forcing water and cellular fluids out into the joint. The fluids absorb oxygen and nutrients and slowly reabsorb into the cartilage. During osteoarthritis, these normal functions decrease and become inadequate for cell nutrition.

Osteoarthritis usually is considered non-inflammatory, but the joint(s) involved can become inflamed and show symptoms of pain, swelling, and increased warmth. This differs from rheumatoid arthritis in which the entire body is affected by the inflammation. However, the development of a hot, red, swollen joint would suggest an infection or possible rheumatoid process and needs the immediate care of a physician.

Three common locations for osteoarthritis include finger joints, spine and weight-bearing joints, especially knees and hips. Osteoarthritis in the finger joints especially seems to run in families.[23] Small, bony enlargement of the distal joint, closest to the fingernail, is called Heberden's nodes. Doctors call similar knobs on the middle joints of fingers Bouchard's nodes. Osteoarthritis also commonly affects the base of thumbs.[24] Symptoms include stiffness, the appearance of "old-age hands" and some pain, especially when Heberden's and Bouchard's nodes are developing. Treatment includes medications, splints and heat treatments. The Arthritis Foundation book, *The Arthritis Helpbook*, includes information on gadgets and aids that assist osteoarthritic individuals deal with problem areas. For example, ergonomic knives and jar openers enable people with decreased finger grip to cook as they once did.[25]

Osteoarthritis in the spine causes stiffness and pain, most commonly in the neck and lower back. Weakness and numbness in the arms and legs can occur if arthritis pressures nerves. Treatment for OA includes medications, heat treatments, and strengthening exercises. A firm mattress may improve an arthritic person's sleep. Severe osteoarthritis of the spine may require surgery if there is instability, nerve pressure, or uncontrolled pain.

OA in weight-bearing joints like knees and hips can cause disability. Knee joints may be "stiff, swollen and painful, making it hard to walk, climb, and get in and out of chairs and bathtubs."[26] Treatments include medications, weight loss, exercise and walking aids. If pain is unrelieved, total knee replacements have proven benefits.

Hip OA pain may be located in the groin and inner thigh, buttocks, or knees. Treatments include medication, walking aids such as canes or walkers, weight loss, and exercise to relieve pain. Total hip replacement brings relief of arthritic pain to many people when conservative treatments do not. Gadgets such as elevated toilet seats, shower seats, and walking aids can simplify activities of daily living, allowing better comfort and independence.

Diagnosis

A diagnosis will be made by a physician who will ask questions about when symptoms began and details about the pain, stiffness, and joint function. The doctor will assess how the arthritis symptoms affect the patient in daily activities. Doctors want to know about the patient's overall health and will ask about routine medications, including herbal and over-the-counter medicines. All medicines taken on a regular basis (daily or several times a week) need to be included. Patients should either take a current list of all medicines or take the medication bottles to each doctor visit. A physical examination will help the doctor diagnose OA. For knee, hip, or spine osteoarthritis, a physician may watch the person walk and pinpoint the location and details of the pain. Early arthritis often does not show on x-rays. After arthritic damage has occurred, x-rays show the damage as decreased joint space and irregularity in the joint.

Blood tests or joint aspiration may be done to rule out other possible disease processes such as rheumatoid arthritis or infection. Joint aspiration involves the physician drawing fluid from inside the painful joint and sending the fluid to a laboratory for testing.

Scientists have identified a chemical they call CTX-II, which results from cartilage, or type II collagen, breakdown. A study conducted in the Netherlands determined the levels of CTX-II in 1,235 adults over the age of 55 and followed them for an average of 6.6 years. Results published in the August 2004 issue of *Arthritis and Rheumatism* reported that patients with the highest CTX-II levels were "six times more likely to experience rapid, destructive progression of OA at the knee and eight times more likely at the hip."[27] More research is needed to verify the accuracy and usefulness of this chemical as a predictor of OA.

Mental and Emotional Effects

Osteoarthritis can cause "depression, anxiety, and feelings of helplessness in individuals."[28] They find themselves limited in daily activities and in their ability to function at work. While struggling to cope with arthritis, individuals may find that their personal lives and family relationships suffer. While 10 percent of the adult American population deals with depression in any given year, people dealing with rheumatoid arthritis and osteoarthritis experience increased rates of depression.[29] One wonders whether the arthritis makes the depression worse or whether the depression makes the arthritis seem worse. Two groups of people are at risk for depression: individuals who lack support from family and friends and those who feel they've lost their ability to participate in valued activities. What can be done to combat the feelings of depression and helplessness? A discussion of successful coping techniques continues in chapter 4, "Taking Charge of Your Life." Studies have shown that people who learn and practice stress management skills, including relaxation techniques and arthritis self-management, found their depression symptoms decreased. Another study showed that 1,001 people with arthritis (mostly OA) and depression benefited from antidepressants and a six- to eight-week psychotherapy session in addition to their arthritis treatment. "After a year, people who had been treated for depression had less pain and better functioning than people in the control group." The control group people received their usual arthritis care.[30] For many people antidepressants help restore sleep cycles and contribute to improved sleep and coping with arthritis while decreasing their depression.

Many people with osteoarthritis suffer and think nothing can be done to help them.[31] To the contrary, the Arthritis Foundation recommends a variety of therapies for osteoarthritis. *The Arthritis Helpbook* focuses on self-management tactics, which enable individuals to take charge of their lives, make positive steps, and improve coping skills. After seeing a physician for a diagnosis and recommended treatment plan, individuals benefit from becoming actively involved in their health.

Conservative Treatment Measures

Conservative measures begin with caring for the whole person. After the doctor has made a diagnosis, the patient wants the pain stopped. Pain medications begin with acetaminophen and non-steroidal anti-inflammatory medications. More information on medications will be found in chapter 6 ("Dealing with Pain") and chapter 9 ("Drug Therapies"). Non-drug strategies for coping with arthritis pain include patient education. The Self-Help Course offered through the Arthritis Foundation can help patients cope. This course, "taught in a group setting, [has] been shown to reduce arthritis pain by 20% and physician visits by 40%."[32]

When Dr. Marion Minor at University of Missouri in Columbia conducted a study in 1989, exercise wasn't a part of arthritis care. Doctors were putting patients on bed rest for bouts of arthritis. The study participants in both aquatic and walking groups significantly improved their ability to perform activities.

They also liked feeling in control of their lives.[33] This research revolutionized the concept of exercise for individuals who have arthritis. Dr. Minor's theory that persons dealing with arthritis would find exercise beneficial was confirmed. The Arthritis Foundation recommends three types of exercise: aerobic, strengthening and flexibility. Find more information about exercise in chapter 8, "Exercising with Arthritis."

What diet does the Arthritis Foundation recommend for persons wanting to eat healthy and lose weight? Can foods make arthritis worse or better? Individuals seeking information on nutrition should refer to chapter 7, "Eating Healthy (Diet and Nutrition)."

The Centers for Disease Control and Prevention (CDC) reports that 36 percent of Americans use alternative therapy, which are defined as "a group of diverse medical and health care systems, practices, and products that aren't presently considered part of conventional medicine."[34] Add health-related prayer to alternative therapies and the number jumps to 62 percent of Americans. Alternative therapies include herbs, massage, acupuncture, and various other strategies.

Surgical Treatments

The American Academy of Orthopedic Surgeons lists the number of total joint replacements at 193,000 hips and 300,000 knees yearly in America.[35] These pain-relieving procedures can help people with arthritis enjoy life when conservative treatments no longer relieve pain.

Surgery should never be taken lightly. While surgery and anesthesia have become safe and commonly performed, people must recognize that anesthesia and surgical risks are present and complications can occur. Surgeons and anesthesiologists discuss these risks with patients before surgery. Past and ongoing efforts by healthcare workers have made surgery safer and improved patient results.

Information regarding how and where to find/research an orthopaedic surgeon and hospital will be discussed in chapter 11, "Preparing for Surgery."

Total knee procedure replaces the weight-bearing surfaces of the femur (thigh bone), tibia (shin bone) and patella (kneecap).*

Total hip procedures replace the hip joint to provide pain-free movement. Surgeons remove the irregular bone of the hip socket, called the acetabulum, and insert a metal cup and high quality liner. They also remove the arthritic femoral head, fit an implant stem down the shaft of the femur (thigh bone) and attach a smooth round implant head to that stem.†

---

*The Arthritis Foundation provides an on-line animation of the total knee procedure at http://ww2. arthritis.org/conditions/SurgeryCenter/surgerycenterflash/totalknee.html
†The Arthritis Foundation animation for total hip procedure can be accessed at http://ww2.arthritis. org/conditions/SurgeryCenter/surgerycenterflash/totalhip.html

The shoulder joint replacement for arthritis is similar to a hip replacement. Because no weight bearing strength is needed, the shoulder replacement implants are smaller, but similar in design to the total hip implants. The "ball and socket" shoulder joint requires an implant stem and head for the humeral shaft and an implant called a glenoid component for the socket portion of the shoulder.*

Other joints affected by arthritis include fingers and thumb, elbow and ankle. Surgical procedures performed on these joints eliminate pain and restore function to the patient.

The World Health Organization initiated the Bone and Joint Decade to emphasize musculoskeletal disorders worldwide. In the United States the Bone and Joint Decade runs from 2002–2011. Goals of the Decade are to "raise awareness and educate the world on the increasing societal impact of musculoskeletal injuries and disorders, empower patients to participate in decisions about their care and treatment, increase global funding for prevention activities and treatment research and continually seek and promote cost-effective prevention and treatment of musculoskeletal injuries and disorders."[36] Around the world more than 50 nations, the World Health Organization, the United Nations and the Vatican endorse this emphasis on health. The Bone and Joint Decade organization works with both the National Institutes of Health (NIH) and Centers for Disease Control and Prevention (CDC) in America.

Ongoing Research

"Major breakthroughs in OA have focused on the end stage of the disease, i.e., improved surgical techniques and synthetic materials to repair or replace joints that are already damaged."[37] The focus is changing and researchers are working to discover the causes of cartilage breakdown. They want to identify and develop tests and treatments that make diagnosis, prevention, and improved treatments possible.

Information to help persons understand research and clinical trials can be found in chapter 17, "Researching Arthritis." The National Institutes of Health, a part of the federal government, funds ongoing research on OA. Many of those clinical trials are recruiting volunteers to participate. Bethesda, Maryland, home of the NIH, is a primary site for research, but programs funded by NIH are held at university medical centers across America.†

In "The Osteoarthritis Initiative: A Knee Health Study," researchers pur-

*The online animation showing total shoulder replacement is available at http://ww2.arthritis.org/con ditions/SurgeryCenter/surgerycenterflash/totalshoulder.html
†People interested in participating should contact NIH's patient recruitment and public liaison office at Bethesda, MD, at 1-800-411-1222 or online at http://clinicalresearch.nih.gov/

sue a prevention strategy as they examine people who have knee OA or are at risk for developing OA. "This study gathers information about the physical changes that occur prior to the onset of arthritis or before OA gets worse."[38] Sites for this study include universities in Maryland, Ohio, Pennsylvania and Rhode Island.

Another study, "The Effect of Weight Loss and Exercise on Knee Osteoarthritis," assigns participants to one of two groups. The weight-loss exercise group participates in a 16-week plan in which they learn a weight-loss plan, strategies to keep it off plus a walking exercise plan. A second group will act as the control and will participate in the weight-loss exercise program four months later after the results are obtained. This study will evaluate the effectiveness of weight loss and exercise for knee OA.[39]

Glucosamine and chondroitin are studied for effectiveness in "Absorption and Distribution of Glucosamine and Chondroitin." The benefits and safety of acupuncture are being evaluated in the study, "Acupuncture Safety/Efficacy in Knee Osteoarthritis."[40]

The Centers for Disease Control (CDC) also conducts research into arthritis and rheumatic diseases. One study being held at Tufts University School of Nutrition Science and Policy involves strength training for older adults. Since people lose bone density and muscle strength as they age, the resulting disabilities complicate their arthritis. Researchers plan to use results of this study to develop safe, effective strength training for older adults.

The Johnston County Osteoarthritis Project is a research project designed to "report contemporary estimates of the prevalence of knee-related osteoarthritis outcomes in African Americans and Caucasians aged 45 or older."[41] The 1991–1998 study results said more African American participants suffered from OA than expected. Other findings pointed to the incidence of overweight people having increased development of OA and that pain limits their activities. The follow-up research began in 1999 and "added studies of genes, body composition, bone density, and complementary and alternative medicine to the baseline surveys and examinations."[42]

The Arthritis Foundation funds research on osteoarthritis. As doctors and scientists learn more about the development of osteoarthritis, they look at different aspects of OA. Researchers at the Northwestern University in Chicago report that being unable to straighten the knee (flexion contracture) apparently increases the worsening of knee symptoms. Boston University researchers show that patellar (kneecap) malalignment contributes to arthritis pain and symptoms.[43]

Scientists search for answers to why the cartilage breaks down during OA. Multiple researchers working with the Arthritis Foundation are studying how specific enzymes break down cartilage. How do cytokines, molecules that help or inhibit communication between other cells, regulate function of cartilage cells, and why do CD44 receptor cells quit signaling for cartilage repair and become a destructive force on the cartilage?

People dealing with OA benefit from exercise. Researchers at Massachusetts General Hospital are evaluating which type exercise is more beneficial for knees: muscle strengthening or training exercises.[44]

Research continues to improve surgical outcomes. University of Maryland researchers compare the wear on different total joint implants. These doctors work to improve the bond between bone and cemented prosthesis. Researchers at the Georgia Institute of Technology aim to improve the cementless implant's attachment to the bone.

Researchers explore vitamins and supplements. Doctors at three universities are studying glucosamine to determine its effectiveness. A researcher discovered that "vitamin C increased the production of cartilage proteins, such as collagen and aggrecans, but high dosages actually worsened OA in guinea pigs."[45] Ongoing research will indicate how to best maximize the benefits while minimizing the negative effects of vitamin C.

Growth factors are being studied. How growth factors trigger "stem cells" to become cartilage or bone cells is the question being studied at the University of California at San Francisco. Growth factor helps maintain healthy cartilage. Researchers at the Harvard Medical School study growth factor to learn more. Doctors at the Hospital for Special Surgery in New York research gene therapy and how to prevent cartilage damage.[46]

The Bone and Joint Decade promises to be exciting as ongoing research yields answers to the cause of osteoarthritis and best treatments. Until the answers arrive, individuals can improve their lives by learning about osteoarthritis, consulting a doctor, and taking charge of their health.

2

Coping with
Rheumatoid Arthritis

Which French Impressionist said, "Why shouldn't art be pretty? There are enough unpleasant things in the world."[1] Pierre-Auguste Renoir dealt with "unpleasant things," battling rheumatoid arthritis the last 25 years of his life. Historians believe Renoir developed rheumatoid arthritis in the prime of life, around age 50. Renoir lived from 1841 to 1919, when few arthritis treatments were available. Renoir had already established himself as a successful painter when rheumatoid arthritis began to affect his body. Instead of giving up, Renoir adapted his painting technique.

> The brushes had to be fixed in his hands by his wife or model and he couldn't hold his palette, so he let it balance on his knees and the edge of the easel. His wheelchair was already of modern design, and he filled the back with cushions to prevent the development of bedsores.[2]

With the help of loving family and friends, Renoir continued his painting and found solace in his art. "When Renoir woke at night because of pain, he asked for painting materials and made small paintings on wood. Painting helped him to endure and forget his pain." In spite of the toll rheumatoid arthritis took on his body, Renoir persevered and "completed more than 400 works of art."[3]

Rheumatoid arthritis (RA) affects 2.1 million people, almost 1 percent of the American population.[4] RA affects people of all ages, including children, but commonly begins between ages 40 and 60, with women outnumbering men three to one. All ethnic groups deal with rheumatoid arthritis and it's found in all countries of the world. "Although RA can run in families and there are certain inherited tissue types that are more common in people with RA, it is not a heritable disease. A child whose parent has RA may be more likely to develop RA than someone else, but he is not doomed to inherit the condition."[5]

Arthritis means inflammation of the joint. How does rheumatoid arthritis differ from osteoarthritis? Rheumatoid arthritis, an autoimmune disease, occurs when the immune system of a person's body goes awry and attacks itself.

15

RA is a systemic disease; it affects the entire body, including the person's heart and lungs. RA may not affect every joint. Joints commonly affected include jaw, neck, shoulders, hips, knees, ankles, and feet. RA may involve the wrist and many joints of the hand but usually not the finger joint next to the fingernails. "Joints tend to be involved on both sides of the body. That is, if knuckles on the right hand are swollen, it is likely that some knuckles on the left hand will be swollen as well."[6]

By comparison, osteoarthritis happens when the articular cartilage of the bones inside joints wears thin and bone rubs on bone, causing pain. The damage to the articular cartilage occurs from injuries, wear and other causes that researchers want to understand. Often osteoarthritis affects a knee or hip on one side of the body instead of the bilateral (both knees or both hands, etc.) joints being affected by rheumatoid arthritis. However, multiple joints can be affected by osteoarthritis.

Physical Symptoms of Rheumatoid Arthritis

Symptoms of RA may be described as follows:

the skin around your joints may become red and your joints feel warm, swollen, painful and difficult to move. You feel sick all over, may lose your appetite, or run a slight fever. You don't have much energy. You may also develop rheumatoid nodules. These are lumps that form under the skin, over bony areas like elbows, feet, or the spine.[7]

According to the American College of Rheumatologists, patients dealing with RA will probably find the stiff joints worse in the morning. This stiffness may go away after an hour or two or it may last all day.[8] Often the onset of symptoms is vague and gradually increases over weeks and months until several joints are involved. Only 10 percent of people have a dramatic onset of the disease.[9] People with RA experience good days and bad days. During periods called flares, times of increased symptoms, people may notice increased joint inflammation, stiffness, and pain. People dealing with RA may become anemic, have decreased red blood cells and oxygen-carrying hemoglobin and feel fatigue and weakness. RA may cause inflammatory changes in the lining of the heart and lungs. Individuals may notice dryness of the eyes or mouth due to inflammatory changes of tear ducts and salivary glands.

Causes of Rheumatoid Arthritis?

The cause of RA is unknown; however, research focuses on three aspects: genetics, infection, and hormones.

Scientists believe the development of RA requires certain genes. However, genetics or inherited makeup only partially explains the development of RA because some people who carry the genes associated with RA never develop the disease. The field of genetics took a giant leap forward when scientists working on the Human Genome Project successfully mapped human DNA. Scientists identified all 3.2 billion base pairs in the human genome and recognized that "there are 30,000–40,000 functional genes among the 46 chromosomes and 20 genes [inherited from the mother] in the mitochondria."[10] Now that the mapping has been completed, researchers believe they can use this knowledge to develop better ways to treat diseases, including RA. Experts speculate that future treatments will involve correcting genetic problems.

Scientists speculate that infection (either bacterial or viral) may be a trigger causing rheumatoid arthritis in people whose genes make them vulnerable.[11] This complex issue isn't solved yet. However, the Arthritis Foundation wants people to know that "rheumatoid arthritis is not contagious."[12]

RA affects women three times as often as men. RA often improves during pregnancy and flares often occur after a woman's baby is born.[13] Scientists study both female and male hormones in their efforts to understand this disease.

Scientists believe "rheumatoid arthritis develops as a result of an interaction of many factors."[14] Multiple ongoing studies search for answers to the question, What causes the body's immune system to attack its own joints?

Rheumatoid Arthritis Affects the Whole Body

Rheumatoid arthritis affects joints when it causes the lining of the joints called synovium to overgrow and destroy the articular cartilage. However, unlike osteoarthritis which mainly affects joints, RA affects the entire body because it's a malfunction of the immune system. Many people with RA become anemic, have a "lower-than-normal number of red blood cells or quantity of hemoglobin which diminishes the capacity of the blood to carry oxygen."[15]

What Happens During Rheumatoid Arthritis

RA is a disease in which the body's immune system harms itself and can destroy its own joints if untreated. Doctors believe a person's genes, especially the genes scientists have named HLA-DR4, HLA-DRB1 and PTPN22, are involved in RA's development. Studies involving twins (identical and fraternal) "support the concept that genetic factors are important for the susceptibility."[16] However, HLA-DR4 occurs in 20–30 percent of the general population and cannot be solely responsible for the onset of RA.[17]

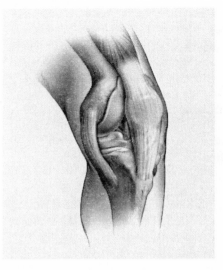

Smooth slick surfaces of knee joints provide pain-free movement (courtesy Zimmer, Inc.).

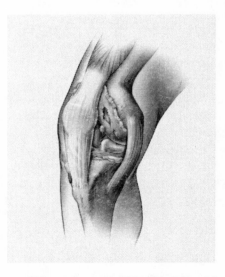

When rheumatoid arthritis and osteoarthritis affect the knee joints, changes occur in the articular cartilage. These craters and irregularities in the articular cartilage can cause pain (courtesy Zimmer, Inc.).

A normal human immune system protects its body from infections and foreign substances that it recognizes as non-self. Doctors call this immunity or immune protection. "An antigen is any substance recognized as foreign (non-self) by the immune system. An antigen can be a microorganism, such as a virus or a bacterium, or it can be a foreign protein or polysaccharide (complex carbohydrate). Tissues or cells from another person, unless it is an identical twin, can also act as antigen."[18]

When the body recognizes an antigen, the body makes antibodies. An antibody is "a specialized immune protein (an immunoglobulin) produced because of the introduction of an antigen into the body."[19] These antibodies can destroy the antigens in a variety of ways: by combining with them, coating, neutralizing, and in some cases blocking them from entering certain areas of the body. Sometimes antibodies assist white blood cells such as macrophages and neutrophils in destroying the antigen.[20] As fighting cells destroy the invader (antigen), they release enzymes that further stimulate the immune system.

In rheumatoid arthritis, the normal process becomes exaggerated and extreme. The protective immune cells move from the bloodstream into the joint. Once inside the joint the immune cells begin producing enzymes, antibodies and cytokines. These chemicals (enzymes, antibodies and cytokines) damage the joint, causing joint stiffness and pain.[21] The synovial lining of joints overdevelops, invades the deeper bone and destroys the cartilage. Doctors call this synovial overgrowth "pannus." Articular cartilage on the ends of bones is eaten away by destructive enzymes and the exposed raw bones rub together, causing pain. The damage becomes visible on x-rays as the joint space becomes narrow and hollow spaces in the bone, called erosions, occur.

Diagnosis

Early RA exhibits some vague symptoms. "For most patients with this disease, especially those who have had symptoms for less than six months), there is no single test that 'confirms' a diagnosis of RA."[22] Doctors use four different techniques to help in diagnosing RA: history, physical exam, lab work and x-ray or imaging tests.

"The history is the story that the doctor puts together by hearing the patient's description of the symptoms and the chronology of their development and by gathering other evidence from previous tests or physician reports."[23] Typically, the patient talks of vague symptoms that developed gradually and became more pronounced. When a doctor hears the patient talk of morning stiffness that lasts more than a few minutes, or pain and joint swelling, the doctor begins to consider RA.

In a physical exam, the doctor examines the individual with special emphasis on joints. The doctor looks for symptoms such as swelling, tenderness in joints and decreased range of motion of the joint. He also notes which joints are affected, and whether joints on both sides of the body are affected.

Doctors may order lab tests such as anti–CCP, rheumatoid factor (RF), complete blood count (CBC), erythrocyte sedimentation rate (ESR), or C-reactive protein (CRP).

The anti–CCP (anti-cyclic citrullinated protein) blood test gained credibility in 2006 when a group of scientists reported that "antibodies against citrullinated proteins do contribute to the development of RA.... Knowing this may allow for the development of targeted therapeutics that inhibit these antibodies or their development."[24]

The rheumatoid factor (RF) test measures the amount of antibody found in the blood. "Approximately 70–80% of people with rheumatoid factor also have rheumatoid arthritis."[25] However, the RF test isn't totally reliable as a diagnostic tool because it's present in people who do not have RA and it's missing from some people who do have RA. RF can be found in people with other rheumatic diseases and "in some patients with infectious diseases, such as infectious hepatitis."[26]

The complete blood count (CBC) blood test checks for anemia by counting the number of red blood cells and their oxygen-carrying ability. This test counts the different types of white blood cells involved in immune functions, including infection fighting. Platelets are the third type of blood cell listed in a

CBC. Platelets function in blood clotting, wound healing and inflammatory responses that occur at the site of injury. After beginning treatment for rheumatoid arthritis, patients will find their doctors checking blood tests periodically.

Two additional blood tests that indicate increased inflammatory process are the erythrocyte sedimentation rate (ESR) and C-reactive protein (CRP). These blood tests don't diagnose RA but indicate an increased inflammation when elevated. Patients with RA will find their doctor ordering these blood tests periodically also to monitor their response to the disease and treatment.

In their efforts to diagnose RA, doctors may recommend a joint aspiration and synovial biopsy. Joint aspiration involves the doctor withdrawing some fluid from the joint and sending the fluid to a laboratory for analysis. Tests done routinely help determine whether the joint is infected and if not infectious, whether an inflammatory process is occurring. Joint aspiration can easily be done in a doctor's office or clinic setting. Synovial biopsy may be recommended. While it may be done in the doctor's office, it's probably done during arthroscopic or open surgical procedure. Arthrosopy can be done on several joints, including knee, shoulder, elbow, ankle, wrist, and hip.

Doctors use x-rays to determine joint space narrowing, which occurs with loss of cartilage. Early RA often doesn't cause x-ray-detectible changes for several months. X-rays can show doctors the progression of joint damage as RA damage occurs.

According to the Arthritis Foundation, MRI scans "detect early inflammation before it is visible on an X-ray, and are particularly good at pinpointing synovitis, inflammation of the lining of the joint."[27]

An arthrogram x-ray procedure may be recommended for post-surgical "painful hip and knee prosthesis to differentiate infection from aseptic loosening."[28]

Mental and Emotional Effects

Everyone experiences feeling down or sadness. Arthritis, especially rheumatoid arthritis, causes depression in many people. Chapter 4, "Taking Charge of Your Life," gives suggestions for grieving the losses that chronic illness may cause. Many coping techniques help people pull themselves out of their sad times. Some of these techniques include: joining a support group, participating in arthritis self-help classes, doing things a person enjoys, and replacing negative thoughts with positive thoughts.

However, when low spirits persist more than two weeks, experts recommend seeing a doctor. A rheumatologist can look at the patient and his symptoms while considering whether any medications or non-arthritis illnesses are causing the depression. Some medications such as prednisone or non-steroidal anti-inflammatory drugs (NSAIDs) cause depression. Some illnesses such as thyroid, diabetes and epilepsy can trigger depression through hormonal changes. Sometimes a change in medication or treatment of an illness will improve the depression.

Symptoms of major depression include: persistent sad, anxious, or "empty" mood, feelings of hopelessness, pessimism, feelings of guilt, worthlessness, help-lessness, loss of interest or pleasure in hobbies and activities that were once enjoyed, including sex, decreased energy, fatigue, being "slowed down," difficulty concentrating, remembering, making decisions, insomnia, early-morning awak-ening, or oversleeping, appetite and/or weight loss or overeating and weight gain, thoughts of death or suicide; suicide attempts, restlessness, irritability, and persistent physical symptoms that do not respond to treatment, such as headache, digestive disorders, and chronic pain.[29]

Early recognition and treatment of depression is recommended. The depressed person may consider treatment of medication and psychotherapy with the goal of obtaining a happier, more fulfilling life. Two types of brief psychother-apy have been recommended as effective for short-term depression of medically ill older persons: talk therapies and cognitive behavioral therapy. Both types involve the person talking with a counselor/therapist in an effort to change neg-ative thoughts and feelings of being helpless.[30]

Medications used to treat depression include three types of drugs: selec-tive serotonin reuptake inhibitors (SSRIs), tricyclics, and the monoamine oxi-dase inhibitors (MAOIs). Patients who begin taking any of these drugs should get drug information from the doctor or pharmacist. The patient needs to know details such as interactions with other medications the person takes and possi-ble side effects the individual may experience. The patient should expect to take the new medication for several months, maybe years. The patient may notice some improvement after taking the antidepressant for a couple of weeks, but full benefit doesn't happen before three to four weeks. According to the National Institutes of Mental Health, patients often are tempted to stop medication too soon. Once the individual is feeling better, it is important to continue the med-ication for the time specified by their doctor to prevent a relapse of the depres-sion.[31] A last bit of advice is to never stop taking an antidepressant without talking to the doctor about how to safely discontinue the medication.[32]

Some people will consider St. John's wort as an optional anti-depressant. An ongoing study done by the National Institutes of Health (NIH) showed patients with major depression rated their "overall functioning was better for the antidepressant [a SSRI anti-depressant] than for either St. John's wort or placebo."[33] This study is continuing to determine the value of St. John's wort in mild depression. Patients taking St. John's wort should not consider this herb safe and without side effects. St. John's wort can prolong the affect of anes-thesia drugs and interfere with drug metabolism. The Food and Drug Admin-istration issued a public health advisory in 2000 notifying people that St. John's wort appears to affect an important metabolic pathway that is used by many drugs prescribed to treat conditions such as heart disease, depression, seizures, certain cancers, and rejection of transplants.[34] Individuals should discuss St. John's wort and all herbal medications with their doctors.

Stress can cause flares, periods of increased symptoms. According to the Arthritis Foundation, "stress packs a powerful wallop for people with autoimmune disease, because some of the biological pathways that ignite the stress response are the same pathways involved in immune-system malfunctions."[35] Stress causes a chemical release that can trigger flares. Cortisol, one of the chemicals released by stress, causes increased danger of heart disease, anxiety, depression and obesity. "Managing your health after this cycle takes hold can seem like jumping for a helium-filling balloon that's floating out of reach."[36] Individuals can use stress management techniques to feel more in control and better protect their health.

Conservative Treatment Measures

According to the Arthritis Foundation, "seeing a rheumatologist is recommended whenever there is doubt about the diagnosis."[37] A rheumatologist specializes in medical treatments of arthritis and other diseases involving bone, muscles and joints. Successful coping with RA begins with an appointment with a rheumatologist, learning about the disease and becoming involved in one's health. The worst thing a person can do about RA is ignore it. RA is "clearly a disease that shortens survival and produces significant disability.... Over 33 percent of RA patients who were working at the time of onset of their disease will leave the workforce within 5 years.... Overall, RA shortens the lifespan of a patient by 5–10 years.[38]

According to the March/April 2005 Arthritis Foundation Research Update, two studies conclude with "further evidence that the widespread inflammation in RA is linked to heart disease and an increased risk of early death."[39] People dealing with RA should ask their physician, "Does the inflammatory process of RA increase my risk for heart attack or other cardiovascular problems?" The researchers recommend early intervention and prevention of cardiovascular disease and mortality.[40] Early intervention begins by discussing a person's risk factors, and may include blood tests such as a lipid panel. The patient and physician will decide whether testing such as electrocardiogram, stress test or angiogram is needed.* New medications and future treatments bring hope to individuals dealing with this disease.

According to the Arthritis Foundation, the goals of treatment for rheuma-

---

*The Arthritis Foundation Disease Center webpage about rheumatoid arthritis can be accessed at http://www.arthritis.org/conditions/diseasecenter/RA/default.asp.

toid arthritis include: "relieving pain, reducing inflammation, stopping or slowing joint damage and improving your functioning and sense of well being."[41] To accomplish these goals, patient education and early treatment are essential. A team of health-care professionals led by the patient's rheumatologist should include occupational and physical therapists, nurses and counselors. Arthritis Foundation chapters around the country provide information, resources and support to patients dealing with RA.* Over the past 20 years doctors recognized that early, aggressive treatment of RA helps prevent joint damage and disability.

Prevention of Osteoporosis

When they hear the word osteoporosis, many people think of stooped, frail elderly women. Facts say that men also develop osteoporosis. About eight million women and two million men in America have osteoporosis. In the over–50 age group, "one in two women and one in six men will suffer an osteoporosis-related fracture at some point in their life."[42]

People coping with RA find themselves at increased risk of osteoporosis. Defined as "thinning of the bones, with reduction in bone mass, due to depletion of calcium and bone protein," osteoporosis puts people with RA at risk for fractures.[43] Studies have shown that steroid medications cause bone loss. When people decrease their activity levels due to pain, osteoporosis can occur. Rheumatoid arthritis can affect bone and is considered a risk factor for osteoporosis.[44] Risk factors for osteoporosis and fractures include

thinness or small frame, family history of the disease, being postmenopausal or having had early menopause, abnormal absence of menstrual periods; prolonged use of certain medications such as glucocorticoids; low calcium intake, physical inactivity, smoking, excessive alcohol intake and anorexia nervosa.[45]

While no one can change the size of his/her body frame or family history of osteoporosis, some of the risk factors involve lifestyle and can be affected. Low calcium intake, smoking, excessive alcohol intake and physical inactivity can be changed by a motivated person.

Prevention of osteoporosis can happen when people recognize their risk factors, talk to their doctors and follow recommendations. Suggested lifestyle changes recommended by the American College of Rheumatology include: getting enough calcium and vitamin D, stopping smoking, limiting alcohol intake, and doing weight-bearing exercises. A conversation with the rheumatologist

*Local chapters can be found at http://www.arthritis.org/.

about RA and osteoporosis-causing medications will educate about prevention and treatment.[46]

Good sources of dietary calcium include dark-green, leafy vegetables, calcium-fortified beverages, and dairy products. One way to boost calcium intake is to add nonfat powdered dry milk to puddings, homemade breads, soups, gravy, or even a glass of milk. Each tablespoon of dry milk "adds 50 mg of calcium and 2 to 4 tablespoons can be added to most recipes."[47] A person should consult with a doctor about calcium supplements because there are multiple brands and dosages available. The National Osteoporosis Foundation recommends 1,000 mg/day from ages 19 through 50, and 1,200 mg after age 51.

Vitamin D plays a major role in calcium absorption and bone health.[48] Vitamin D can be produced in the skin when a person is in sunlight. However, because of skin cancer concerns more people are using sunblock, covering up and avoiding the sun. These actions make food sources of Vitamin D more important.[49] Major food sources of vitamin D are egg yolks, vitamin-D-fortified dairy products, liver and saltwater fish. If a vitamin D supplement is recommended, the normal amount is 400 international units (IU) daily. Massive amounts of vitamin D, more than 800 IU, should not be taken because fat-soluble vitamins store in the body and can be harmful.[50]

Weight-bearing exercise recommendations should be discussed with an individual's rheumatologist or family doctor. Persons dealing with RA and osteoporosis should increase their activity in a manner that protects their joints and prevents fractures. The National Osteoporosis Foundation (NOF) recommends two types of exercise: weight-bearing and resistance exercises. Weight-bearing exercises involve a person using his muscles and bones to work against gravity.[51] Walking and climbing stairs count as weight-bearing exercises. Resistance exercises include weight lifting with free weights or by using weight machines. The NOF gives this caution: "If you are frail, have had a fracture, fall frequently or have osteoporosis, you should take extra caution. Certain movements like twisting of the spine, high impact aerobics or bending from the waist can be harmful. NOF recommends that before starting any exercise program, you should consult with a knowledgeable physician about your fracture risk."[52]

Diagnosis of osteoporosis involves one of several bone density studies used to diagnose osteoporosis. Unfortunately, too many individuals find out their bone is fragile and osteoporotic when the bone breaks. Treatment of osteoporosis involves the medications available. Several medications are approved by the Food and Drug Administration (FDA) for prevention and/or treatment of osteoporosis. Whether a post-menopausal woman, a man or a patient dealing with RA and glucocorticoid drugs, a variety of medications can prevent and treat osteoporosis.[53]

Ongoing Research

Coffee lovers, drink up. Researchers looking at 83,000 participants in the Nurses' Health Study found that drinking coffee, decaffeinated coffee or tea didn't increase the risk of developing RA. However, the study did confirm that smoking tobacco might be "associated with an increased risk of RA.[54]

Researchers such as Dr. Julia Ying Wang at Brigham and Women's Hospital and the Harvard Medical Center report that a complex carbohydrate called glycosaminoglycans (GAG) may be involved in the development of rheumatoid arthritis. GAG is found normally in the articular cartilage of joints and is not influenced by a person's diet. "While studying immune responses to carbohydrate antigens, we discovered that aberrant immune responses to glycosaminoglycans (GAGs), a major component of connective tissue, can cause RA."[55] Doctors found they could cause GAG-induced arthritis. This research proposes that the development of RA may involve the GAG carbohydrate and infection caused by bacteria, fungi or viruses. Ongoing research by these scientists offers hope of future vaccines or anti-toxins to prevent and/or treat RA.

The words "stem cell transplants" bring hopes for cures. Stem cells, called the building blocks of the body, can mature into different types of cells, depending on their environment.[56] Scientists and patients dream of the day when the human body will be able to renew and repair itself using stem cells. Then diseases such as Parkinson's, diabetes, genetic diseases and auto-immune diseases, including rheumatoid arthritis, will be treated and cured through stem cell transplants.

Stem cell transplants become controversial in America when the stem cells come from human embryos and fertilized cells. The stem cell research discussed in this book doesn't involve embryonic stem cells.

One type of stem cell transplant is being performed for rheumatoid arthritis. This procedure, commonly called bone marrow transplant, has been used for several years to treat certain types of cancer. Bone marrow transplants happen when the patient's own bone marrow cells, are harvested. The patient then undergoes either radiation or chemotherapy to suppress the immune system and then receives bone marrow cells returned in a blood transfusion autologous graft. Then the patient waits for his immune system to become strong again. "A major consequence of stem-cell transplants is suppression of the immune system which means the body's defense mechanisms are completely wiped out. Therefore, the common cold or a normally harmless virus could lead to a serious, and even life-threatening infection."[57] The patient stays in the hospital for several weeks to months. A second risk is that the person's immune system could be impaired or non-existent if the transplanted cells do not survive and successfully transplant.

A small study reported in 2004 in the *Annals of Rheumatology* looked at bone marrow transplants for children. Several children with severe unsuccessfully treated juvenile rheumatoid arthritis have undergone bone marrow (stem cell) transplants in Europe.[58] Thirty-four children received the stem cell transplant and 18 of the 34 (53 percent) achieved complete remission (with a post-procedure follow-up of 12 to 60 months.) Six more of the 34 children showed a partial response and seven children had unsuccessful transplants. The doctors pointed out that the procedure "carries a significant mortality risk." Five of the children died, three due to the transplant and two due to their disease. Infection problems were common.[59] The doctors involved offered suggestions for improvements in future procedures.

The second source of autogenous, or self-produced stem cells is the peripheral blood stem cell. A small number of stem cells circulate in the blood and can be easily accessed through drawing a sample of blood. Obtaining a sufficient number of stem cells for transplantation is difficult with peripheral blood stem cells.[60]

Allograft stem cells come from other people. Donation of stem cells by an identical twin would be the least likely to cause rejection problems. Those from a donor other than an identical twin pose the same potential risk of rejection as an organ transplant.

In 1988, a successful stem cell transplant for a child with anemia used umbilical cord blood collected when his sibling was born. Prior to that time, umbilical cord blood was discarded. In 1992, umbilical cord blood was used to successfully treat a leukemia patient. Since then, more than 6,000 transplants for immune disease have used cord blood as a stem cell source.[61] Umbilical cord blood has positive aspects. "Umbilical cord blood stem cell transplants are less prone to rejection than either bone marrow or peripheral blood stem cells."[62] Again, the quantity of stem cells found in umbilical cord blood is too small an amount for many people who need a transplant. Also, umbilical cord blood stem cells take longer to engraft, take up residence and repopulate the bone marrow. This prolongs the recovery time period when the patient has no protection from infection.

Scientists continue searching for other sources for stem cells, including fat cells and hair cells. If successful, Americans could forge onward in stem cell research without the moral and ethical dilemmas involved with fetal tissue use. Many hope that stem cells can be used to prevent and treat rheumatoid arthritis and to repair the damaged articular joints found with osteoarthritis.

People dealing with early morning stiffness that lasts more than two hours, warm and swollen joints, often on both sides of the body, and feeling tired or sick should see their doctor. These vague symptoms need to be investigated and the person treated. The Arthritis Foundation says, "Rheumatoid arthritis is a serious disease. It is crucial that you get an early diagnosis and work with your doctor to find the best treatment for you so you can live well with it."[63]

3

Remembering the Past: A Brief History of Arthritis and Methods of Prevention and Treatment

History of Osteoarthritis

Early evidence of osteoarthritis in humans was found in a skeleton of Neanderthal man showing arthritic changes in the knees and spine. Eight thousand B.C. era Egyptian mummies demonstrate osteoarthritic changes. Egyptian royal family mummies from the period of 1570 B.C. to A.D. 324 were x-rayed and studied. Scientists found three out of the twelve had arthritis in their knees, hips, or spines. A group of 400 skeletons from medieval Roman and England society were studied and "nearly half of the specimens" had osteoarthritis.[1] Through the ages until modern times, arthritis continues to afflict mankind.

Arthritis has been studied and explored for centuries. William Heberden, an 18th century English physician, was the first to study and record his observations about arthritis involving the hands. Heberden's nodes, the bony arthritic bumps found on the distal (closest to fingernail) joint of fingers, were named after him. Dr. Heberden's observations read as below:

> What are those little hard knots, about the size of a small pea, which are frequently seen upon fingers, particularly a little below the top near the joint? They have no connection with the gout, being found in persons who never had it, they continue for life; and being hardly ever attended by pain, or disposed to become sores, are rather unsightly than inconvenient, though they must be some little hindrance to the free use of the fingers.[2]

In 1884, Dr. Charles-Jacques Bouchard described similar bony bumps that develop on the proximal joints (closest to wrist) of fingers. Doctors now call those Bouchard's nodes.

Throughout the 19th and early 20th centuries, doctors worked on describing and recognizing the differences in osteoarthritis and rheumatoid arthritis. Sir William Osler wrote *The Principles and Practice of Medicine* in 1909 and described "arthritis deformans" as a "chronic disease of the joints of doubtful etiology, characterized by changes in the synovial membranes and peri-articular structures, and in some cases by atrophic and hypertrophic changes in the bones."[3] Osler recommended that treatment of osteoarthritis consist of "fresh air," a good diet, hydrotherapy, range-of-motion exercises, and massage.[4] Several of these treatments are still used in modern-day therapy.

In 1944, two doctors, R. M. Stecher and A. H. Hersh, concluded from their studies that osteoarthritis has a familial (inherited) tendency.[5] Recent studies agree with this theory that inherited genes may not cause but are a factor in the development of OA.

In 1986, the American Rheumatism Association (now called the American College of Rheumatology) published guidelines for diagnosing osteoarthritis. These guidelines did not require x-rays or invasive procedures.

History of Rheumatoid Arthritis

The first description of rheumatoid arthritis is credited to Augustin-Jacob Landre-Beauvais who in 1800 called it a type of gout, "goutte asthenique primitive." "A. B. Garrod coined the term rheumatoid arthritis (RA) in 1858 and differentiated RA from gout in 1892."[6]

The painter Renoir (Pierre Auguste) is believed to have suffered from rheumatoid arthritis. After he suffered a bicycle accident in 1897 and broke his right arm, the arm healed. Soon afterward he began suffering arthritis pain. By 1911, Renoir was forced to give up walking but continued his beloved painting until the day he died.[7]

"When a patient with arthritis walks in the front door, I feel like leaving out the back door."[8] With these words, Sir William Osler (1849–1919) described the frustrations of doctors who had few successful treatments for rheumatoid arthritis.

Orthopedic Surgery, written by Dr. James E. Moore and published in 1898, uses the term "rheumatoid arthritis." Dr. Moore said, "This affliction is a polyarticular disease of adult life, usually running a sub acute course from the first, and is extremely chronic. All joints of the body may be affected."[9] Dr. Moore declared, "The prognosis is bad under any treatment, but the patient's chances are very improved by residence in a warm, dry climate. When the joints are not too sensitive, massage with passive motion is followed by improvement."[10] Pain medications available included opiates (narcotics), which weren't recommended for persons dealing with chronic pain. Braces and splints were utilized to relieve deformity and pain. "Braces should be light, strong, and well-fitting, for, at best, they're more or less a burden, and when ill-fitting may be as great a source of suffering as the disease for which they are applied." Regarding operative treatment, Dr. Moore said, "There are but few operations coming under the head of orthopedic surgery."[11]

Orthopaedic Nursing, a book written by Robert V. Funsten, MD, and Carmelita Calderwood, RN, and published in 1949, lists treatments for RA such as diet, heliotherapy (sunshine), rest and prevention of deformity, chrysotherapy (gold shots), physical therapy, traction, and psychotherapy. No special diet was recommended, but rather a healthful variety of foods. "Rest is so essential in the treatment of the disease that without it any other treatment is likely to be fruitless."[12] Splints and braces were used to rest sore, inflamed joints. Gold shots were "thought by some physicians to be exceedingly promising" in 1949. Injections of gold were given intramuscularly (shots into the muscle) and spaced several days to a week apart. "A course of gold therapy treatment may extend to twenty weeks or longer, after which the patient rests for six to eight weeks. A second course may then be given."[13] Physical therapy included heat, cold, massage, and traction. Psychotherapy was considered important because "the pattern of the arthritis patient's life has been so altered by this particularly harassing disease, the adjustments he has had to make have been so profound, that it seems impossible that any nurse could fail for one moment to extend toward him the most wholehearted understanding."[14]

History of Ergonomics and Preventing Injuries

Ergonomics is defined as "the science of adapting working conditions to the needs of the worker."[15] Contrary to popular belief, ergonomic principles have been used for many years. Dr. Bernardino Ramazinni (1633–1714) wrote about work-related injuries his patients suffered in a 1713 publication, *De Morbis Artificum* (*Diseases of Workers*).[16] During the Industrial Revolution, machines such as the spinning jenny, used to make cloth, and rolling mills, used to flatten iron ore into flat sheets, improved work processes.

The term "ergonomics" was coined by Wojciech Jastrzebowski in 1857.[17] During the early 20th century, Frank and Lillian Gilbreth worked to make jobs more efficient and less tiring to workers. They studied bricklayers. By doing time-motion analysis and standardizing tools, materials and job activities for the bricklaying job, Frank and Lillian developed tools and techniques that decreased the needed movements in laying a brick from 18 movements to four and a half. This new efficiency increased the speed of bricklaying from 120 to 350 bricks/hour.

World War II brought interest in human and machine interaction. "Design concepts such as fitting the machine to the size of the soldier and logical/understandable control buttons evolved."[18] After World War II, worker safety, not just productivity, became a priority. Researchers began looking at how much muscle force is required to perform manual tasks, the amount of force exerted on a person's lower back during lifting, and the cardiovascular response to heavy labor. Industry, government and workers continue in their efforts to improve "the science of adapting working conditions to the needs of the worker."[19]

History of Pain Management

Pain historically was considered a punishment or means of atonement. The Greek word *poine* and Latin word *poena* both mean punishment.[20] Ancient peoples believed they were being punished with pain. The sorceress, priestess, or shaman negotiated with spirits who caused illness and pain. These religious leaders performed rituals and treated people suffering from pain using various medicines, as well as applications of heat, cold, friction, and pressure.[21] The first society to use opium as a pain treatment was probably the Mesopotamian culture (A.D.).

The Egyptians believed pain resulted from spirits of the dead entering the living through their ears and nose (nares). Their treatments purged the body, using herbs to cause vomiting, sweating, sneezing, and urinating. The Egyptians treated pain with TENS (transcutaneous electrical nerve stimulation) when they placed an electric fish from the Nile River on wounds.

Ancient Buddhists considered emotions and pain to be closely related and believed frustrated desires caused pain. Both Ancient Buddhists and Hindus considered chanting a valuable coping skill for pain. Modern-day relaxation and biofeedback techniques provide similar diversions.

Ancient Chinese used willow plant, which contains salicylic acid (main ingredient of aspirin), for rheumatic pain. The Chinese believe that two opposing forces—yin (negative/passive/feminine) and yang (positive/active/male)—maintain a balance and energy (chi) within the body. Stress, illness and pain cause and result in imbalances in yin and yang forces. Acupuncture was developed to restore balance to the body. Using small needles, acupuncturists alter organ function to restore balance and health.

The Ancient Greeks used topical medicines applied locally to treat pain, dry secretions, and promote healing. Aristotle described pain as the opposite of pleasure. He recognized our five senses as sight, hearing, taste, smell, and touch. He thought pain began in the heart and resulted in increased touch sensitivity.

The first documented "pain" pills were used by 1st-century Romans. They recognized that some nerves in the human body were sensory (involved with five senses and include pain) and some nerves were motor (control movement).

Historians believe massage, exercise, and drinking alcohol were also used as pain management techniques throughout ancient times.

The Middle Ages saw little progress in treatment of pain. During the Renaissance ether was developed. When opium and alcohol were combined, laudanum resulted and helped relieve pain. Physical therapies such as massage and exercise were popular.

Major progress in pain management occurred in the 19th century when ether was used for general anesthesia. Morphine was isolated from raw opium in 1803 as an effective pain reliever. In 1884 cocaine was recognized as effective for local anesthetic. Surgery was made possible by these anesthesia and pain medications.

The 20th century saw major advances. Biofeedback and drugs including nonsteroidal anti-inflammatory (NSAIDs), serotonin-altering drugs (SSRIs) and steroids were developed.

Pain clinics called "nerve block centers" were first set up after World War II by anesthesiologists, medical doctors specializing in anesthesia and pain management. These clinics have evolved and developed into multidisciplinary centers that offer much help to people suffering from pain. Today's centers strive to educate patients in causes and treatments for pain, help patients develop skills to manage their pain successfully, and create a support group for patients coping with pain.

During the 20th century, national and international organizations such as the International Association for the Study of Pain (IASP) and the American Pain Society (APS) developed to study and treat people suffering from pain.[22] The Internet is a great resource for people dealing with pain.*

During the late 20th century, government agencies such as the U.S. Department of Health and Human Services Agency for Health Care Policy and Research and state government agencies became involved in directing pain management research and treatments. The accrediting body for hospitals, the Joint Commission on Accreditation of Healthcare Organizations (JCAHO), set standards of care regarding pain management and requires hospitals to meet those standards.

The Decade of Pain Control and Research began January 01, 2001, and ends in 2010. This declaration by the United States Congress signed into law by President Clinton focuses attention on education, research, and clinical management of pain.[23]

*Three reputable sites include the American Pain Foundation web site (http://www.painfoundation. org/), the National Chronic Pain Outreach Association (http://www.chronicpain.org/) and the American Chronic Pain Association (http://www.theacpa.org/).

Nutrition and Diet

"Two hundred and fifty years ago, any man who joined the crew of a seagoing ship knew he had only half a chance of returning alive, not because he might be slain by pirates or die in a storm, but because he might contract the dread disease scurvy."[24] No one knew or understood why sailors on long ocean voyages came down with scurvy. A British physician, James Lind, performed the first nutrition experiment in 1747. He discovered that lack of citrus fruits, vitamin-C-containing foods, caused scurvy. After the cook on the ship used up all the fresh fruits and vegetables, he served cereals and meats and the crew became vitamin-C deficient. When the British navy began requiring that sailors receive lime juice daily, a source of vitamin C, the sailors avoided scurvy and were nicknamed "limeys."

The first American cookbook, *American Cookery*, written by Amelia Simmons and published in 1796, began the love affair with food and cookbooks. These cookbooks provided recipes and became sources of health information. "Discontented with the lack of effective nineteenth century medical treatment options and sometimes less than desirable bleeding and blistering and induced purging and vomiting sessions, physicians and health enthusiasts of the time began to search for and offer alternative solutions."[25] As early as the 1800s, advocates for a healthy diet included people like Sylvester Graham, a minister who emphasized whole grains and the benefits of uncooked food. Dr. Russell Trall objected to some medical practices of his time and promoted a vegetarian diet. Dr. Trall spoke at the 1860 American Vegetarian Society meeting on the topic of "The Scientific Basis of Vegetarianism." In 1865, Dr. Mary Cox recommended that people quit eating rich foods and return to fruits, vegetables and whole-grain foods. Dr. Cox published a cookbook in 1865 entitled, *The Hygienic Cook Book, or How to Cook Without the Use of Salt, Butter, Lard, or Condiments.*[26] Throughout the 19th and 20th centuries, cookbooks provided nutrition information mixed with recipes.

The American government first published nutritional guidelines in 1894. This first publication was entitled *Farmers' Bulletin* and suggested diets for American males. Specific vitamins and minerals weren't yet discovered. A 1916 United States Department of Agriculture (USDA) publication, *Food for Young Children*, first recommended five food groups: milk and meat, cereals, vegetables and fruits, fats and fat foods, and sugary foods.

A 1930s Depression version of the government guidelines gave "food plans at four cost levels to help people shop for food."[27] The plan could be utilized to provide a healthy diet on a limited budget.

President Franklin Roosevelt called the National Nutrition Conference for Defense in 1941. From this conference came Recommended Dietary Allowances (RDAs), recommendations for calorie intake and intake of nine essential nutrients (calcium, iron, protein, vitamins A, C, D, and the B vitamins, thiamin, riboflavin, and niacin). This wartime conference also gave a plan called the Basic Seven to help people eat nutritiously in spite of war-time rationing and shortages. *Dietary Goals for the United States* in 1977 "shifted the focus from obtaining adequate nutrients to avoiding excessive intakes of food components linked to chronic diseases."[28]

Emphasize Health

"Let food be your medicine and medicine be your food."[29] Hippocrates, honored as the father of modern medicine, is credited with this quote from 2,400 years ago.

Throughout history, most cultures have regarded fatness as a sign of success, health, and beauty. Less than 100 years ago, Americans equated body fat with money, and excess fat was described as a "snug balance in the body bank and a comfortable reserve in the case of emergencies." A 1908 *Harper's Bazaar* article gave advice on "how to get plump."[30]

Even as late as the 1950s and 1960s, full-figured women such as Jane Russell, Marilyn Monroe and Jayne Mansfield were considered beautiful movie stars of the ideal size.

During the 1960s American opinions about beauty and the ideal female size changed. Thin was in. When the Barbie doll was introduced in 1959 by a fledgling company called Mattel, the American public began a love affair with this 11½ inch doll and her buddies that continues to present day.[31]

The medical community changed their opinion regarding ideal body size also. In 1926, Dr. Woods Hutchinson, former president of the American Academy of Medicine, warned that "the longed for slender and boyish figure is becoming a menace, not only for the present, but for future generations."[32] By 1951 the U.S. government and medical establishment began a campaign against obesity.[33]

During the 1950s Jack LaLanne's show introduced fitness to the American household. The word "aerobics" was added to Webster's Dictionary in the late 1960s. Several books written about diets become best sellers: *The Doctor's Quick Weight Loss Diet* by Erwin Stillman and Samm Sinclair Baker in 1968, *Dr. Atkins' Diet Revolution* by Robert C. Atkins in 1972 and *The Complete Scarsdale Medical Diet* by Dr. Hermann Tarnower and Samm Sinclair Baker in 1979.[34]

When Karen Carpenter died from heart failure due to anorexia nervosa in February 1983 at the age of 32, national attention focused on eating disorders. By 1996 the "National Association of Anorexia Nervosa and Associated Disorders estimates that 8 million Americans, mostly young Caucasian women, suffer from either anorexia or bulimia."[35]

Drugs

German chemists identified and manufactured aspirin from the willow bark plant in 1899. Aspirin's main ingredient, salicylate, had been used in its herbal form, willow bark, since 500 B.C. to relieve painful joints. Aspirin was brought to the market in 1925 by the company that became F. Bayer & Co.[36]

Acetaminophen (Tylenol, Datril, others) was introduced in 1955 as Tylenol Elixir for children as an aspirin-free analgesic. "Researchers had discovered giving aspirin to children who had influenza or the chicken pox were at greater risk of contracting the deadly Reye's syndrome. Reye's syndrome is an acute neurologic illness that results in fatty degeneration of the liver and fatal swelling of the brain."[37] Between 20 and 30 percent of the children who developed Reye's syndrome died. Aspirin-free Tylenol was recommended and consumers learned to trust acetaminophen (Tylenol).

People called cortisone a miracle drug when it was discovered. Two Mayo Clinic doctors, Edward Kendall and Phillip Hench, and a Swiss doctor, Tadeus Richstein, shared the Nobel Prize for Physiology and Medicine in 1950 for discovering cortisone. As often happens in medicine, the accumulated work of several doctors contributed to the knowledge. One hundred years earlier, a Scottish doctor, Thomas Addison, had recognized a connection between the adrenal glands and a disease of adrenal insufficiency, named after him as Addison's disease. Work by an English physician in 1894 confirmed the presence of hormones in the adrenal cortex. During the 1930s Dr. Kendall isolated six different compounds from the adrenal gland. In 1936 Dr. Richstein isolated as many as seven adrenal substances. During World War II, rumors that Germans were researching cortisone to help the Luftwaffe pilots fly at high altitudes spurred the U.S. government to make this research a high priority.[38] In 1944, a tiny amount of cortisone was produced from the bile of 2,500 cows.

The first DMARD (disease-modifying antirheumatic) drug became available when doctors began giving gold shots.

Alternative Therapies

Acupuncture practitioners trace their roots back to the Han Dynasty in China (second century B.C.). Two ancient books, *Huang Di Nei Jing* (*Yellow Emporer's Inner Classic*) and *Nan Jing* (*Classic of Difficult Issues*) are considered major sources of acupuncture theory.[39] The Chinese philosophy believes vital life energy (qi or chi, pronounced "chee") flows through the body via pathways called meridians. A person's health is disrupted when the blockages in the energy flow occurs. Pain and illness result from these blockages. "Acupuncture works to reprogram and restore normal functions by stimulating certain points on the meridians in order to free up the Chi (qi) energy."[40] For centuries, the Chinese studied and refined the practices of acupuncture. A book published in 1601, the Zhen Jiu Da Cheng (*Great Comprehendium of Acupuncture and Moxibustion*) became the source of information for Europeans. Acupuncture arrived in the U.S. during the 1970s when President Nixon visited China. When an American reporter had emergency surgery under acupuncture, attention focused on acupuncture practices and its applications.[41]

Steps Toward Successful Surgery—Hygiene and Aseptic Technique

As far back as the ancient Hindus in 2000 B.C., hygiene was recognized as important. Hippocrates (460–370 B.C.) recommended cleanliness and hand-washing by surgeons. He used pure boiled water to clean wounds and advocated clean bandages.[42]

Galen (A.D. 131–201), a respected Greek physician, expressed the idea that pus was an essential part of the healing process. This erroneous idea was accepted for centuries and caused doctors to allow wounds to become contaminated. The first attack on the theory of "laudable pus" was made in the 13th century A.D. by Theodoric of Cervia.

John Pringle, an army surgeon, coined the term "antisepsis" in 1751 to describe "substances which resisted putrefaction in wounds."[43] Conditions in 18th-century hospitals were horrendous, as shown by a shocking mortality statistic from a hospital in Dublin, which had survival rate of only 45 infants out of the 10,339 babies born there from 1775–1796.[44]

Another huge step forward in preventing infection came when several different doctors recognized that doctors and midwives could be carrying infection from one patient to another in the form of puerperal fever, post childbirth infection. Alexander Gordon practiced medicine from 1786 to 1795. He advocated that doctors and nurses wash themselves after caring for women with puerperal fever before caring for another patient. This theory offended some doctors, but mounting evidence continued to support this idea.

Ignaz Semmelweiss practiced medicine in Vienna, Austria during the 1840s. He noticed that pregnant women with high infection rates (9.92 percent) were being attended by medical students. Medical students routinely dissected dead people in the cadaver lab and then examined the patients without washing their hands. The women attended by midwives not involved with the cadaver lab experienced an infection rate of 3.38 percent. In 1847, "a colleague of Semmelweiss died of septicemia [blood-borne infection] resulting from a cut to his hand during a post-mortem exam [examination of a dead person]. Semmelweiss noted that the cause of death of his colleague was identical to puerperal [post childbirth] fever."[45] Semmelweiss believed that infected material from the cadavers was caus-ing the infections in the pregnant women and began to insist that everyone, including medical students leaving the cadaver lab, wash their hands in chlo-rine water or chlorinated lime. With this new hand washing procedure, mater-nal mortality (death of mothers) sharply declined in Vienna.

Patients undergoing surgery in the mid–1800s continued to die at a rate of almost 50 percent. A common report by surgeons read: "Operation success-ful but the patient died."[46] One early theory regarding germs said "sepsis was a kind of combustion caused by exposing moist body tissue to oxygen."[47] Search-ing for a better way, Joseph Lister heard of the germ theory of Frenchman Louis Pasteur who believed that "germs" or microorganisms caused infection. When Lister heard that carbolic acid succeeded at killing disease-causing parasites in sewers, he began cleaning and dressing surgical wounds with a solution of car-bolic acid, a phenol. Initial resistance by the medical community was overcome when Lister announced that the "wards at the Glascow Royal Infirmary had remained clear of sepsis for nine months."[48] A giant step forward in surgical care had been accomplished. Lister became "Baron Lister of Lyme Regis" in 1897 after caring for Queen Victoria who honored his medical advances.[49]

Another giant step forward occurred when a German surgeon, Ernst von Bergmann, introduced steam sterilization and the idea of asepsis (absence of germs) in 1891.[50] Modern standards for American surgery grew out of the idea of asepsis. Surgical instruments and equipment are sterilized before use on patients. Drapes, supplies, and many implants arrive at the hospitals sterilized and ready to implant. Surgeons, operating room staff, and medical supply com-panies continue in their efforts to decrease the number of infections. In their opinion, one infection is too many.

In 1928 Sir Alexander Fleming, a London researcher, noticed that bacte-ria growing in his petri dish didn't grow around the mold called *Penicillium*. Flem-ing recognized the mold inhibited the growth of the *Staphylococcus aureus* germ and called it Penicillin.[51] Since its discovery, this first antibiotic and subsequent antibiotics have saved countless lives of people.

The antibiotic treatments called medical miracles during World War II have become routine treatment for infections.[52] Antibiotics first saved lives of soldiers who would have died from infected wounds during World War II. Through the years, antibiotics have become expected treatment, prescribed by physicians and demanded by patients for infections whether the infection was caused by germs or viruses. Antibiotics cannot kill viruses. Along the way, some bacteria have mutated, changed and become immune to antibiotics that killed them in the past, hence, the term "super germs." With increased knowledge and understanding, patients understand why their doctor doesn't order antibi-otics when antibiotics aren't needed. When antibiotics are prescribed, the patient should take the antibiotic as prescribed and for the entire dosage.

"Patients often stop taking the drug too soon because symptoms improve. However, this merely encourages resistant microbes to proliferate."[53]

Seeing Through Flesh—Radiology

U.S. newspaper headlines screamed, "New light sees through flesh to bones!"[54]

This medical advance involved x-rays. In 1895, Wilhelm Conrad Roentgen, a German physics professor, developed the first x-ray. He was working on light phenomena and the emissions that occurred when electrical current was discharged in special glass tubes. During this work, he discovered that he could see the bones inside his hand.

Fascinated by this new technology, Thomas Edison (1847–1931) worked to obtain a brain x-ray. He developed a hand-held fluoroscope. X-ray technology was accepted by the public very quickly. Studios opened where people could have "bone portraits." Detectives advertised Roentgen (x-ray) devices as tools to help follow unfaith spouses, and "lead underwear was manufactured to foil attempts at peeking with X-ray glasses."[55] Within a month of newspaper announcements of this new technology, doctors found patients demanded x-rays be taken for broken bones and foreign bodies. By 1904 medical doctors were using x-rays to differentiate between osteoarthritis and rheumatoid arthritis. "Never before or since has a new medical technology been accepted as quickly."[56]

Anesthesia Advances

The days of "biting a bullet" while a surgeon operated is long past. Individuals undergoing surgery today expect to hear a calm voice telling them to "pick out a good dream. We'll be here with you all the time and you will wake up in the recovery room." When the individual wakes up in the recovery room (post-anesthesia care unit), soreness may be experienced but people expect to be comfortable.

Anesthesiology is "the branch of medicine specializing in the use of drugs or other agents that cause insensibility to pain."[57] Anesthesia is administered by Medical Doctor Anesthesiologists (MDAs), medical doctors with specialty training in anesthesia, and certified registered nurse anesthetists (CRNAs) who have a master's degree in Nursing with Anesthesia specialty.

Anesthesia caregivers consider the whole person when planning and giving the anesthesia. They consider all the body systems of their patients. Mr. Jones, who had a heart attack three weeks ago, faces a greater risk of complications from the surgery and anesthesia than a healthy person. Mrs. White's out-of-control diabetes puts her at higher risk of problems. The more complicated the patient's health problems, the higher the risk of complications. The astute MDA and CRNA know the potential problems and plan the anesthesia to reduce the complications to the lowest level possible.

Before anesthesia became available, surgeons considered pain inevitable and patients dreaded the experience. "In those dark days, many patients approached surgery as though facing execution, an often appropriate assessment of uncontained risks, including pain, hemorrhage, shock, and post-operative infection. While awaiting even a minor elective procedure, patients often put their estate and personal affairs in order in the anticipation that their wealth would soon be passed on to the next of kin."[58]

Early uses of both ether and nitrous oxide were mostly recreational. Diethyl ether (ether) is very old, possibly dating back to an 8th century Arabian philosopher named Jabir ibn Hayyam. For many years poor people used ether as an inexpensive recreational drug when they drank small amounts of it or held ether-soaked towels to their faces. Observers noted that the revelers fell asleep and awakened unharmed. The first documented use of ether for anesthesia happened in 1842. William E. Clarke used ether to provide anesthesia to a young woman named Hobbie while a dentist pulled her tooth. A few months later, Dr. Crawford Williamson Long gave ether to a patient who needed two tumors excised from his neck. Afterwards, the patient reported "he was unaware of the removal of the tumor." In the first known fee for anesthesia, Dr. Long charged $2.00 plus $.25 for the ether.[59]

Nitrous oxide was prepared in 1773 by a British scientist and clergyman, Joseph Priestley. During his chemistry research, Priestley also created the first carbonated beverage by adding carbon dioxide to water and he recognized that oxygen exists in a pure gas form. Another British researcher, Humphry Davy, did much research on nitrous oxide and published a 580-page book entitled *Nitrous Oxide* in 1800. Davy noticed nitrous oxide relieved pain and coined the name "laughing gas" to describe the hilarious and uninhibited behavior it caused.

Chloroform, another anesthesia gas, was gaining popularity and credibility among obstetricians seeking to improve childbirth experiences for mothers. John Snow, credited as being the first anesthesiologist, gave Queen Victoria chloroform for her last two childbirth deliveries. Queen Victoria wrote in her journal, "Dr. Snow gave that blessed chloroform and the effect was soothing, quieting, and delightful beyond measure."[60] Besides being a respected physician, Dr. John Snow conducted research and published his findings about ether and chloroform.

Dr. Frederick Hewitt became Sir Frederick Hewitt when he was knighted in 1909 after giving anesthesia to King Edward VII. When King Edward VII suffered an appendix rupture and abscess, he needed surgery. After the monarch's recovery, both surgeon and Dr. Hewitt were honored.

Many doctors, dentists and chemists have contributed to anesthesiology. Dr. Francis Hoeffer McMechan contributed much to the written practice of anesthesia in spite of his own health problems from rheumatoid arthritis. He became editor of the first professional magazine devoted to anesthesia, *Current Researches in Anesthesia and Analgesia*. Ralph W. Waters became one of the leading teachers and fathers of academic anesthesiology. "At that time, the custom of becoming a self-proclaimed specialist in medicine and surgery was not uncommon."[61] Dr. Waters helped establish high standards for anesthesia training and the formal examination process for anesthesiologists.

Before anesthesia gases such as ether and nitrous oxide, dentists "regularly met patients who refused restorative treatment for fear of the pain that would be inflicted by the dentist."[62] Dentists who contributed to anesthesia include Horace Wells and Gardner Q. Colton. Wells recognized the value of nitrous oxide in anesthesia. In 1839, Colton used nitrous oxide to provide safe, painless tooth extractions. Dr. Colton's advertising slogan "31½ Miles Long" described a scroll containing 55,000 signatures of patients treated in his dental clinics across America. Nitrous oxide had been administered to provide painless tooth extractions to these patients.

Advancements in anesthesiology have made anesthesia safer for surgical patients. Prior to 1900, medical care often happened at the patient's home. Most early doctors carried their equipment in their pockets and black medical bag when they made house calls. As doctors recognized the need for anesthesia equipment and ways to monitor the patients, they worked to design those items. "Physicians of 60 years ago who practiced anesthesia with just a rag and bottle would be amazed to observe modern techniques in which fresh gas flows are metered precisely."[63]

Anesthesia machines began to be used in operating rooms around 1900. Through the efforts of men like Dennis Jackson, Ralph Waters and Brian Sword, the carbon dioxide absorber anesthesia machine was developed. Professor Lucien Morris at the University of Wisconsin developed the copper kettle vaporizer and increased patient safety by controlling the amount of anesthesia gas being given. Blood pressure monitoring was first proposed by Dr. George W. Crile and Harvey Cushing in 1902. EKG (electrocardiogram) monitoring wasn't routinely used until after World War II due to the risks of explosive anesthesia gases and the cathode ray oscilloscopes.

Modern-day patients find a variety of options in anesthesia. General anesthesia, commonly called "being put to sleep," means being completely unaware during the time of the surgery. Regional anesthesia includes spinal, epidural, and various nerve blocks of extremities. This type of anesthesia provides pain control when the anesthesia provider injects medicines that block specific nerves for a specific time frame. The patient having a regional block can be awake, sedated, or under general anesthesia. Anesthesiologists utilize a variety of anesthesia gases and drugs to keep the patient comfortable and safe.

Orthopaedic Specialty

Modern-day orthopaedic surgeons are doctors with an additional five to seven years of specialized training. They use surgical and non-surgical treatments to correct musculoskeletal problems.

Nicholas Andry, a professor of medicine at the University of Paris, coined the term "orthopaedic" from the Greek words "straight" and "child." In 1741 Andry published a book entitled *Orthopaedia: Or the Art of Correcting and Preventing Deformities in Children*.[64]

Jean-Andre Venel, the father of orthopaedics, established the first orthopaedic hospital to treat children in 1780. Plaster of Paris cast material was developed in 1851 by a Dutch military surgeon, Antonius Mathysen.[65]

Many orthopaedic advancements have happened during wartime. World War I developments involved plaster casts and splints for fractures. World War II advances involved intramedullary rods to treat broken leg bones, both upper (femur) and lower (tibia). The Vietnam War found American doctors adapting and refining the external fixator. A Russian doctor, Gavril Ilizarov, had developed the external fixator during the 1950s. Dr. Ilizarov found himself in Siberia caring for soldiers with crooked, unhealing fractures. Utilizing bicycle parts, Dr. Ilizarov "achieved healing, realignment and lengthening to a degree unheard of elsewhere."[66] Out of these and many more contributions by scientists and doctors, advancements in care of arthritic joints developed.

Total Hip Surgery

Surgeons have long recognized that arthritis in the hip joint causes patients pain and increasing disability. For over a century, efforts were made to treat hips with procedures such as fusion, osteotomy and debridements. Unpleased with the results of these procedures, surgeons and scientists kept working.

In 1925 a procedure called mold arthroplasty was tried by Dr. M. N. Smith-Petersen, in which he "molded a piece of glass into the shape of a hollow hemisphere which could fit over the ball of the hip joint and provide a new smooth surface for movement."[67] While the glass didn't hold up, this unique idea moved doctors a step closer to modern-day joints. In 1936, scientists manufactured a cobalt-chromium alloy. This strong metal resists corrosion and was successfully made into total hip stems. Cobalt-chromium femoral stems are still used today.

Two surgeons, Dr. Frederick R. Thompson of New York and Dr. Austin T. Moore of South Carolina, were independently developing hip prosthesis. The hip prosthesis consisted of a metal stem that fit inside the canal of the femur and a large metal ball that fit the inside of the hip socket (acetabulum). Today, this design is still used successfully for fractures. However, it didn't fix the arthritic hip socket (acetabulum). Dr. Edward Haboush from New York City utilized a "fast setting dental acrylic" to glue the implants to the bone.[68]

Sir John Charnley gained fame when he combined some of these advances with his own ideas. He revolutionized total hip replacements despite questioning by some of his colleagues. Sir John used the dental glue called methylmethacrylate to hold the implants in place. His first attempts at resurfacing the acetabulum socket utilized Teflon implants. Teflon was unsuccessful but his next choice, polyethylene or plastic, worked well. When Sir John "glued" in the metal stem with head and plastic acetabular cup, the modern total hip was born. This technology revolutionized the surgical care of arthritic hips. The Queen of England knighted Sir John Charnley in 1977. A report of "survivorship on Sir John Charnley's patients between 20–25 years was astounding, rounding off at around 85%." This means at 20–25 years, 85 percent of Sir John Charnley's total hip replacement implants were still secure and doing well.[69]

Despite the good results obtained from cemented prosthesis, doctors recognized that loosening of cemented components sometimes happened. They worked with implant companies to develop implants out of metals such as titanium, trabecular metal and ceramics in efforts to develop an implant that would last the patient's lifetime. They've worked on improving the plastic acetabular component and made it a two-piece (metal and plastic liner) component. The plastic liner could be replaced if needed. They've improved the quality of the plastic liner to withstand many years of wear. Porous implants that the bone can grow into and hold firm have been developed. The idea of a metal head sitting in a metal acetabulum shell/liner has been around for many years, but early metals were imperfect and caused problems. With modern-day machining and different metals, the metal-on-metal components have gained popularity for total hip implants.

Total Knee Replacements

As early as the 1860s, doctors were trying to treat knee arthritis by removing the arthritic knee joint (resection arthroplasty). They tried to put tissues such as skin, muscle, fat and pig bladder between the ends of the bone to relieve arthritic pain. During the 1940s and 50s, doctors tried several designs with limited success. During the 1960s, Dr. Frank Gunston developed total knee implants out of metal and plastic. Utilizing the methylmethacrylate "glue" successfully used in total hip replacements, Dr. Gunston implanted the first modern total knee in 1968.[70] In 1973 Dr. John Insall designed a prosthesis still popular today. This modern-day design resurfaced all three knee surfaces, the femur (thighbone) with an all-metal component, the tibia (shinbone) and patella (kneecap) with all-plastic components. A 1993 study reported results on Dr. Insall's knee components at 94 percent survivorship at 15-year follow-up.[71]

Over the years, surgeons learned more about the complex movements of the knee and worked to improve implants. One improvement was modularity; the tibial component was manufactured in two pieces, a metal baseplate and a plastic surface on top of the baseplate. The rationale was that the plastic surface could be replaced in the future when it became worn, a retreading type of procedure that has extended the life span of many total knee joints. While the patient does have to return to the operating room for this retreading or revision surgery, it's easier to pop out the tibial plastic surface and replace it with a new one than removing and replacing all the components.

Porous implants that the bone grows into and holds firm have been developed for total knee replacement also. Both porous implants and the cemented versions of total knee implants have been used successfully. Annually, doctors perform over 300,000 total knee replacements for patients dealing with arthritis pain.[72]

4

Taking Charge of Your Life

When the doctor says a person has arthritis (or rheumatoid arthritis), the response will be as varied as people. Some individuals will shrug it off and go on. Others will feel the words as a punch in the stomach. To these people, the diagnosis may feel like a pronouncement of death. That person may think of Aunt Suzie's gnarled fingers that forced her to give up playing her piano. Or visualize Uncle George whose arthritis and aging years took a strong erect-postured man down to a shrunken, fragile old man using a walker to get to the bathroom. For these persons, grief must be dealt with before they can take charge of their health.

Dealing with Grief

"That doctor must be wrong. He can't be talking about me." Even as that person stumbles out of the doctor's office, his mind doesn't accept that life-changing diagnosis. Denial is the first stage of dealing with a loss.

We think grieving is something we do when a loved one dies, but people deal with grief when they suffer the loss of a life goal or expected opportunity. For some people, this occurs with a diagnosis of chronic disease such as arthritis. The expectation to travel to exotic places or take up a sport could be affected by the arthritis. There are steps of grieving that must be worked through before this person can successfully cope.

People experiencing grief find they lack concentration and are apathetic or they may be angry—at themselves or at God. Other common experiences include "sleep disturbances, loss of appetite, withdrawal from others, irritability, intense sadness or tears when a memory is triggered, numbness, loneliness, or a sense of separateness from others, and loss of life's meaning."[1]

J. William Worden, a psychologist, discusses four "tasks of grieving" that the grieving person must complete. These tasks are: "1. accept the reality of the loss, 2. work through the pain of grief, 3. readjust to the environment after the loss, 4. reinvest energy in the present and future."[2]

Task 1. Individuals need to accept that their health will be different than expected. With proper treatment and therapies, the health will probably be quite good. However, there are no guarantees and self-image will probably suffer at least temporarily. This reality may be painful to individuals whose dreams and expectations were dashed by this diagnosis. A young mother would not want to hear the doctor say she has rheumatoid arthritis and she may deny the reality. "Coming to an acceptance of the reality of the loss takes time since it involves not only an intellectual acceptance but also an emotional acceptance. The bereaved person may be intellectually aware of the finality of the loss long before the emotions allow full acceptance of the information as true."[3]

Task 2. Grieving people experience both physical and emotional pain. Successful coping requires recognizing this pain and working through it. Avoiding or suppressing the pain only prolongs the process and may result in depression. Individuals must "indulge the pain of loss—to feel it and know that one day it will pass."[4] Experts recommend expressing this pain through crying. "Crying in the presence of a supportive, caring friend and being heard fully is the best medicine for the griever."[5] Many persons will find a support group helpful. The local arthritis group consists of people who have dealt with this diagnosis and understand the grief. It's likely that local members will be at varying stages of coping with their own illnesses. Their understanding and support plus their knowledge of the disease will be valuable to new group members.

Task 3. Individuals must recognize that their world has changed and must be dealt with. "The bereaved person searches for meaning in the loss and its attendant life changes in order to make sense of it and to regain some control of his or her life."[6] A sports activist may find this new diagnosis directly affects self-image. Chronic illness such as arthritis will be unwelcome and adapting that self-image will be necessary for successful coping. An athlete might channel his knowledge and love of sports into a free-lance writing career. Instead of high-impact sports, the athlete might choose less strenuous, gentle-to-joints, activities such as swimming, walking, and bicycling.

Task 4. The person grieving will deal with "reinvesting energy in the present and future." During this last task, people should hang on to the good memories and move on. "One never loses memories of a significant relationship."[7] Persons dealing with loss of dreams and goals could consider those dreams being saved for "when I have time" or "someday." The early retiree whose health has changed due to arthritis might want to make plans for that cruise to Alaska after talking to the physician.

Experts in grieving tell us the grieving process lasts months and often years. The time required varies from person to person. Experts also say going through the grief process is a circular, not linear, process. Persons will feel they've accomplished steps until something triggers a painful response, plunging that person back into prior tasks of grieving. Knowing this is a normal part of the process, that person will continue dealing with the grief until successful coping occurs.

People who find the grieving process too painful may get stuck and want to avoid dealing with tasks. "Effective grieving is an intentional moving into the pain so the wound of loss can heal. Deep physical wounds are frequently left open in order to heal from the inside out.... Similarly, people need to find ways to feel and express the pain they've locked away—to open the wound so it can heal from the inside out."[8] Suggested things to help with healthy grieving include:

"Don't expect the process to be easy or impossible; avoid both extremes.

Don't compare the time it takes you with the time it has taken someone else.

Draw on your preexisting support structures, that being your family, friends, and family of faith in church.

Deal with issues, don't avoid them. Despite the temptation to give up or at least procrastinate, move ahead with necessary actions.

Deal with belongings; avoid extremes.

Expect unusual emotions. You may experience confusion more than ever before. Often people speak of feeling a weight upon their shoulders or their chest, holding them back.[9]

When you feel a good cry coming on, make it a positive experience by reflecting upon good times."[10]

How can a person know when the grieving process is accomplished? "Successful resolution of the grief response is thought to have occurred when a bereaved individual is able to remember comfortably and realistically both the pleasures and disappointments of [that which is lost]."[11]

Once the grieving process is underway, the person with arthritis needs to consider the future. What can be done for the arthritis? Over half of people with arthritis think "nothing." This dooms them to toughing it out, which will work for a short time but is not a good long-term solution. At present, arthritis has a lifelong impact; there's no cure. The good news involves many treatments and strategies that improve quality of life.

Making a Decision

Whether or not to take charge of one's health is a choice everyone makes. Taking charge begins with seeing a physician or nurse practitioner. A primary care doctor, family doctor, or health clinic doctor should be the first doctor a person sees. Nurse Practitioners (NP) are advanced practice nurses with a masters' degree who function with the physician's oversight. This doctor or NP

Ten Steps from Patient to Person

Courtesy of the American Chronic Pain Association

STEP 1: **Accept the Pain**
Learn all you can about your physical condition. Understand that there may be no current cure and accept that you will need to deal with the fact of pain in your life.

STEP 2: **Get involved**
Take an active role in your own recovery. Follow your doctor's advice and ask what you can do to move from a passive role into one of partnership in your own health care.

STEP 3: **Learn to Set Priorities**
Look beyond your pain to the things that are important in your life. List the things that you would like to do. Setting priorities can help you find a starting point to lead you back into a more active life.

STEP 4: **Set Realistic Goals**
We all walk before we run. Set goals that are within your power to accomplish or break a larger goal down into manageable steps. And take time to enjoy your successes.

STEP 5: **Know Your Basic Rights**
We all have basic rights. Among these are the right to be treated with respect, to say no without guilt, to do less than humanly possible, to make mistakes, and to not need to justify your decisions, with words or pain.

STEP 6: **Recognize Emotions**
Our bodies and minds are one. Emotions directly affect physical well being. By acknowledging and dealing with your feelings, you can reduce stress and decrease the pain you feel.

STEP 7: **Learn to Relax**
Pain increases in times of stress. Relaxation exercises are one way of reclaiming control of your body. Deep breathing, visualization, and other relaxation techniques can help you to better manage the pain you live with.

STEP 8: **Exercise**
Most people with chronic pain fear exercise. But unused muscles feel more pain than toned flexible ones. With your doctor, identify a modest exercise program that you can do safely. As you build strength, your pain can decrease. You'll feel better about yourself, too.

STEP 9: **See the Total Picture**
As you learn to set priorities, reach goals, assert your basic rights, deal with your feelings, relax and regain control of your body, you will see that pain does not need to be the center of your life. You can choose to focus on your abilities, not your disabilities. You will grow stronger in your belief that you can live a normal life in spite of chronic pain.

STEP 10: **Reach Out**
It is estimated that one person in three suffers with some form of chronic pain. Once you have begun to find ways to manage your chronic pain problem, reach out and share what you know. Living with chronic pain is an ongoing learning experience. We all support and learn from each other.

looks at the individual as an entire person and would take care of the individual's cold or bronchitis. Patients should continue to see this primary doctor or NP on a routine basis and keep the doctor informed of improvements, problems and changes. Often the patient will be sent to a specialist, such as a rheumatology doctor or surgeon.

Specialists are physicians (doctors) with extra training in specific areas. The specialty doctors should be considered valuable resources because they know the latest, best information about their specialty. The vast amount of medical knowledge cannot be known by any single person, so specialty doctors use their expertise to benefit patients. Specialty physicians include rheumatologists and surgeons, psychologists and physiatrists. Rheumatologists treat arthritis and rheumatic diseases using conservative measures such as medicines and therapies. Orthopedic surgeons offer conservative measures and perform surgery on bones, muscles and ligaments of the human body. These doctors offer a variety of surgeries, including arthroscopy and total joint replacements. Psychologists help patients cope with life and their health condition in their home and work environment. People dealing with depression and difficulty coping would probably find a psychologist helpful. Physiatrists (rehabilitation specialists) are doctors who "help patients make the most of their physical potential."[12]

Other Resource People

RNs—registered nurses—show up in doctors offices, community-based programs and hospitals in every city and town. Registered nurses "trained in arthritis care can assist your doctor with your treatment program and can answer many of your questions."[13]

An Occupational Therapist (OT) evaluates "the patient's ability to perform activities of daily living, provides assistive devices as needed, and teaches joint protection techniques and energy conservation skills."[14] Occupational therapists offer tips and aids to simplify household tasks and cooking. An OT visit would evaluate the individual to identify problems, needs, and goals.

Physical Therapists (PT) believe exercise gives people "the physical strength and vitality they need to cope with day-to-day living."[15] A PT teaches how to protect joints while exercising. They actively involve persons with arthritis in their treatments.

Pharmacists do more than fill prescriptions written by physicians. Researchers at Ohio State University found that patients who discussed their medical condition and medications with pharmacists had 60 percent fewer medication-related problems.[16] Many pharmacies provide written information of a person's drugs that should be kept for the patient's future reference. Individuals should use the same pharmacy for all their prescriptions because pharmacists keep records of medications prescribed and alert people to potential problems that can occur from medication interactions. Pharmacists are easily "accessible health care professionals"[17] and share their knowledge of resources in the community.

Social workers are professionals who "assist patients with social challenges caused by disability, unemployment, financial hardships, home health care, and other needs resulting from medical conditions.[18] They know details of programs, both service and financial, which will provide needed resources to citizens.

Dietitians teach good nutrition and help patients make healthy choices in their diets. The dietitian and individual can incorporate a weight loss plan into the life style of those individuals who need and want to lose weight.

Caring for All Aspects

Empowerment begins when people take charge of their health. Successful coping means the person recognizes all aspects of self and needs: physical aspects of the body, mind or thoughts, emotions or feelings and spirit. Holistic healing "considers all aspects of a person's internal and external environment that may contribute to health and well-being, and being willing to entertain a wide variety of options to help that person heal.... The words healing and holy both come from the root word hal (hale) which means to make whole."[19] As people become aware of all parts of their being and better care for themselves, life becomes more fulfilling.

Caring for Physical Aspects

The patient's physician makes the diagnosis of osteoarthritis or rheumatoid arthritis. Individuals make the choice to cope successfully. What can be done to care for the physical aspect of a person?

Most people want the pain stopped, so they ask the doctor for pain medication and receive advice regarding acetaminophen, aspirin and other NSAIDs (non-steroidal anti-inflammatory) medications. If the first medication doesn't decrease the pain level, then the patient should contact the doctor for another drug. During a conversation with the doctor, the individual should get his/her opinion about non-drug options that can make life better. Glucosamine chondroitin supplements bring pain control for some individuals. Touch therapy benefits people by relaxing the person and relieving pain. Acupressure, acupuncture and massage are included in the chapter on alternative therapies (chapter 10).

Exercise has proven beneficial for arthritis patients. People may decrease their activity levels because of pain but they need to keep moving. Exercise builds strong muscles that protect joints while decreasing pain and stiffness. Exercise increases flexibility and endurance. Other benefits of exercise include improved sleep, increased energy, and more normal body weight for those who exercise. These benefits result in a more positive mental outlook. But what exercise is beneficial and safe? The person dealing with arthritis should talk to the doctor about what exercises to start doing. Three types of exercise are recommended by the Arthritis Foundation: flexibility, strength and aerobic exercises. Flexibility exercises include range of motion and stretching exercises. Strength exercises such as weight lifting make muscles stronger. Aerobic exercises, also called cardiovascular exercises, include walking, swimming, dancing and bicycling.[20] Experts recommend starting slow and enjoying the activities. Chapter 8, Exercising with Arthritis, gives more information about exercise.

Sixty-one percent of Americans fit the overweight or obese classification. According to the United States Department of Health and Human Services, obesity and being overweight contribute to arthritis.[21] Amid all the diet trends and fads, confusion reigns. Nutrition, diets and healthy eating are discussed in chapter 7.

Caring for Mental Aspects

Look on the bright side. Optimistic people live longer than pessimists. A thirty-year-long study conducted by the Mayo Clinic shows pessimistic people are 19 percent less likely to live a normal life expectancy, which leads author David Niven to conclude "Your focus is not merely a personality quirk, but a way of life."[22] Everyone has seen cancer patients whose positive outlook and enjoyment of life keeps them living and enjoying life long past the projected life span. These inspiring people make a person wonder at their secret, the decision they made to look on the bright side. It's easy to say but harder to accomplish, especially when a person hurts. People endeavoring to be optimistic use a variety of strategies.

Write it down. People with chronic conditions such as asthma and arthritis wrote about their lives and thoughts in a journal for one hour per week as part of a North Dakota State University study. The participants showed a 47 percent measurable improvement in their symptoms over the months they participated.[23]

Find something to get involved in. The individual who wants to return to college will find many adults, including retirees attending college. People who dream of traveling should call a travel agent, grab the spouse or good friend, and take that trip. One who dreams of a beautiful garden will find it therapeutic to dig in the dirt. A pair of gardening gloves, a trowel, and a few plants will result in a beautiful garden and therapy for the individual.

Consider volunteering. Schools welcome volunteers in "foster grandparents" programs. Agencies, hospitals, and hospice programs need and welcome volunteers. Lonely individuals could find themselves too busy in worthwhile projects to be lonely. Volunteering promotes good feelings and gratitude for what we have.

Animal lovers with the resources to care for an animal might adopt a dog or cat. Local humane society facilities are good sources for a new member of the family. Petting an animal decreases a person's blood pressure, a healthy benefit to pet ownership. If the new animal possesses a gentle temperament, pets and their owners are welcomed at many health-care facilities. Anyone interested in pet therapy should contact the facilities for information.

Caring for Emotional Aspects

How can a person foster emotional health? Researchers recognize that humans, plants and animals thrive when loved. Support could be a "pet, a church group, family, a feeling of connection to a Higher Power, plants people care for, a social group, or wherever one feels loved and accepted."[24] Arthritis Foundation local chapters would be excellent support, as many members cope with similar adjustments. Positive effects of support include improved feelings of self-worth and coping with the changes occurring due to arthritis. When people feel more in control, their stress hormone levels decrease, the immune function improves, and overall health improves. Lack of social support brings on a reverse situation with progressive illnesses of many types. "Love and caring create a connection over time and great distances, affecting physical change."[25] Modern technology fosters long-distance communications. Cellular phones, e-mails, and Internet private messenger programs enable family and friends to utilize this support connection.

Scientists rank "hope as crucial to human wellness and successful coping." While they believe hope is shaped during childhood and young adulthood, they recognize individuals can cultivate hope. Research by Dr. Anthony Scioli, a psychology professor in New Hampshire shares his assessment of hope and 14-step practices at www.gainhope.com/hope/test_form.cfm.[26]

How does one nurture one's spirit? Eighty-six percent of Americans believe in God or a universal spirit.[27] In a study of nearly "600 severely ill hospital patients aged 55 and older, researchers measured 47 ways of coping and discovered patients who sought a connection with a benevolent God as well as support from clergy and church members were less depressed and rated their quality of life as higher, even after taking into account the severity of their diagnosis. The researchers also found that patients who gave spiritual support to others by praying for them or encouraging their faith also fared better emotionally."[28]

Many studies have found that church participation helps people feel more attached to their community. Becoming active in church encourages people to get involved in civic organizations, from local school activities to professional and political activities. "Congregations foster volunteering through emotional attachments to friends and family, and through the emotional satisfaction of 'giving back' or expressing one's spirituality," the researchers stated.[29]

Arthritic people deal with sexual intimacy. *The Arthritis Helpbook* reminds readers, "Sex is more than the act of sexual intercourse, it is also the sharing of physical and emotional sensuality."[30] This book gives excellent, practical suggestions to dealing with this aspect of life.

Successful coping with arthritis begins when individuals see the physician and learn about the disease. Choosing to make the most of their health continues this process. People who want to enhance their health must take the holistic view and consider all parts of life. Taking charge means individuals care for themselves in all aspects: physical, mental, emotional and spiritual.

Considering Resources

Arthritic persons should count their family and friends as valuable resources and appreciate them. Individuals should remember that their spouses or significant others and close family/friend unit may be suffering their illness with them. Good communication with support persons will enhance life for everyone. The Arthritis Society suggests, "You'll need the help and support of a network of people, all of whom have a need and a right to know more about how you're feeling than you may have ever shared before.... The person you're communicating with has to understand what you're trying to say; in other words, you have to learn to communicate clearly and effectively."[31]

Arthritic fingers struggle to open a jar of spaghetti. Which gadget works best? Chapter 9 of *The Arthritis Helpbook*, entitled "Self-Helpers: 100+ Hints and Aids," gives valuable information on gadgets and aids.

Many resources provide information for people coping with arthritis. The premier organization, the Arthritis Foundation, funds research into causes and cures for the 100+ diseases and syndromes the Arthritis Foundation claims. Reliable and up-to-date information is available through local chapters and regional centers, and online.*

Many excellent books have been written for and recommended by The Arthritis Foundation, including the booklet, "Take Charge: Money Matters and Your Arthritis."

What financial resources are available to help people with arthritis cope? Prescription drug spending rose 15.7 percent to $140 billion in 2001.[32] What

*http://www.arthritis.org.

10 Things to Know about Evaluating
Medical Resources on the Web

(source: National Center for Complementary and Alternative Medicine)
NCCAM, Frequently Asked Questions,
http://www.nccam.nih.gov/health/webresources (accessed 04/02/2008)

1. Who runs this site?
Any good health-related Web site should make it easy for you to learn who is responsible
for the site and its information. On this site, for example, the National Center for Complementary and Alternative Medicine (NCCAM) is clearly marked on every major page of
the site, along with a link to the NCCAM homepage.

2. Who pays for the site?
It costs money to run a Web site. The source of a Web site's funding should be clearly
stated or readily apparent. For example, Web addresses ending in "gov" denote a federal
Government-sponsored site. You should know how the site pays for its existence. Does it
sell advertising? Is it sponsored by a drug company? The source of funding can affect what
content is presented, how the content is presented, and what the site owners want to accomplish on the site.

3. What is the purpose of the site?
This question is related to who runs and pays for the site. An "About This Site" link appears
on many sites; if it's there, use it. The purpose of the site should be clearly stated and should
help you evaluate the trustworthiness of the information.

4. Where does the information come from?
Many health/medical sites post information collected from other Web sites or sources. If
the person or organization in charge of the site did not create the information, the original source should be clearly labeled.

5. What is the basis of the information?
In addition to identifying who wrote the material you are reading, the site should describe
the evidence that the material is based on. Medical facts and figures should have references
(such as to articles in medical journals). Also, opinions or advice should be clearly set apart
from information that is "evidence-based" (that is, based on research results).

6. How is the information selected?
Is there an editorial board? Do people with excellent professional and scientific qualifi-
cations review the material before it is posted?

7. How current is the information?
Web sites should be reviewed and updated on a regular basis. It is particularly important
that medical information be current. The most recent update or review date should be
clearly posted. Even if the information has not changed, you want to know whether the
site owners have reviewed it recently to ensure that it is still valid.

8. How does the site choose links to other sites?
Web sites usually have a policy about how they establish links to other sites. Some med-
(continued on next page)

(10 Things to Know, *continued***)**

ical sites take a conservative approach and don't link to any other sites. Some link to any site that asks, or pays, for a link. Others only link to sites that have met certain criteria.

9. What information about you does the site collect, and why?
Web sites routinely track the paths visitors take through their sites to determine what pages are being used. However, many health Web sites ask for you to "subscribe" or "become a member." In some cases, this may be so that they can collect a user fee or select information for you that is relevant to your concerns. In all cases, this will give the site personal information about you.

Any credible health site asking for this kind of information should tell you exactly what they will and will not do with it. Many commercial sites sell "aggregate" (collected) data about their users to other companies—information such as what percentage of their users are women with breast cancer, for example. In some cases they may collect and reuse information that is "personally identifiable," such as your ZIP code, gender, and birth date. Be certain that you read and understand any privacy policy or similar language on the site, and don't sign up for anything that you are not sure you fully understand.

10. How does the site manage interactions with visitors?
There should always be a way for you to contact the site owner if you run across problems or have questions or feedback. If the site hosts chat rooms or other online discussion areas, it should tell visitors what the terms of using this service are. Is it moderated? If so, by whom, and why? It is always a good idea to spend time reading the discussion without joining in, so that you feel comfortable with the environment before becoming a participant.

---

can consumers do to decrease their drug costs? Chapter 9 discusses several options for decreasing drug costs. Consider generic drugs instead of name-brand drugs. Comparing prices between pharmacies can save money. Comparing prices between prescription drugs and their over-the-counter (OTC) version may save dollars for some older drugs available OTC. Internet pharmacy (mail order) services may offer savings.

Federal resources help people with arthritis. Medicare federal insurance coverage provides help with hospital and doctor fees for many people with arthritis.*

---

*For more information regarding Medicare coverage, contact http://www.medicare.gov. For those eligible for Medicare a drug discount program (Medicare Part D) was instated on January 1, 2006 as an option for prescription drugs. Details of benefits and how to apply for this program can be obtained through their website: http://www.medicare/gov/ or at 1-800-MEDICARE (1-800-633-4227). The Medicare-Approved Drug Discount program (Part D) began after January 1, 2006. Counselors provided through the State Health Insurance Assistance Program (SHIP) will assist consumers with Medicare questions or problems. This free service provides toll-free and local telephone numbers for access to counselors. The SHIP numbers can be accessed through 1-800-MEDICARE or http://www.medicare.gov/contacts/static/allStateContacts.asp. Consumers often find community-based programs locally to assist them regarding these programs.

For people who are ineligible for Medicare but who cannot afford their medications, patient assistance programs from pharmaceutical companies offer help with prescription drugs.*

Vocational rehabilitation programs educate and train people who can no longer perform their jobs and want job training. The U.S. Department of Education grants money to state programs to provide "employment related services for individuals with disabilities, giving priority to individuals who are significantly disabled."[33] State level vocational rehabilitation office phone numbers can be located under that state's education department or at http://www.ed.gov/about/contacts/state/index.html.

If a person's ability to work and function diminishes to the point of disability, Social Security and Supplemental Security Income disability programs provide assistance. Qualifying for these programs requires that an individual has worked a specified time frame and paid Social Security taxes. Qualifying persons who find themselves unable to work receive benefits that equal a portion of the monthly income they earned while working.[†]

For those persons eligible for Medicaid, a program called Cash and Counseling Demonstration has been tested in several states—Arkansas, Iowa, New Jersey, New York and Florida. A similar program called Independence Plus will soon be available in South Carolina and New Hampshire. Operated by the states, these programs provide funds that the individuals use to hire assistance for daily living activities such as "cooking and bathing. These programs allow recipients to hire whomever they wish, including relatives and friends."[34] The research group monitoring the results reported the Cash and Counseling Demonstration trial to be successful. Those participating "loved it, in part because they were able to hire people they trusted."[35]

Centers for Disease Control (CDC) funded educational programs are being conducted in several states.[‡] The Arthritis Self-Help course, a six-week program, teaches persons dealing with arthritis better coping skills. The Arthritis Self-Help Course has been shown to reduce arthritis pain by up to 20 percent and physician visits by 40 percent.[36]

The Missouri Arthritis Rehabilitation Research and Training Center (MARRTC) was founded in 1971 as the only federally funded rehabilitation research and training center in America. MARRTC conducts "cutting-edge rehabilitation research that addresses the needs of people with arthritis in general, as well

*The Arthritis Foundation Website recommends the Partnership for Prescription Assistance at www.pparx.org or 888-477-2669.
†More information is available at http://www.socialsecurity.gov or 1-800-772-1213 (toll free). Twenty-four-hour access to recorded information and services is available for callers with touch-tone phones. Operator-assisted service is available from 7 A.M. to 7 P.M. Monday through Friday.
‡For more information about arthritis programs funded by CDC, visit http://www.cdc.gov/arthritis/state_programs/index.htm.

as the specific needs of minority populations, who are particularly vulnerable to the devastating effect of arthritis."[37]

The Farmers and Arthritis program, sponsored by MARRTC and the U.S. Department of Agriculture, focuses efforts on helping farmers and agriculture workers with arthritis. AgrAbility, another program based at the University of Missouri–Columbia and co-sponsored by Lincoln University, provides "assistance adaptive technology and education materials to farmers with disabilities."[38]*

Social service workers provide information regarding resources. Many cities will have programs to help people with arthritis continue to live independently. Finding the programs is sometimes a challenge and social workers have knowledge about these programs.

The Arthritis Foundation's seven Principles of Arthritis Management[39] include:

1. Each person is an individual and should be viewed as a person with a type of arthritis, rather than a type of arthritis seen in a person.

2. There is no best treatment for everyone who has a particular type of arthritis, as each individual may respond differently to different treatments.

3. No single type of arthritis is always better or worse than another type.

4. Information and input from a person with arthritis can be as valuable in diagnosis and management as information from laboratory tests and x-rays.

5. In arthritis management, the emphasis is on improving function of joints and relieving pain.

6. Your doctor and health-care team need your involvement to help you to the fullest extent. People with arthritis and health professionals are partners in care.

7. Something can always be done to improve your situation with arthritis.

Individuals dealing with chronic illness and pain could find themselves unhappy with their circumstances. Each individual will make the choice: to let circumstances and health status rule or to take charge of his health. Build a team of professionals, including doctors, pharmacists, and others who can guide health decisions. Enrich life by becoming involved with worthwhile, fulfilling projects and spending time with supportive family and friends.

*For further information, visit http://marrtc.missouri.edu/media/releases/farm-7-31-02.html

5

Prevent Arthritis?

Prevent rheumatoid arthritis (RA)? Until scientists determine the cause of RA, prevention hovers beyond our reach. With many research projects happening around the world, researchers hope to identify the cause, prevention and better treatments for RA. Doctors do know that stress can cause flares (periods of increased symptoms). "Stress packs a powerful wallop for people with autoimmune disease, because some of the biological pathways that ignite the stress response are the same pathways involved in immune-system malfunctions. For people with arthritis and other inflammatory diseases, stress prompts the release of chemicals in the brain and body that can trigger flares, inflammation and pain. To make matters worse, some of those chemicals, like cortisol, increase the risk of developing other chronic health conditions, such as heart disease, obesity, anxiety and depression, which can create more stress."[1] Persons dealing with RA should find stress-reducing behaviors and incorporate these into their lives. Exercise, yoga, meditation, massage therapies and other stress-reduction behaviors can be found in this book, through various Arthritis Foundation programs, and at www.arthritis.org.

Prevent osteoarthritis? Because osteoarthritis involves joint cartilage wearing thin, prevention of injuries and damage can help avoid the onset and severity of OA. The Centers for Disease Control (CDC) and American College of Rheumatology recommend prevention behaviors such as "maintaining ideal weight, taking precautions to reduce repetitive joint use and injury on the job, avoiding sports injuries by performing warm-ups and strengthening exercises using weights, and by choosing appropriate sports equipment."[2]

Prevention Strategies

Maintaining ideal weight is a battle for many people. While it's true that added weight increases the pressure on lower extremity joints, people struggle with this issue. More information for diet and nutrition can be found in chapter 7.

Employers and industry seek ways to keep workers healthy and avoid repet-itive injuries through ergonomics. *Ergonomics* is defined by Webster's Dictionary as "the science of adapting working conditions to the needs of the worker."[3] The word *ergonomics* brings to mind well-designed tools and equipment that enhance the comfort and productivity of workers.

"Blackberry thumb," one of the most recent musculoskeletal injuries, involves the thumb. Users of handheld computers with miniature keyboards scroll and type rapidly with their thumbs, a repetitive awkward action that results in pain. Recommendations for avoiding "Blackberry thumb" include "sending very short e-mails and replying in kind, and taking frequent breaks from thumb-ing. The eraser tip of a pencil can be a handy thumb substitute."[4] Some users avoid this injury by attaching an external keyboard to their mini-computer when typing long messages.*

According to the American Academy of Orthopaedic Surgeons, "research studies have shown that cold muscles are more prone to injury." Suggested warm-ups for many sports include this advice: "Warm up with jumping jacks, station-ary cycling or running or walking in place for 3 to 5 minutes. Then slowly and gently stretch, holding each stretch for 30 seconds."[5] Proper warm-up before sports helps protect players from injury.

In 2002, University of Missouri athletic trainers began to teach injury pre-vention and warm-up exercises to area elementary school children. Research indicated that "children who play sports without doing warm-up exercises end up injured and develop arthritis when they're older.... Children between the ages of 5 and 14 account for more than one-third of all sports-related injuries, according to the Arthritis Foundation."[6] Parents and team coaches should learn approved warm-up exercises and incorporate these behaviors into children's team activities.

Experts believe that stronger muscles help protect joints. "Deconditioning of the musculoskeletal system is seen with joint injury, obesity and aging, all known risk factors for osteoarthritis."[7] In other words, weak muscles cannot protect joints and may contribute to osteoarthritis. Strengthening (weight lifting) exer-cises build strong, healthy muscles and protect joints. Strengthening exercises involve isometric and isotonic exercises. Isometric exercises tighten muscles with-out moving the joint. Isotonic exercises move the joint. Strengthening exercises can be done by using the person's own body weight, elastic bands and weights. People who are beginning strengthening exercises should get specific recommen-dations from their trainer/physical therapist/physician. Good advice is to start exercising with very light weights and increase very gradually. As individuals

---

*Resources for ergonomic equipment and devices are available from many sources. The National Insti-tute for Occupational Safety and Health (a branch of Centers for Disease Control) provides infor-mation at http://www.cdc.gov/niosh/topics/ergonomics/

begin exercising, they should feel they're not working hard at all. Pain after exercising may indicate the person is putting too much stress on muscles and should be avoided.

General safety tips for strengthening exercises include the following: remember to breathe normally while doing exercises. A person should be able to talk while exercising and should not hold his breath at any time. Good posture is important to help protect the body while exercising. A plastic bottle of water can be substituted for free weights if a person doesn't want to purchase elastic bands or free weights. Other recommendations involve alternating exercises to give muscles a rest. For example, serious exercisers often exercise leg muscles on Monday and Wednesday and do upper body arm exercises on Tuesday and Thursday so their muscles rest. A word of caution involves not exercising sore muscles. Wait until soreness decreases before resuming strength training.[8]

Choosing sports equipment appropriate to size and sport helps protect the body and prevent injuries. No one expects a professional quarterback to play a Sunday game without appropriate equipment. Amateur athletes and children should also utilize appropriate equipment to decrease the risk of injuries.

Additional Suggestions from the Arthritis Foundation

The Arthritis Foundation suggests these tips for protecting joints and preventing OA: "Stand up straight ... use the big joints ... pace yourself ... listen to your body ... don't be static ... forget the weekend warrior ... ask for help."[9]

Good posture or standing up straight protects many joints such as neck, spine, hips and knees. Utilizing the big joints and muscles of the legs while lifting and carrying protects the spine and prevents back injuries. Pacing oneself involves alternating rest with exercise, while paying attention to pain helps prevent injuries. "Pain after activity or exercise can be an indication that you have overstressed your joints."[10] Avoid static positions by moving and changing positions frequently to reduce joint stiffness.

The advice to "forget the weekend warrior" reminds a person to start slowly and protect the body from injury due to overuse. Stretching a springtime chore of landscaping over several days or weekends will increase the pleasure and help avoid sore, aching muscles that hurt on Monday morning. Get help with large jobs and avoid injury. People who lack the financial resources to pay for help might trade skills such as cooking meals or watching a friend or neighbor's child in exchange for yard labor.

Plan to Prevent Injuries

Women, throw away those high-heel shoes. A study from the University of Virginia documented that when women wear high-heel shoes, the pressure on their knees increases over 23 percent compared to wearing flat shoes.[11] Dr. Casey Kerrigan and colleagues at the Harvard Medical School and Boston's Spalding Rehabilitation Hospital looked at 2-inch-heel shoes of both wide-heeled and narrow-heeled varieties. Both caused increased pressure on the wearer's knees. By comparison, these researchers found that "strain on the knee joint when walking barefoot is no different for men and women, eliminating any question of knee stress resulting from gender differences."[12] Researchers believe the increased pressure contributes to osteoarthritis in women's knees and recommend, "Don't wear heels."[13]

Shoes matter. Many people don't think about the 26 bones and more than 30 joints in their feet until pain happens. "With every mile we walk, 200,000 to 300,000 pounds of stress bears down on our tootsies, and by the time we're 50, most of us have walked 75,000 miles."[14] Shoes that fit poorly can contribute to feet problems. Many doctors believe ill-fitting shoes contribute to bunions, hammertoes and neuromas.[15] The American Academy of Orthopedic Surgeons' (AAOS) recommendations include the following: "Wear shoes that are comfortable and fit your feet properly ... place cushions in your shoes for additional comfort and support. Exercise regularly to lower your body mass index ... stretch your leg and calf muscles daily ... see a physician sooner rather than later, if you are experiencing persistent foot and ankle problems."[16] Tips for sizing shoes include: "Buy shoes shaped like your feet."[17] The individual wanting better-fitting shoes will look for shoes squared or rounded and roomy for toes. One suggestion involved tracing the shoe onto a piece of paper and standing barefoot on the tracing. If the foot or toes stick out past the traced shoe pattern, that shoe won't give the comfort and fit needed. Other tips for improving shoe comfort include: Consider a good arch support in shoes and rubber soles that give more cushion. Shoes should allow enough room to stick a finger between the heel and back of the shoe.

Does prolonged squatting contribute to osteoarthritis? A team of researchers examined squatting to see whether it contributes to knee OA. The researchers concluded that "prolonged squatting is a strong risk factor for tibiofemoral knee OA among elderly Chinese subjects in Beijing, and accounts for a substantial proportion of the difference in prevalence of tibiofemoral OA between Chinese subjects in Beijing and white subjects in Framingham."[18] The results were published in the April 2004 *Arthritis and Rheumatology*. The study included 2,269 persons older than 60 years. It compared persons who had at age 25 squatted more than an hour/day (Chinese) to persons who reported that at age 25 they had squatted 30 minutes or less per day (non–Chinese). "Chinese women were

9.5 percent more likely to be afflicted with tibiofemoral OA (a form of knee OA) than their white American counterparts. Chinese men were 7% more likely than white American men to have tibiofemoral OA."[19]

Parents' Guide to Prevention

Children who participate in sports activities benefit physically and emotionally from the activity. Physical activity helps children maintain proper weight, build strength and coordination and incorporate habits of exercise and healthy eating into their lives. Emotionally healthy children build social skills while gaining self confidence and a sense of well-being. Since the benefits of sports and physical activities are desirable, how can parents help their child avoid sports injuries and arthritis in later life?

How many adults can trace their arthritic joint pain to a specific injury? How many men could tell a story similar to this? "Yeah, I tore my ACL during my senior college year. We won that game 10 to 7 in the last couple minutes when I made the winning TD. Now that was a game to remember! Unfortunately, when that safety hit me, he wiped out my knee. It's never been the same."

According to an *Arthritis Today* article, "Safe or Sorry: A Parent's Guide to Sports Injury Prevention," prevention of osteoarthritis begins with children's sports.[20] "According to one study, a single knee injury early in life can put a person at five times the risk for osteoarthritis in adulthood; likewise a hip injury could more than triple the risk."[21] Surprisingly, two-thirds of the sports-related injuries in children involve soft tissue injuries such as sprains and strains. Broken bones account for only five percent of injuries.[22] Two types of injuries can occur: acute injury, which is caused by sudden trauma, and overuse injury caused by multiple small injuries that add up.

The Arthritis Foundation recommends several strategies for safer sports participation for children.

The "American Academy of Pediatrics recommends team sports only for children six years and older."[23] Children younger than six may not be physically, mentally and emotionally ready for team sports.

Look for coaches who teach prevention, recognition and care for injuries. Parents can choose coaches/teams through a variety of school and community leagues. By talking to other parents, concerned parents can identify coaches who stress safety in sports.

Parents can be role models and practice injury prevention. Parents can learn warm-up exercises from the coach/trainer and do those exercises with their child before sports. Parents can let their children see them do appropriate exercises before their own exercise routine.

"Notice the basketball players warming up and doing their stretching exercises." Parents can emphasize injury preventive behaviors of sports idols.

Other suggestions include: Repeat the safety rules over and over because children have a short attention span. Kids will more likely use safety equipment if they get to pick out the color and style they like and want. Ease into new activities and build strength slowly. Sports equipment should be in good shape and fit properly. "A runner's sneakers should be replaced every 250 to 500 miles."[24]

First aid should be available at every game and practice. Children should be taught to stop playing and seek help when in pain. Parents should remember pain means something is wrong and needs to be investigated for proper treatment and prevention of additional injury. In the heat of the game, sometimes coaches and parents forget this. Parents and coaches should work together to encourage safe play.

After the game, cooling down exercises help loosen muscles. If injuries do occur, first aid, proper care by physicians and trainers, and rest helps with healing. "When a joint has been injured, minimize long-term damage by allowing the affected area to heal completely before participating in the sport again. It's important not to push your child to play while in pain. This could make the injury worse."[25]

Sport Specific Tips

The Parents' Guide to Prevention includes basic suggestions. Sport-specific recommendations follow. Safe sports participation always includes appropriate warm up exercises and readily available first-aid and medical care.*

Baseball, America's favorite pastime, accounts for almost half a million injuries treated in hospitals, doctors offices and various health care facilities every year.[26] Tips specific to preventing baseball injuries include wearing appropriate equipment, including well-fitting shoes. Batting helmets should be worn while batting, running bases, and when waiting for turn at bat. Facial protective devices attached to batting helmets can help prevent facial fractures if the ball hits the batter's face. Catchers should use a catchers' mitt and wear protective gear: a helmet, face mask, throat guard, long-model chest protector, shin guards and protective supporter. Protect the pitcher's arm. The AAOS recommends, "Count the number of pitches thrown and use 80 to 100 pitches as a maximum in a game, and 30–40 pitches in a practice."[27] The baseball field

---

*Reliable sources include the American Academy of Orthopaedic Surgeons (AAOS). Online information on prevention of injury can be found at http://orthoinfo.aaos.org/menus/safety.cfm. Play It Safe! sponsored by several orthopaedic organizations, including the AAOS, provides information at 800-824-BONES.

should be inspected, debris or glass removed, and holes filled to prevent injury. The American Academy of Pediatrics recommends "using break-away bases, which come loose more easily when struck from the side, and eliminating the on-deck circle to prevent injuries."[28]

Basketball causes more than 1.6 million injuries every year treated in hospitals, doctors' offices and other healthcare facilities.[29] Tips for preventing basketball injuries include wearing appropriate equipment. Protective knee and elbow pads protect against abrasions and bruises. The players' teeth and mouths can be protected by a mouth guard. Players should not have gum or candy in their mouths during game and practice. Players should leave jewelry at home. If players wear glasses, glass guards or safety glasses better protect the eyes. Non-skid shoes that fit snugly and provide ankle support helps prevent sprained ankles. "High-tops don't physically do much to brace the foot or ankle, but the pressure of the fabric helps remind the brain of what the foot is doing. This lets a player react more quickly when his foot begins to twist in a difficult position."[30] Players who are aware of the locations and movements of other players can better avoid colliding with them. Both indoor and outdoor courts should be clean of debris and hazards to prevent injury.

Cheerleading ranks as "the number-one sport responsible for female direct catastrophic injuries, and accounts for more than half the catastrophic injuries in high school and collegiate female athletes."[31] Cheerleading maneuvers that result in injury include the basket toss and the pyramid. "The basket toss is a stunt in which a cheerleader is thrown into the air—often between 6 and 20 feet—by three or four tossers. In the pyramid drill, the cheerleader at the top is most often injured after falling and landing on a hard surface."[32] New safety measures required by the governing bodies for both high school and collegiate athletics have been instituted to make cheerleading safer.

Football causes more than 400,000 injuries that require treatment in various healthcare facilities such as hospitals and doctors' offices every year.[33] "Before adolescence, serious football injuries are actually quite rare."[34] Wearing the protective equipment helps prevent injuries. Equipment needed for tackle football includes helmet with face guard and chin strap, a mouth guard to protect teeth and absorb blows to the head, pads for shoulder, hip, tail and knee, and athletic supporter. Players who wear eyeglasses should have non-shattering glasses or contact lenses. Parents and coaches should teach children/youth who want to play football to always block and tackle with the head up. College-age football players have the highest risk of catastrophic or severe injury. "Head injuries are the most common direct cause of death among football players; athletes who use their head to make contact dramatically increase their risk of sustaining serious injury. However, there has been a dramatic decrease in brain injury-related fatalities since the late 1960s and research concluded the improved helmet design and establishment of safety standards ... are largely responsible for this decline."[35] Dehydration and heat-related illnesses can be prevented when the players drink enough fluids and take breaks to cool off.

Soccer accounts for more than 470,000 injuries treated in hospitals and various other healthcare facilities, including doctors' offices, annually.[36] A recent *Current Opinions in Rheumatology* article states, "Knee osteoarthritis in young adults is common after knee injury. In women who sustained an anterior cruciate ligament injury in soccer, 51% (mean age 31) had radiographic changes after 12 years. Men, 41% (mean age 36) had osteoarthritis after 14 years."[37]

Prevention of soccer injuries includes protecting lower legs with shin guards and wearing proper shoes. "Wear shoes with molded cleats or ribbed soles. Shoes with screw-in cleats often are associated with a higher risk of injury. However, shoes with screw-in cleats should be worn when more traction is needed, such as on a wet field with high grass."[38] Children should be taught not to sit on the goal or hang from the net, as players have been injured when goals fall on them. Soccer goals should be properly padded and secured to prevent injuries to players. The playing field should be appropriately cared for and free of debris or holes to prevent injury. The recommended soccer ball for wet playing fields is a synthetic, nonabsorbent one. A water-logged, heavy leather ball can injure players.[39]

Volleyball injuries number more than 187,000 each year and require treatment at various health care facilities.[40] Prevention of volleyball injuries begins with proper equipment. Knee pads protect a player's knees and "defensive pants, which are padded from hip to knee, can protect you from floor burns and bruises."[41] Proper shoes are lightweight, provide strong ankle and arch support, and good shock absorption. "The volleyball court should have 23 feet of overhead clearance. Objects such as portable basketball goals, lighting fixtures, and tree limbs should be cleared from the space above the court."[42] Any volleyball net supporting wires should be covered. Players should be taught to avoid grabbing the net and hanging from it, which could cause it to topple over and injure a player. Players should "call" the ball to avoid collisions with each other.

Gardening yields beautiful flowers, delicious fresh vegetables and fruits, and health benefits for the gardener. Researchers at the University of Arkansas found gardening "ranks as high as weight training for strengthening bones."[43] Flexibility, range of motion, and quality of life are all benefits of gardening. However, gardeners can cause themselves overused muscles, aches, and pains.

Prevention of injuries from gardening involves warm-up, pacing oneself, and working smart. The person just coming out of a winter's hibernation should not try to accomplish everything in one day or one weekend. Gardeners will feel better when they pace themselves and avoid overdoing. Working smart involves using proper equipment to prevent injuries. A wheelbarrow or dolly should be used to move heavy bags of soil, flowers, and tools. Gardening shears should be used to open bags rather than stressing fingers trying to tear open heavy bags. Proper gardening tools take the stress off a person's body. Long-handled rakes and hoes allow gardeners to work with a straight back, which decreases stress. A garden hose unrolled from its hose holder simplifies watering plants.[44]*

Golf, an increasingly popular sport, finds 109,000 injuries being treated in health care facilities yearly.[45] Prevention of injuries begins with learning how to make a proper swing. The AAOS recommends that individuals "take golfing lessons and begin participating in the sport gradually."[46] A bad swing can cause injuries to elbow, spine, knee, hip, and wrist, but the two most common injuries involve the elbow and lower back. Prevention of golfer's elbow focuses on strengthening the forearm muscles and slowing the swing. Rowing and pull-down exercises are recommended by AAOS for preventing low back injuries.†

Golfers should always practice courtesy and safety when driving a golf cart to avoid injuries to self or others. All extremities (hands, arms, feet and legs) should stay inside the golf cart while it is moving. Golfers should be alert to the dangers of overheating and dehydration and avoid those problems by drinking adequate amounts of water and electrolyte-replacement fluids.

Prevention of injuries helps people avoid pain now. The experts believe that preventing muscle and joint injuries may have long-term benefits when joint cartilage stays healthy and arthritis doesn't develop.

*These and other tips to simplify gardening can be found in "The Arthritis Foundation's Tips for Good Living with Arthritis" or at www.arthritis.org/resources/Home_Life/tips.asp.
†On-line information about avoiding golf related injuries can be found at http://orthoinfo.aaos.org/topic.cfm?topic=A00137&return_link=0.

6

Dealing with Pain

Words such as *throbbing, piercing, burning,* and *aching* describe pain. Pain sends people to doctors more often than any other complaint. Pain is defined as "an unpleasant sensory and emotional experience associated with actual or potential tissue damage or described in terms of such damage."[1] An easier-to-understand definition says "pain is whatever the experiencing person says it is, existing whenever he says it does."[2]

Doctors describe pain as acute or chronic. Acute pain is either new pain (pain not occurring at this site previously) or pain that has a sudden onset. It's a valuable alarm that the pain site needs attention. "Acute pain warns of tissue damage."[3] Acute pain begins with an injury or disease and ends with healing. Chronic pain is the same pain that persists for a longer time frame. Chronic pain is long-lived and bothers a person for a long period of time, weeks, months or years. People who deal with chronic illnesses such as arthritis routinely deal with chronic pain.

The National Chronic Pain Outreach Association suggests that chronic pain affects approximately one in ten Americans and costs the U.S. economy more than $90 billion annually in medical costs, disability costs and lost productivity. "Pain makes it hard to work, hard to play, hard to get support from others, and hard to live a happy life. Chronic pain shatters productive lives."[4] One source of chronic pain is arthritis.

Pain Involves the Physical

The physical aspect of pain involves the three parts of our nervous system: the peripheral nerves, spinal cord and brain. Peripheral nerves start at your spine and extend out to the skin and muscles. These nerves branch and become smaller as they go to the farthest reaches of fingers and toes. When an injury or problem occurs, the peripheral nerves are stimulated. Nociceptors (no-sih-SEP-turs) are receptors located at the end of nerve fibers that stimulate the person to withdraw from sharp objects, electrical current, or heat and cold (about

10 degrees C above or below skin temperature).[5] Nociceptors could be called pain receptors; they recognize potential and actual tissue damage to the body. Millions of nociceptors reside in skin, bones, muscles and joints as well as protective membranes of internal organs. The largest numbers of nociceptors are found in areas prone to injury such as fingers and toes.

When nerve fibers carry pain messages to the spinal cord, chemicals called neurotransmitters are released. These neurotransmitters help move the messages to the spinal cord where specialized nerve cells filter the message. Messages carrying news of severe pain or the chance to avoid pain speed up to the brain. The body withdraws or jerks quickly to avoid the pain and damage. Less intense messages from a chronic problem would be blocked out and priority would be given to the acute injury message. In addition, chemicals released at the spinal level may intensify the pain signal. At the site of the injury, an inflammatory reaction occurs with symptoms of swelling, redness, warmth and additional pain. This reaction sounds like a negative situation. However, it promotes healing by increasing blood flow and bringing the body's defenses to that site.

Pain messages arrive at the thalamus, "a sorting and switching station located deep inside the brain. The thalamus forwards the message simultaneously to three specialized regions of the brain: the physical sensation region (somatosensory cortex), the emotional feeling region (limbic system) and the thinking region (frontal cortex)."[6] Using all these functions, the brain can identify "where" the pain is occurring and send a message to motor muscles to withdraw from the painful stimuli. Also, an emotional and thinking response follows.

The "basic sensation of hurtfulness, or pain, occurs at the level of the thalamus" in the brain.[7] The brain can also send messages to body cells, which release natural painkillers (endorphins and enkephalins.) Doctors believe these messages from the brain to body cells influence our perception of pain, the emotional and psychological aspect. Many of the treatments and interventions recommended by doctors interfere with pain messages and result in decreased or no pain.

Pain Involves the Emotional and Psychological

How a person interprets pain and tolerates pain can be affected by the person's culture. Culture is defined as "the beliefs, values and practices shared by a group or community of people. This learned behavior is passed down from one generation to the next."[8] Upbringing, attitude, memories of past pain experiences, beliefs and values contribute to a person's responses to pain. Pain results in emotions that are expressed or suppressed. Stoic patients suffer in silence, rarely complaining. Persons who express their pain speak up about it and may display moaning and crying.

Symptoms of Acute Pain

Acute pain serves as a protection and warning that injury exists. Acute pain occurs for a short duration and usually a cause can be found. For example, a person undergoing surgery expects some pain to result. Surgeons write prescriptions for pain medications because they don't want their patients to suffer needlessly.

Physical response to acute pain involves the "fight or flight" response. This response allows the body to run away from danger or fight to protect itself. The body releases chemicals called catecholamines, which send the blood away from non-vital organs to the vital organs. This causes the heart, lungs, and skeletal muscles to receive increased blood circulation. The rate of a person's breathing and heart rate increase, while muscle tension increases. The person is primed for action. This same response occurs when a person experiences acute pain. Even though there's no external threat for the person to fight or to run away from, the body reacts the same way. Because the circulation has been diverted to vital organs, the person suffering acute pain will have a dry mouth and may experience nausea and vomiting. This occurs because the body's blood supply has been temporarily moved away from the gastrointestinal (GI) system by the catecholamines. The person's skin may become pale and cool. People suffering from acute pain may find themselves anxious. Anxiety has been defined as "worry or uneasiness about what may happen."[9] People display pain non-verbally by facial expressions such as frowning and grimacing, biting their lips, and clenching their teeth. The facial expressions are the basis for one of the pain assessment scales, the Wong-Baker Faces Pain Rating Scale. After the person's acute pain is relieved, the person will relax and the physical symptoms disappear.

Chronic Pain

When pain persists past the time of healing, medical people describe it as chronic. The Latin word chronos means "time." Chronic pain can be intermittent or continuous and accomplishes nothing. For people with arthritis, chronic pain occurs due to inflammation in joints and damage to joint tissues. Researchers explain chronic pain using the word *sensitization*. Consider a car stereo turned up to maximum volume so the music is loud and distorted. If sensitization occurs, the pain message becomes amplified, distorted, and out of proportion. The sensitization itself can cause inflammatory changes. The nociceptors become extra sensitive and respond too quickly, too easily and at too great a response. The spinal cord, brain and all pain-processing centers in the body become affected. "Chronic pain especially can set up a perpetual state of physical and mental tension, and unrelenting stress is like running all of your systems as hard and fast as they will go. Eventually, the systems begin to break down."[10]

Chronic pain researchers are studying the science of sensitization with plans to identify better treatments.[11]

Symptoms of Chronic Pain

Chronic pain serves no useful function. Unlike acute pain, there's no impending danger to avoid. The symptoms of "fight or flight" that the person displayed when experiencing acute pain quickly wear the body down and the symptoms may no longer be obvious. Patients dealing with chronic pain may be irritable. If pain is unrelieved, these people can sink into depression and despair. This person could then lose his/her outgoing and caring attitude toward others and only worry about "himself/herself." Appetite for food may either increase or decrease. Sleep habits may be disturbed and decreased. Relationships may suffer as the person withdraws from family and friends. He/she may worry about family finances, which medical costs will adversely affect.

Successful Management of Pain

Management of pain begins with an assessment of the pain by a physician or a nurse practitioner. The doctor may ask for specific information such as history of the pain event. Important information includes date, time and the events surrounding the onset of pain. Did the knee pain begin after a fall on the ski slope last November? Did the knee pain begin without any known injury? The healthcare provider will want to know what improves or worsens the pain. A list of x-rays and tests and their results may be needed. The doctor will want the person's medical history, including a list of allergies and medications, whether prescribed, herbal or over-the-counter. The doctor may have the patient keep an around-the-clock diary with activities and associated pain levels.[12] A physical examination will probably be done. Additional lab work or x-rays may be ordered by the physician to complete the pain assessment. During discussions of pain, doctors and nurses will ask patients to rate their pain. One method is to give the pain a number on a scale of one to ten with "one" being almost none and "ten" being unbearable. Another method of rating pain is to use the Wong-Baker Faces Pain Rating Scale. These six faces demonstrate a range from no pain to worst pain.

Treatment of Acute Pain

Treatment of acute pain is mainly accomplished by analgesic drugs such as nonsteroidal anti-inflammatory drugs including aspirin, acetaminophen (Tylenol) and narcotics. For selected post-operative acute pain, nerve block techniques can extend the pain-free postoperative time frame. For example, a shoulder block for post-operative shoulder pain and epidural lumbar block for post-operative pain after total hip or knee replacements are two techniques used to avoid acute pain after surgery. Other treatments such as applications of heat and cold, splinting or casting may be used to relieve acute pain.

Treatment of Chronic Pain

Physicians prefer their patients to be pain free. However, doctors face the concerns that patients can become addicted or habituated to narcotics when those drugs are used for chronic pain. Also, patients who use narcotics for pain control could take too large a dose, which is called an "overdose." Overdose amounts of narcotics slow a person's respirations, lower blood pressure and can cause death. Also, long-term usage of narcotics can cause problems of pain control whenever the person needs narcotics to control acute pain after surgery or injury. Because the person's body is accustomed to large doses of narcotics, pain relief may be difficult to achieve. Physicians and organizations such as the Arthritis Foundation and various pain foundations focus on coping with arthritis and other causes of chronic pain. Because people are complex creatures with multiple dimensions, successful coping strategies must deal with physical, mental, spiritual, and emotional aspects of humans.

Insomnia

"Miserable" would describe a sleepless, full-of-pain night. A person who is tossing and turning wonders if his pain is caused by something worse than arthritis. That person's night lasts forever. Seventy-five percent of people with arthritis/rheumatic disorders experience sleep problems.[13] People suffering from osteoarthritis may suffer from unrefreshing sleep, pain and fatigue symptoms. "Light, restless sleep is common among patients with osteoarthritis."[14] People dealing with rheumatoid arthritis may find sleep disturbances cause fatigue and pain, and may lead to anxiety and depression. Lack of sleep causes decreased energy, lack of concentration, depressed mood and greater risks of accidents. When a person can't sleep, he/she can become irritable and relationships can suffer. Work performance may be affected. Pain seems worse because of lack of sleep.[15]

Scientists describe normal sleep in five stages. Stages 1 through 4 are progressively deeper stages of non-rapid eye movement (NREM) sleep. When people fall asleep, they start at stage 1. As sleep deepens, they progress through

---

States and Stages of Sleep

Reprinted with permission from the National Sleep Foundation

NREM: 75% of night*	As we begin to fall asleep, we enter NREM, which is composed of Stages 1–4.
Stage 1	Light sleep; between being awake and entering sleep
Stage 2	Onset of sleep, becoming disengaged with the environment, breathing and heart rate are regular and body temperature goes down.
Stage 3 and 4	Deepest and most restorative sleep; blood pressure drops, breathing slower, energy regained; and hormones are released for growth and development.
REM: 25% of night	First occurs about 90 minutes after falling asleep and increasing over later part of night; necessary for providing energy to brain and body; brain is active and dreams occur as eyes dart back and forth; bodies become immobile and relaxed; muscles shut down, breathing and heart rate may become irregular; important to daytime performance and may contribute to memory consolidation.

Time spent in these states and stages of sleep varies by age.

---

stages 2, 3 and 4, with stage 4 being the deepest, most restful sleep. Stage 5 is rapid eye movement (REM) sleep in which dreams occur. REM sleep normally occurs about 90 minutes after a person falls asleep and should account for 25 percent of a person's sleep time.

Sleep problems combined with aging and chronic health problems equal sleep disorders for many older people. Research shows people need the same amount of sleep as they age that they needed as young adults.[16] As people age, they tend to spend less time in the deeper stages of sleep, stages 3 and 4. Scientists believe many older people progress through the stages of sleep more quickly and enter REM sleep sooner. Studies suggest that aging people take longer to fall asleep. "One study found that after age 65, 13% of men and 36% of women reported taking more than 30 minutes to fall asleep."[17] Among the elderly, sleep tends to be lighter and interrupted by frequent trips to the bathroom. Researchers believe decreased levels of melatonin and growth hormone in aging people contribute to poor quality sleep. Body temperature cycle changes also cause increased sleep problems. Lack of exercise and decreased mental activity in older people also may complicate sleep difficulties. These situations contribute to lack of rest, daytime sleepiness and nighttime insomnia.

Another sleep stealer is called movement disorders such as restless legs syndrome (RLS) and periodic limb movements disorder (PLMD). Restless legs syndrome (RLS) causes constant leg movements when the person is at rest. People dealing with RLS describe their symptoms as an "uncomfortable sensation in the foot, calf or upper leg that feels like something is crawling or moving inside the limbs, or a tickling or aching deep inside them. This sensation is yoked with a compulsion to move the legs. Movement resolves the symptoms, but the syndrome is unrelenting. Within seconds or minutes, the sensations return. If the legs are not moved, they frequently jump involuntarily. Since rest brings on symptoms, and walking offers relief, suffers are often called nightwalkers."[18] The cause of RLS is unknown, with possible culprits being anemia caused by iron deficiency, kidney dialysis, neuropathy or pregnancy. Symptoms for PLMD include periodic leg movements and jerks during sleep, as often as every 20 to 40 seconds. These leg kicks wake up the person afflicted and the spouse or bed partner. A trip to the primary care physician and/or neurologist will bring relief for both these movement disorders. Medications prescribed by these doctors should control both RLS and PLMD as well as restore rest.

The newspaper columnist physician, Dr. Peter Gott, shares comments from his readers who recommend placing a bar of unscented soap between the sheets where the person sleeps at night as a treatment for RLS. No one, including Dr. Gott, can explain how or why a bar of soap between their sheets would help decrease the symptoms of RLS. However, some people swear this safe and inexpensive practice decreased their RLS symptoms. One person contributed these comments: "Did this sound ridiculous? You bet. But I gave it a try. Did it work? Yes, indeed. I haven't had a cramp since. The proper technique is simple. Unwrap a fresh bar of soap (don't use Dove or Dial) and discard the wrapper. It doesn't need to be a huge, bath-size bar; even the small bars common in hotels work for most people. Then place the unwrapped bar directly under the bottom sheet or on the bed where the legs are usually located. That's it."[19]

Sleep apnea and snoring contribute to sleep problems. Forty percent of the adult population snores. Sleep apnea occurs when a partial blockage of the airway happens during sleep. Twenty-eight percent of men and 24 percent of women over the age of 65 experience sleep apnea. Symptoms of sleep apnea include "loud snoring punctuated by multiple, nightly brief episodes of breathing cessation."[20] Being overweight contributes to the incidence of sleep apnea. Diagnosis of sleep apnea involves an overnight sleep study with non-invasive monitoring. Treatment for mild sleep apnea may involve recommendations to lose weight, sleep lying on one's side, and avoid alcohol and sedatives. For moderate to severe sleep apnea, CPAP (continuous positive airway pressure) is the treatment of choice. A CPAP face mask is attached to a machine that blows moist air onto the person's nose and airway, helping keep the internal airway open.[21] People with treated sleep apnea report that when they use the CPAP machine at night, they wake up the next morning feeling more rested.

The National Sleep Foundation gives recommendations people can use to overcome insomnia problems.[22] Another help for sleep problems would be the

Healthy Tips for Better Sleep
(reprinted courtesy of the National Sleep Foundation)

1. Maintain a regular bed and wake time schedule including weekends.
Our sleep-wake cycle is regulated by a "circadian clock" in our brain and the body's need to balance both sleep time and wake time. A regular waking time in the morning strengthens the circadian function and can help with sleep onset at night. That is also why it is important to keep a regular bedtime and wake-time, even on the weekends when there is the temptation to sleep in.

2. Establish a regular, relaxing bedtime routine such as soaking in a hot bath or hot tub and then reading a book or listening to soothing music.
A relaxing, routine activity right before bedtime conducted away from bright lights helps separate your sleep time from activities that can cause excitement, stress or anxiety which can make it more difficult to fall asleep, get sound and deep sleep or remain asleep. Avoid arousing activities before bedtime like working, paying bills, engaging in competitive games or family problem-solving. Some studies suggest that soaking in hot water (such as a hot tub or bath) before retiring to bed can ease the transition into deeper sleep, but it should be done early enough that you are no longer sweating or over-heated. If you are unable to avoid tension and stress, it may be helpful to learn relaxation therapy from a trained professional. Finally, avoid exposure to bright light before bedtime because it signals the neurons that help control the sleep-wake cycle that it is time to awaken, not to sleep.

3. Create a sleep-conducive environment that is dark, quiet, comfortable and cool.
Design your sleep environment to establish the conditions you need for sleep—cool, quiet, dark, comfortable and free of interruptions. Also make your bedroom reflective of the value you place on sleep. Check your room for noise or other distractions, including a bed partner's sleep disruptions such as snoring, light, and a dry or hot environment. Consider using blackout curtains, eye shades, ear plugs, "white noise," humidifiers, fans and other devices.

4. Sleep on a comfortable mattress and pillows.
Make sure your mattress is comfortable and supportive. The one you have been using for years may have exceeded its life expectancy—about 9 or 10 years for most good quality mattresses. Have comfortable pillows and make the room attractive and inviting for sleep but also free of allergens that might affect you and objects that might cause you to slip or fall if you have to get up during the night.

5. Use your bedroom only for sleep and sex.
It is best to take work materials, computers and televisions out of the sleeping environment. Use your bed only for sleep and sex to strengthen the association between bed and sleep. If you associate a particular activity or item with anxiety about sleeping, omit it from your bedtime routine. For example, if looking at a bedroom clock makes you anxious about how much time you have before you must get up, move the clock out of sight. Do not engage in activities that cause you anxiety and prevent you from sleeping.

(continued on next page)

(Healthy Tips for Better Sleep, *continued***)**

6. Finish eating at least 2–3 hours before your regular bedtime.

Eating or drinking too much may make you less comfortable when settling down for bed. It is best to avoid a heavy meal too close to bedtime. Also, spicy foods may cause heartburn, which leads to difficulty falling asleep and discomfort during the night. Try to restrict fluids close to bedtime to prevent nighttime awakenings to go to the bathroom, though some people find milk or herbal, non-caffeinated teas to be soothing and a helpful part of a bedtime routine.

7. Exercise regularly. It is best to complete your workout at least a few hours before bedtime.

In general, exercising regularly makes it easier to fall asleep and contributes to sounder sleep. However, exercising sporadically or right before going to bed will make falling asleep more difficult. In addition to making us more alert, our body temperature rises during exercise, and takes as much as 6 hours to begin to drop. A cooler body temperature is associated with sleep onset.... Finish your exercise at least 3 hours before bedtime. Late afternoon exercise is the perfect way to help you fall asleep at night.

8. Avoid caffeine (e.g., coffee, tea, soft drinks, chocolate) close to bedtime. It can keep you awake.

Caffeine is a stimulant, which means it can produce an alerting effect. Caffeine products, such as coffee, tea, colas and chocolate, remain in the body on average from 3 to 5 hours, but they can affect some people up to 12 hours later. Even if you do not think caffeine affects you, it may be disrupting and changing the quality of your sleep. Avoiding caffeine within 6–8 hours of going to bed can help improve sleep quality.

9. Avoid nicotine (e.g. cigarettes, tobacco products). Used close to bedtime, it can lead to poor sleep.

Nicotine is also a stimulant. Smoking before bed makes it more difficult to fall asleep. When smokers go to sleep, they experience withdrawal symptoms from nicotine, which also cause sleep problems. Nicotine can cause difficulty falling asleep, problems waking in the morning, and may also cause nightmares. Difficulty sleeping is just one more reason to quit smoking. And never smoke in bed or when sleepy!

10. Avoid alcohol close to bedtime.

Although many people think of alcohol as a sedative, it actually disrupts sleep, causing nighttime awakenings. Consuming alcohol leads to a night of less restful sleep.

If you have sleep problems...

Use a sleep diary and talk to your doctor. Note what type of sleep problem is affecting your sleep or if you are sleepy when you wish to be awake and alert. Try these tips and record your sleep and sleep-related activities in a sleep diary. If problems continue, discuss the sleep diary with your doctor. There may be an underlying cause and you will want to be properly diagnosed. Your doctor will help treat the problem or may refer you to a sleep specialist.

doctor who, after reviewing health status and medications, may prescribe a sleep aid, pain pill or anti-depressant drug. Several possibilities for helping people achieve more restful sleep exists.

The Three M's—Massage, Meditation and Music Therapy

Coping with arthritis successfully involves caring for physical, emotional and mental aspects of a person. Emotional dimension involves how a person feels. This can be achieved through activities such as massage and music therapy. Meditation treats a person's mental dimension.

Massage

Mrs. H. swears that her monthly massage increases her flexibility and decreases her arthritic pain, especially in her neck and shoulder areas. She makes her monthly appointment and considers it a treat to herself. People with arthritis will find the benefits of massage includes stretching tight muscles and improving flexibility while decreasing pain, stress and depression.[23]

Dr. Tiffany Fields established the Touch Research Institutes (TRI) at the University of Miami medical school in 1992, and over 90 studies have been conducted into the physical and emotional benefits of massage. Massage therapy benefits people of all ages, beginning with premature babies. The babies who were gently massaged daily "gained 47 percent more weight, became more socially responsive, and were discharged 6 days earlier."[24] People benefit from massage therapy because it "reduces stress hormones, alleviates depressive symptoms, reduces pain, and improves immune function."[25]

Does massage benefit children with mild to moderate juvenile arthritis? The study group parents massaged their child for 15 minutes daily for 30 days while the control group children engaged in relaxation therapy. The study group children suffered less anxiety and their stress hormone levels measured at a lower level. The children, their parents and doctors all reported the children experienced less pain when compared to the control group during the 30-day period.[26]

One study compared elderly volunteers giving massages to infants vs. the volunteers receiving a massage. The study group gave massages to the babies, while the control group received massages themselves. After a month of giving massages to the babies, the study group reported less anxiety, lower pulse rates, and decreased cortisol levels. They experienced improved mood, felt better about themselves and made more positive social contacts.[27] The volunteers who received the massages themselves (the control group) had positive results but at a lesser level. Ask any grandparent if they would agree that giving a massage to a baby is better than receiving a massage.

Pain therapists have learned that active tactile stimulation (rubbing) decreases the intensity of pain experienced by patients. This decreased pain intensity may last from minutes to hours.[28] This pain-relieving rubbing could be harnessed in "do it yourself massage."[29] The Arthritis Foundation recommends learning how from a massage therapist and enjoying the double benefits. "The part you are massaging will feel better, and so will your hands that are doing the work."[30] Tips for a good self-massage can be found in *The Arthritis Foundation's Guide to Alternative Therapies.*

Massage is defined as "manual or mechanical manipulation of parts of the body, as by rubbing, kneading, slapping or the like, used to promote circulation, relax muscles, etc."[31] Massage has been practiced in many cultures through the ages. The ancient healing tradition of India, ayurveda, originated over 5,000 years ago. This massage, which involves warm oil and herbs, is a small portion of the Indian detoxification and rejuvenation program called panchakarma.[32] Old Chinese records from three thousand years ago discuss the use of massage. Other oriental types of massage, including Shiatsu (Japanese) and Thai acupressure techniques, will be discussed in chapter 10 with acupuncture therapy. Swedish/European massage involves stroking and kneading muscle and skin with oils or lotions. This technique is easily recognizable to many who've enjoyed a massage.[33] This type of massage can be gentle for those suffering from pain or vigorous for those wanting a vigorous massage.

Deep-tissue massage uses more vigorous technique useful for low back pain and some arthritic joint pain. Strong pressure, often against the grain of the muscles, relaxes muscle and deep tissue. Trigger-point therapy occurs when the therapist uses deep finger pressure on the specific pain points, where the knotted-up tissue is found. Both deep-tissue massage and trigger-point therapies can cause pain while it's being done and isn't for everyone.

Massage, once considered a luxurious spa treatment, has become an approved method of coping with arthritis by the Arthritis Foundation.[34] The Arthritis Foundation recommends people talk to their doctor and ask if massage is safe for them. Other suggestions from the Arthritis Foundation include: avoiding massage during arthritis flare episodes or during times of fever and infection, and avoiding massage over open sores. Massage may cause a person to experience peace and contentment or strong feelings such as sadness. Another suggestion involves being comfortable with the massage therapist. The person receiving the massage should feel comfortable and safe. If that person feels threatened, she should speak up or stop the session and leave.[35]

Reflexology techniques have been practiced for thousands of years in China and Egypt.[36] The therapist puts pressure on specific areas of the foot, hands, or ears believing that it will affect the entire body. This pressure "promotes a response from an area far removed from the tissue stimulated via the nervous system and acupuncture meridians."[37] Reflexology achieves "total body relaxation leading to the balancing of all internal and external body systems; improving circulation via stimulation to the nervous and subtle energy system."[38] Therapists may use oil or lotion while massaging and putting pressure on the specific area. Persons wanting pain relief in the hip, knee and lower leg would find the outer, posterior portion of their foot being rubbed. The modern version practiced in the U.S. is based on the idea that energy channels originating in the foot are connected to specific areas of the body. No studies involving reflexology and arthritic pain have been done. The warnings regarding reflexology involve talking to a person's doctor before using reflexology, especially if the patient has recent or healing fractures, gout, or unhealed wounds. People with arthritic feet and ankles or severe circulatory problems in feet and legs should also consult their doctor before using reflexology.[39]

Meditation

Meditation treats a person's mental dimension. The earliest religions, both Eastern and Western, included meditation as a way to gain peace, insight and enlightenment. The verb *meditate* has been defined as "self-regulation of attention to suspend the normal stream of consciousness."[40] While practicing meditation, people sit quietly, comfortably and focus the mind. The goal of meditation is to reach of state of "thoughtless awareness, during which a person is passively aware of sensations at the present moment."[41]

Techniques such as saying a sound repeatedly or visualizing an image help the person focus his/her attention. Transcendental meditation uses a mantra (a sound, word or phrase) spoken aloud or silently and repeated. Through this single focus, the person reaches the state of "relaxed awareness." Visualization or imagery involves focusing on an image. The person using this technique might visualize himself sitting in the sunshine on a beautiful beach, pain free and relaxed. The scene visualized will be unique to each person involved and can be beneficial. Two major American universities have done work on meditation in terms of "mindfulness," which is defined as "learning to pay attention to what is happening to you from moment to moment."[42] Both the Mind/Body Medical Institute at Harvard University in Massachusetts and Center for Mindfulness in Medicine, Health Care, and Society at the University of Massachusetts use the term *mindfulness* and other universities follow their lead.

Studies have documented that meditation can decrease stress and relieve pain. A study of 90 chronic pain patients who learned mindfulness meditation in the University of Massachusetts program found "significant reductions" in the patient's perception of pain, anxiety, and depression.[43]

The Mind/Body Institute at Harvard found "chronic pain patients reduce their physician visits by 36%" after practicing meditation. People suffering from insomnia benefited from meditation. One hundred percent of the insomnia patients reported sleep improvement and 91 percent were able to eliminate or reduce medication use.[44]

A 2005 study looked at the Mindful-Based Stress Reduction (MBSR, a combination of meditation, yoga and relaxation exercise) program for 63 rheumatoid arthritis patients. "When the study began, both groups showed moderate levels of disease activity and above normal levels of psychological distress. Two months later, there was no change in disease activity, but the MBSR group showed a 20 percent reduction in psychological distress compared to the control group. At the end of the six month observation period, there was a 33 percent reduction in psychological distress, an 11 percent decrease in rheumatoid arthritis disease activity and a 46 percent decrease in erythrocyte sedimentation rate (indicating less inflammation) in the MBSR group compared to the control group, all of which were statistically significant."[45]

Music Therapy

Music has been considered a "healing influence which could affect health and behavior" ever since the writings of Aristotle and Plato.[46] According to the American Music Therapy Association, music can do the following: "promote wellness, manage stress, alleviate pain, express feelings, enhance memory, improve communication, and promote physical rehabilitation."[47]

Multiple studies have shown that listening to music decreases people's anxiety levels and their perception of pain. A study conducted by Florida-based nurses and published in the *Journal of Advanced Nursing* examined 66 older people who suffer from osteoarthritis. One group, the study group, listened to music for 20 minutes a day while the control group sat quietly without music. The study group who listened to music reported a 66 percent decrease in pain while the researchers measured a 50 percent reduction in pain (the music listeners perceived their paid level dropping more than the researchers could verify). The researchers speculate that music helps the body release endorphins, the body's painkiller.[48] Other benefits include decreasing blood pressure, heart rate, respiratory rate and oxygen consumption.

Another study done by nurses compared 60 women ages 25 to 45 who underwent laparoscopic gynecological surgery. One group of patients listened to music and the other patients listened to a blank CD before surgery. These patients received the same pre-operative medications and treatments. Both groups of patients had significantly lower anxiety scores and lower post-operative pain scores. The music group had "significantly lower pre-operative respiratory rate and used significantly fewer doses" of pain medication post-operatively. The researchers concluded that "giving patients periods of peaceful, undisturbed rest before and after surgery is beneficial with or without music."[49]

While many people enjoy and can benefit from music in their personal activities, music therapy as a profession has specific functions, which include assessing a patient's emotional and mental coping, physical health and communication skills. The therapist then designs music sessions for individual or group sessions based on the needs recognized. Activities include listening to music, song writing, performing and learning from music.

To harness this pain-reducing option, each person should choose the type of music he enjoys. One day a person may want the music pouring out of the speakers to be classical and the next day the listener's favorite jazz saxophone may wail. Joy and sorrow can be experienced with the emotions music brings out. The person should sit back and enjoy the music, knowing that stress and pain will decrease.

Doctors and scientists search for cures for pain. Meanwhile, organizations like the National Chronic Pain Outreach Association send a message, "You can lead a fulfilling life despite the pain."[50]

7

Eating Healthy:
Diet and Nutrition

"If we could give each person the right amount of nourishment and exercise, not too little and not too much, we would have found the safest way to health."[1]

We Americans bounce from one diet to the next, searching for the magic diet that will let us eat what we want and be healthy and slim. Low-fat, high-fat, low-carb, high-carb diets abound and all promise health and nutrition. Meanwhile, obesity reaches epidemic proportions. Confusion reigns and people throw up their hands and eat what they want whether it's good for them or not.

Food Provides Fuel and Pleasure

Food serves as fuel and provides building blocks that our body uses to build, maintain, and then repair aging tissues. Every day at different times, individuals make decisions on what food/fuel they consume, often without considering the long-term results. When people choose healthy foods, they provide health and nutrition for their bodies. People eating food lacking in good nutrition may suffer long-term results.

People choose what they eat for many reasons, including pleasure. People eat foods they enjoy. Personal preference refers to the type of food people like, whether sweet or salty, hot and peppery, or spicy curry flavors. Comfort foods bring to mind Grandma's cream of tomato soup that she fixed on cold winter days. Comfort foods bring an emotional response to the person enjoying it. People eat out of habit, often eating the same food for breakfast and simplifying the early morning rush to work and school. Food often means a social event and many social occasions involve food whether at a public restaurant or at someone's home. Convenience factors into busy working people's lives when they return home after work and don't have the desire or energy to cook elaborate meals. Food involves our values when foods are avoided or included because of religious, cultural or political beliefs. People choose what they eat for many reasons.

Diet and Arthritis

A diet that will prevent or treat rheumatoid arthritis and osteoarthritis is still a mystery. People have tried some exotic, crazy diets trying to find relief from their pain with varying success. "As recently as two decades ago, many experts believed that no bona fide relationships between foods and arthritis even existed. Most claims about food and arthritis were widely considered to be folklore or forms of quackery."[2]

Research into diet and how foods affect arthritis symptoms is in its infancy. Many factors complicate this research. Arthritis symptoms appear to be unpredictable, sometimes flaring for no apparent reason and then disappearing for a long time. Does diet directly affect a person's arthritis? Do weight gains or loss affect a person's symptoms? Can the placebo effect, a person's expectations that a diet or treatment will help, explain improvements?

"Nutritional research is still in its infancy as far as understanding how plant chemicals and antioxidants work individually and in concert to prevent and treat diseases such as arthritis."[3] Three areas of food being studied for links to arthritis include vitamins and minerals, omega-3 fatty acids, and how food allergies may affect arthritis symptoms.* Present recommendations include "grounding yourself in good health with an overall nutritious diet rather than chasing food fads for an arthritis fix."[4]

Researchers at Tufts University in Boston conducted a study to answer the question, "Should folks with RA increase their caloric intake to make up for their increased resting energy expenditure?" This study involved forty women, twenty healthy and twenty with RA. The results showed that "even though their basal metabolism is revved up, people with rheumatoid arthritis tend to be less active than people without—which reduces their caloric needs."[5] The researchers recommend that persons with RA eat healthy and try to add physical activity to their day. "Such a regime will help them improve their physical function and quality of life and maintain a healthy weight."[6]

Nutrition and Healthful Eating

"Your skin, which seems to have covered you since birth, is replaced entirely by new cells every seven years. The fat beneath your skin is not the same fat

*The latest research and recommendations from the Arthritis Foundation will be found at http://www. arthritis.org.

that was there a year ago. Your oldest red blood cell is only 120 days old, and the entire lining of your digestive tract is renewed every 3 days. To maintain your 'self' you must continually replenish from foods, the energy and nutrients you deplete in maintaining your body."[7]

The body of a person weighing 150 pounds contains approximately 90 pounds of water, 30 pounds of fat, and 30 pounds of compounds made of protein, carbohydrates, minerals and vitamins.[8] Not surprisingly, the substances the body uses to provide energy, maintain life, and repair tissues include those same nutrients: carbohydrates, fat, protein, vitamins, minerals and water.

Carbohydrates provide half the energy the body uses. Excess carbohydrates are stored in the liver as glycogen until needed and then the body converts glycogen back to glucose, the ready-to-use energy of the body. Dietitians and physicians recommend eating complex carbohydrates. People trying to improve their nutrition can do so by choosing whole-grain products when they choose breads, cereals, pasta and rice.

Carbohydrates containing table sugar, honey, syrups, and jellies add calories and flavor but little nutrition and should be included in small quantities only. Candy lovers won't want to hear that advice.

Fats or lipids provide "the body with continuous fuel supply, keep it warm, and protect it from mechanical shock; their component fatty acids serve as starting materials for important hormonal regulators."[9] The omega-3 fatty acid being studied is an essential fatty acid called linolenic acid. This nutrient cannot be made by the body but must be obtained from food. Healthy sources of fats include vegetable oils such as canola and olive oils, certain fish, and nuts.

Proteins function as the building blocks for bone, ligaments, and tendons. Proteins act as enzymes and enable the body to break down worn structures and rebuild new ones. Proteins act as hormones (such as insulin) and as antibodies, which protect against disease. Complete proteins include meats, poultry, fish, eggs and milk products. The vegetable sources of proteins, seeds, nuts, legumes, tofu and grains, provide incomplete proteins. If a person eats the right amounts of vegetable protein sources, the body can convert them into complete proteins.

Major nutrients needed in a healthy diet include vitamins, minerals, and water. Vitamins "assist enzymes which release energy from carbohydrates, fats, and proteins."[10] Minerals function in many roles within the body, including the balance of water. Water makes up 60 percent of the adult body and an even larger amount of a child's body. "Water becomes the fluid in which all life processes occur."[11]

"Healthy eating does not mean that you can never eat your favorite foods again, or that you have to 'diet' or buy 'special' foods. Rather, it means learning to make healthier choices in the foods we eat, preparing it in new or different ways, and eating in moderation."[12]

Elaine, a 52-year-old female who exercises fewer than 30 minutes most days of the week, would find her daily recommended calorie count at 1,600. Like many other Americans, Elaine admits she eats too much meat and refined carbohydrates, but not enough fruits and vegetables. As a working woman, Elaine recognizes her best diet happens when she packs her own snack and lunch instead of eating in the cafeteria at work. When she pre-plans and packs her own food, she takes a small entrée or whole-wheat sandwich, and a couple of different vegetables such as carrot sticks, small tomato or celery sticks. Dessert will be an apple or handful of grapes. Elaine also recognizes she likes soda and her diet isn't perfect yet. She has consciously made choices that improve her diet by adding more fruits and vegetables and more whole-grain breads and pastas while decreasing the amount of fried foods she eats.

MyPyramid

Arthritis Foundation recommendations for nutrition follow the United States Department of Agriculture (USDA) MyPyramid. The 2005 Dietary Guidelines for Americans recognizes that a person's age and activity level affect food requirements. Important parts of MyPyramid include activity or exercise, moderation, portion size, and variety in the foods chosen. MyPyramid encourages citizens to improve their eating habits and lifestyle.[13]

For healthy individuals, the MyPyramid recommendations can improve nutrition and health. Persons with chronic health problems should consult with their physician before making dietary changes. Individuals trying to lose weight should consult their physician about recommended calorie intake.

The program recommends 5 ounces of grains daily. At least three ounces of the five should be whole grains. Whole-grain foods include brown rice, oatmeal, popcorn, whole-grain breads, whole-grain crackers or pasta, and wild rice. Refined grains include white breads, white rice, crackers, cornbread, grits, and white pastas. Check labels for the words *whole grain* or *whole wheat*. One ounce of grain equals one slice bread, 1 cup ready-to-eat cereal, or ½ cup cooked rice, pasta or cooked cereal.

Doctors believe dietary fiber helps prevent high cholesterol and heart disease. Whole-grain fiber helps prevent constipation and diverticulosis. Several B vitamins found in whole grains, such as niacin, thiamin, riboflavin, and folate play important roles in metabolism. Whole grains provide a feeling of satisfaction and fullness while containing fewer calories.[14]

The MyPyramid program also suggests people eat plenty of vegetables. Elaine should eat 2 cups of vegetables daily. Over the period of a week she should eat 2 cups of dark green vegetables, 1½ cups orange vegetables, 2½ cups dried beans and peas that have been cooked, 2½ cups starchy vegetables, and 5½ cups other vegetables. One cup of raw or cooked vegetables or vegetable juice, or 2 cups of raw leafy greens can be considered as 1 cup. Elaine finds a wide variety of vegetables that she likes: dark green vegetables (broccoli, spinach, raw leafy greens including several types of lettuce), orange vegetables (carrots, sweet potato, pumpkin, and winter squash), dry beans and legumes (also included in the meat/protein section), starchy vegetables (corn, green peas, and white potatoes), and other vegetables (cabbage, cauliflower, celery, cucumbers, peppers, onions, tomatoes, green and red peppers, and zucchini squash).

As a group, vegetables provide nutrients such as potassium, dietary fiber, folate (folic acid), and vitamins A, C, and E. According to MyPyramid.gov, a diet rich in fruits and vegetables "may reduce the risk for stroke and cardiovascular disease, ... type 2 diabetes, ... certain cancers such as mouth, stomach and colon-rectum cancer."[15]

Fruits are also part of a healthy diet. Elaine should eat 1½ cups of fruit daily. The recommendation is to "go easy on fruit juices" because of added sugar. Healthy choices of fruits include apples, oranges, bananas, grapes, grapefruit, pears, strawberries, and melons of all kinds. Canned fruits such as fruit cocktail, pineapple, mandarin oranges and pears provide another source of fruit. Elaine can enjoy an easy-to-take snack of dried fruits (consider ½ cup of dried fruit as a serving) on her most hectic day if she plans ahead.

Fruits provide many nutrients such as potassium, vitamin C, folate (folic acid), and dietary fiber without added fat, sodium, or calories. Nutritionists recommend fruits as part of a healthy diet that "may reduce risk for stroke and perhaps other cardiovascular diseases, ... type 2 diabetes, ... certain cancers, such as mouth, stomach, and colon-rectum cancer."[16]

The MyPyramid section limits fats and oils. Elaine's allowance includes 5 tsp of oil daily. Fish, nuts, and healthy vegetable oils provide fats and oils.

Oils important in the diet contain "essential fatty acids," which can only be gotten from foods. MyPyramid.gov recommends polyunsaturated and monounsaturated oils as the more healthy oils. Because oils and solid fats contain 120 calories per tablespoon, and small amounts add up to large calories, "the amount of oil consumed needs to be limited to balance total calorie intake."[17]

Milk is another key part of the pyramid. Elaine should have 3 cups of low-fat or fat-free milk or milk products daily. One cup of milk or yogurt, 1½ oz of natural cheese, or 2 oz processed cheese are considered equal amounts. Low-fat or fat-free milk is recommended.

Milk and milk products provide calcium, which the body uses to build bones and teeth. Doctors recommend calcium and vitamin D to help prevent and treat osteoporosis. Potassium found in milk may help prevent high blood pressure.[18]

Meat and beans are the final component. Elaine should eat a total of 5 oz of meat and beans daily. Protein foods included in this group will be meat, poultry, fish, dry beans or peas, eggs, nuts, and seeds. This food group provides proteins, several B vitamins, vitamin E, iron, zinc, and magnesium.

The body uses proteins broken down into amino acids to build muscle, bones, cartilage, skin, and blood. Amino acids make up enzymes, hormones, antibodies, and help in fluid and electrolyte balance.[19] The body uses vitamins found in meats and beans in a variety of functions.

Diet and Healthful Lifestyle

A person who wants to be healthy adds healthy food and exercise to the daily routine.

"During 1999–2000, the diets of most people (74 percent) needed improvement. Only 10% of the population had a good diet; 16% had a poor diet.... Only 17% of the people consumed the recommended number of servings of fruit per day, and only 30 percent met the dietary recommendation for milk."[20]

The word *diet* brings to mind a plan of eating certain foods, usually for the purpose of losing weight. That's only one definition for a word that also means "what a person or animal usually eats or drinks."[21] Using this definition, every person is "on a diet" whether healthy or unhealthy.

When discussing whether a person is underweight, normal weight or overweight, two indicators are used. One is called the waist circumference. Whether a person carries excess weight around the abdomen or through the thighs seems to matter. When a person carries excess weight around the waist, often referred to as having an apple shape, obesity-related health problems are more likely to occur. A person who carries excess weight around thighs would be described as "pear" shaped. In this reference, pear shaped is healthier than apple shaped. "Women with a waist measurement of more than 35 inches or men with a waist measurement of more than 40 inches have a higher health risk because of their fat distribution."[22]

The second way of measuring size is called the Body Mass Index.* A person can fill in height and weight and the computer will calculate BMI. A person can figure BMI with a mathematical formula (BMI = kg/m^2). A third way to determine BMI using pounds and inches is to multiple your weight (in pounds) by 703, then divide the result by your height in inches, and divide that result by your height in inches a second time. Elaine can figure hers. Elaine's weight (145 lbs × 703) divided by height (Elaine's height 5'3" or 63 inches) and divided by height (63 inches) a second time = 25.7 BMI.[23] When Elaine looks at the following BMI chart, she recognizes she's in the overweight category.[24]

*The Body Mass Index (BMI) calculator can be found at http://www.doctorsforadults.com/topics/ dfa_obes.htm and can be used to calculate body mass.

The BMI Categories

18.5 or less	Underweight
18.5–24.9	Normal
25.0–29.9	Overweight
30.0–39.9	Obese
40 or greater	Extremely Obese

Persons in the underweight and normal categories would be considered by many to be doing well and be healthy. Some people never gain weight no matter what they eat. Whether because of genetics, an active lifestyle, or for reasons unknown, these people do not gain weight. People who struggle with being overweight would consider those people lucky. According to a study published in the *Journal of the American Medical Association* (JAMA), "underweight and obesity, particularly higher levels of obesity, were associated with increased mortality relative to the normal weight category."[25] However, even a "normal weight" does not automatically mean a person enjoys health. A healthful diet is a crucial component of health.

Underweight and normal weight persons need healthful diets. People with a small frame face a risk of osteoporosis. Osteoporosis occurs in 8 million women and 2 million men in America. Risk factors for developing osteoporosis include "thinness or small frame, family history of the disease, abnormal absence of menstrual periods, prolonged use of certain medications such as glucocorticoids; low calcium intake, physical inactivity, smoking and excessive alcohol intake."[26] Dietary intake of calcium and vitamin D through low fat dairy products, dark green, leafy vegetables, and calcium-fortified beverages can help prevent osteoporosis and fracture-prone bones.*

Anorexia and Bulimia Disorders

A person who has an eating disorder such as anorexia or bulimia faces health risks, whether at a normal weight or underweight. Eating disorders like anorexia and bulimia bring to mind images of young women, but the problem affects more people than young women. "Contemporary western culture consistently values women's bodies and appearance above other attributes, sexualized images of female bodies saturate mass media, shaping the prevailing ideal. Of course, women of all ages who live in this culture are affected." Statistics agree. "Approximately 43 million adult women in the United States are dieting to lose weight at any given time; another 26 million are dieting to maintain their

---

*More information about osteoporosis, its prevention and treatments can be obtained at the National Osteoporosis Foundation at www.nof.org.

weight. Body image dissatisfaction in midlife has increased dramatically, more than doubling from 25% in 1972 to 56% in 1997."[27] Comparable levels of dieting and disordered eating are found across the spectrum of young and elderly women. When asked what bothered them most about their bodies, a group of women aged 61 to 92 identified weight as their greatest concern. Men also deal with eating disorders. "The incidence of eating disorders in males has also increased; in fact, a 1994 report by Powers and Spratt suggested the number of males with bulimia nervosa surpassed the number of females with anorexia nervosa. Males also account for 25% of the cases of binge-eating disorders."[28]

Some people will become obsessed with his or her weight and suffer from anorexia nervosa or bulimia. Anorexia nervosa occurs when a person restricts their food intake or binge eats and purges to lose weight. This person will refuse to maintain a normal body weight and may exercise excessively. "The hallmark of anorexia nervosa is a preoccupation with food and a refusal to maintain minimally normal body weight. One of the most frightening aspects of the disorder is that people with anorexia nervosa continue to think they look fat even when they are bone-thin."[29] Anorexia can result in starvation and death.

Bulimia combines binge eating with inappropriate measures to control weight such as self-induced vomiting, abuse of laxatives, diuretics, enemas, or non-purging behaviors such as fasting or excessive exercise. "Constant concern about food and weight is a primary sign of bulimia. Common indicators that suggest the self-induced vomiting that persons with bulimia experience are the erosion of dental enamel due to the acid in the vomit and scarring on the backs of the hands due to repeatedly pushing fingers down the throat to induce vomiting."[30] Purging can cause serious health problems such as electrolyte imbalance, dehydration, heart complications, and sudden death.

Persons suffering from anorexia nervosa or bulimia can be helped through treatment. Treatment involves physical restoration to a normal weight and health and therapy to treat eating behaviors.

Being a few pounds overweight should not cause problems. However, being overweight or obese causes problems due to "the strain it puts on organs and joints."[31] The higher a person's BMI, the greater the strain on organs and joints. When talking osteoarthritis, "a modest weight loss of 5 kg (11 lb) will reduce a woman's risk for development of knee OA over the subsequent years by 50%."[32]

Traditional thoughts regarding being overweight include: the person needs to lose the excess weight. The problem occurs when people try to accomplish this task. If it were easy, everyone would master the weight problem. Instead, Americans grapple with problems of overweight and obesity. Successful weight loss means permanent changes in eating habits or the person regains those pounds. A diet does not work when a person follows it for a few weeks and loses weight, only to regain that weight when the diet ends. Beware of diet plans called elimination diets, because they exclude an entire food group. Leaving out an entire food group may deprive the person of needed nutrition. Good resources for information about weight loss include registered dietitians and physicians.*

A Different Thought Regarding Diet and Health

"Faced with the dismal track record of dieting, the rising prevalence of obesity, and the premise that obesity itself may be relatively benign compared with health habits, nutritionists began to look for a more effective way of dealing with the health risks. One common-sense approach is known as Health at Every Size (HAES)."[33] HAES affirms that people naturally come in different sizes and shapes and promotes "feeling good about oneself, eating well in a natural, relaxed way, and being comfortably active."[34] This philosophy teaches one to quit counting calories and start paying attention to feelings of hunger and fullness.[35] The third portion of HAES involves physical activity. When a person adds enjoyable activities into the daily routine, health improvements follow.

This philosophy was studied at UC Davis when 78 female participants were assigned to either a dieting or non-dieting group. All participants received instructions and participated in 24 weekly treatment sessions followed by six monthly support groups. Over the two-year study time frame, 92 percent of the non-dieters stuck with the program vs. 58 percent of dieters. While early results from the dieters and non-dieters were about the same, over the two-year study non-dieters had better results by decreasing their total cholesterol levels, and LDL (bad cholesterol) levels. The non-dieters increased their activity levels and sustained those levels through the two years. Non-dieters lowered their systolic blood pressure numbers and sustained the decrease. "In summary, while the non-dieters did not lose weight, they succeeded in improving their overall health, as measured by cholesterol levels, blood pressure, physical activity, and self-esteem. The dieters, on the other hand, were not able to sustain any of the short-term improvements they experienced and worsened in terms of their self-esteem."[36]

The HAES philosophy says, "Thin is not intrinsically healthy and beautiful, nor is fat intrinsically unhealthy and unappealing. People naturally have different body shapes and sizes. This naturally occurring range may be increased as a result of lifestyle factors, including physical inactivity, unhealthy eating and dieting. Dieting usually leads to weight gain, decreased self-esteem, and increased risk for disordered eating. Health and happiness involve a dynamic interaction among mental, social, spiritual, and physical considerations."[37]

Dr. Jon Robison, a supporter of the Health at Every Size philosophy, states,

---

*The official website for dietitians, www.eatright.org, provides information on weight loss. A review of popular diets can be found at http://www.eatright.org/ada/files/Popular_Diets_Reviewed_2007.pdf. Persons considering a weight loss program can find information on selecting a weight loss program at www.nhlbi.nih.gov/health/public/heart/obesity/lose_wt/wtl_prog.htm.

"The focus on weight is at best, misleading, and at worst, an obsession. A person's health is not determined by weight. Rather than focusing and obsessing about weight, we suggest that people focus on the really important things in life, which are people's relationships, work, health and yes, physical activity and nutrition as well. But take the focus off weight because it's a self-defeating focus."[38]

Adopt a Healthy Lifestyle

The person wanting to adopt a healthy lifestyle can do several things to help oneself. Go for a walk. According to *Arthritis Self-Management* magazine, walking has a variety of potential health benefits. Walking, as with other forms of aerobic exercise, causes the heart and lungs to work more efficiently. Walking lowers the bad (LDL) cholesterol and raises the good (HDL) cholesterol. Walking decreases stress and by releasing endorphins helps ward off depression. It strengthens muscles, makes bones stronger, and helps protect joints.[39] Walking burns calories and helps with weight loss. Other types of exercise recommended for people with arthritis can be found in chapter 8.

Get enough sleep. Researchers reported, "Sleep deprivation alters hormones and increases appetites."[40] They found lack of sleep caused altered levels of leptin and ghrelin, two appetite-suppressing hormones. This small study reported in the *Annals of Internal Medicine* involved 12 healthy young men for a two-day span of time. More research is needed to support or disprove these findings. If it's true, loss of sleep could be contributing to America's weight gain. Nevertheless, a good night's sleep contributes to a person's health.

The newly released MyPyramid offers concrete information about eating healthy. *Dietary Guidelines for Americans* is another resource for healthy eating and can be accessed at http://www.healthierus.gov/dietaryguidelines/.

The complex carbohydrates, vitamins, and fiber found in whole grains add health to a person's diet. Substitute whole grains for refined grains and cereals. The researchers at Brigham and Women's Hospital looked at dietary habits of 74,091 U.S. female nurses, ages 38 through 63. "Women who consumed more whole grains consistently weighed less than did women who consumed less whole grains. Over 12 years, those with the greatest increase in intake of dietary fiber gained an average of 1.52 kg less than did those with the smallest increase in intake of dietary fiber."[41]

Some people say healthy food costs more. The United States Department of Agriculture offers advice on how to make a healthy diet affordable.* One suggestion is to buy fresh fruits and vegetables in season when they cost less.

The document, "Preparing Nutritious Meals at a Minimal Cost," provides free menus and recipes at their website and can be accessed at http://www.nal.usda.gov/fnic/pubs/USDAnutritious_meals.pdf.

Much attention turned to dairy foods and calcium when the question arose, "Does calcium/dairy foods help with weight loss?" The results of studies contradict each other. For now, the recommended daily allowance (RDA) for calcium is 1,000 mg for younger adults and 1,200 mg for persons 51 and older. Persons who consume adequate calcium and vitamin D intake help prevent osteoporosis, the silent thief of bone health.

Drink water. "More than one in three Americans over the age of 60 may not be consuming enough total water from all sources."[42] Water could be called the "silent nutrient" because it acts as "solvent, coolant, lubricant, and transport agent."[43] How much water should a person drink? For years the rule-of-thumb recommendation for healthy adults has been 8 8-oz glasses per day plus an additional amount equal to all caffeinated drinks. Concerned scientists don't all agree with that amount.[44] They do agree that adequate water is essential to health and wellness. The body loses water every day through urine, perspiration and body functions people don't think about. "To replace this loss, you should consume at least 6 full glasses of water a day—a minimum of 48 ounces. Of course, foods are 70–90 percent water, so don't count just the glasses you drink in a day."[45] People with kidney failure, congestive heart failure, and other health issues who are instructed by their doctors to drink less fluids should do so.

The amount of water a person needs also depends upon activity levels and climate. Naturally, a person exercising on a hot, humid day loses more fluid through perspiration. Persons who sweat while exercising need to drink extra water prior to, during, and after the exercise to help replenish the fluids. Cold winter weather can cause a person to sweat due to heavy insulated clothing. That person needs extra water also. If a person loses more water and fluids than they take in from food and water, dehydration sets in. "Signs and symptoms of dehydration include: excessive thirst, fatigue, headache, dry mouth, little or no urination, muscle weakness, dizziness and lightheadedness."[46] Individuals should recognize that we often perceive thirst as hunger. A person should drink water instead of automatically going for a snack. "Thirst is not always a good indicator of the body's need for water. It's important to drink regularly, even if you don't feel thirsty. This is especially true with the elderly because the sensation of thirst becomes weaker as people age. Also, intense dehydration may impair the usual strong desire to drink."[47] A person can check on his/her state of hydration by watching the color of urine. "A pale yellow color and low odor indicates proper hydration."[48]

Three nutrient-poor food groups, sweets and desserts, soft drinks and alcoholic beverages, contributed almost 25 percent of all the energy consumed in the U.S. population.[49] A person wanting to improve health and nutrition will consider these foods a treat to be enjoyed in small quantities.

Watch portion size. Food portions served in restaurants have grown larger.

Consequently, when Americans eat out, they face the likelihood of more calories and larger portions. A bagel of 20 years ago measured 3 inches in diameter and contained 140 calories. Today's bagel measures 6 inches in diameter and contains 350 calories.[50]

Vitamin Supplements

The American Dietetic Association (ADA) recommends Americans use the MyPyramid to improve their diet and get all the nutrition needed. However, many Americans eat high-calorie, low-nutrition foods and cheat themselves of the nutrition they need.*

Persons who choose to take a multivitamin and mineral supplement should heed these recommendations:

"Watch out for too much A." Vitamin A, a fat-soluble vitamin, can become toxic and harmful. Take no more than "100% of the daily value (5,000 IU) of vitamin A and only 4000 IU, or 80% daily value (DV) from retinol. Lower retinol amount—around 2500 IUs—are even better. Too much retinol may increase your risk of bone fractures."[51] In fact, all fat soluble vitamins which include A, D, E, and K are stored in the body if taken in larger than recommended amounts and can become toxic and harmful. Unless recommended by a physician, people should not take doses of fat soluble vitamins larger than the recommended daily amounts.†

"Pay attention to iron." Iron is needed for young women of childbearing age. Healthy men and post-menopausal women generally do not need iron unless prescribed by their physician for a specific reason. "Don't overload on trace minerals." Four trace minerals, iron, zinc, iodine, and selenium, have been studied and assigned a recommended daily allowance (RDA). Nutritionists have established safe daily intake numbers for five more trace minerals, copper, manganese, fluoride, chromium, and molybdenum. Four additional trace minerals, arsenic, nickel, silicon, and boron, are recognized as essential to animals, but their value to humans is being studied. Check the multivitamin and avoid high levels of trace mineral unless recommended by a physician.[52]

Other advice from *Arthritis Today's Vitamin and Mineral Guide* includes: "Beware of extras" such a bonus nutrients and trace minerals, which increase the cost while adding little value. If not needed, those extras may be harmful. Look for the United States Pharmacopeia (USP) logo, which sets standards "for disintegration, dissolution, strength and purity." Never swallow expired vitamin/

*People interested in improving their diet can access information at the ADA's website, http://www. eatright.org.

†The Arthritis Foundation provides a free brochure about vitamin and minerals, which can be accessed at http://ww2.arthritis.org/resources/arthritistoday/2005_archives/2005_09_10/Vitamin_Min eral_Guide.

mineral supplements. Check the expiration date and throw away expired supplements. Vitamins with chelated or colloidal minerals claim better absorption, but no scientific evidence supports this claim. Lastly, which is better—natural or chemical vitamins? "With the exception of vitamin E which is better absorbed in its natural form—buying vitamins and minerals in their 'natural' state doesn't make a difference. Both synthetic and natural vitamins are equally potent. In the case of folic acid and vitamin B-12, synthetic forms are actually better absorbed than natural forms."[53]

Food and diet is one of the most complicated healthcare issues Americans face. People who deal with osteoarthritis or rheumatoid arthritis join the millions of Americans facing issues of diet and health. By using commonsense guidelines, anyone can make healthy choices and improve his lifestyle.

8

Exercising with Arthritis

When Dr. Marion Minor of the University of Missouri conducted a study in 1989, doctors were putting patients on bed rest for bouts of arthritic pain. Dr. Minor's premise that persons dealing with arthritis would find exercise beneficial was confirmed. The participants in aquatic and walking groups significantly improved their ability to perform activities. They also liked feeling in control of their lives. This research revolutionized the concept of exercise for arthritic patients.[1]

Benefits of Exercise

"Physical fitness for people is much like good maintenance and proper use for an automobile. Both allow you to start when you want, enjoy a smooth and relaxed trip, get to your destination without a breakdown, and have some fuel in your tank when you arrive."[2] Physical fitness involves many parts of the human, including cardiovascular (heart, lungs and blood vessels), muscular strength, endurance, and flexibility. People dealing with arthritis benefit from fitness. "Exercise reduces joint pain and stiffness, builds strong muscle around the joints, and increases flexibility and endurance. But it also helps promote overall health and fitness by giving you more energy, helping you sleep better, controlling your weight, decreasing depression, and giving you more self-esteem. Furthermore, exercise can help stave off other health problems such as osteoporosis and heart disease."[3]

Researchers at the University of Kansas Medical Center looked at the benefits and safety of an aerobic program for women dealing with rheumatoid arthritis. They found that after a 12-week program, those women showed no worsening of symptoms. The women reported improved flexibility with decreased pain and fatigue. Blood tests indicated a decrease in levels of inflammation and disease status for some of the participants. These blood tests involved C-reactive protein, sedimentation rate, and interleukin-6 levels.[4]

Researchers in Israel looked at men undergoing treatment for cardiovascular disease. After 12 weeks of aerobic exercise, the participants had higher levels of infection-fighting T-cells than the non-exercising men.[5]

Preventing Falls

Exercise can help individuals improve their balance. According to Webster's dictionary, "balance is an even distribution of weight ensuring stability."[6] Impaired balance increases a person's risk of falling. "More than one third of adults 65 and older fall each year in the United States. Among older adults, falls are the leading cause of injury deaths. They are also the most common cause of nonfatal injuries and hospital admissions for trauma."[7]

What enables people who stand on two legs to keep their balance? A motor-cycle cannot stand still on two wheels and keep its balance without a kickstand. How can humans keep this balance and not fall over during activities such as walking, running, and climbing?

An amazing set of senses within the body enable a person to maintain balance. A combination of visual and auditory senses (seeing and hearing), complex senses called proprioception (sensing stimuli within the body) and the inner ear (vestibular) senses work with the human brain to enable people to keep their balance. When balance is affected, the person wobbles and may injure himself while falling.[8]

Pathological (disease) conditions that can cause balance problems include inner ear problems, head injuries, some movement disorders such as Parkinson's and dystonias and diabetic neuropathy (impaired nerve function) in the feet. "Pain, stiffness, poor posture, limited mobility, and weakened muscles can all contribute to balance disturbances in people with arthritis. Aging is a factor, too."[9]

Balance can be improved through exercises. Studies show that falls decreased when the persons worked at fall-prevention exercises. One study showed an 11 percent decrease in falls while another study showed a 35 percent decrease in falls.[10] Explanations and pictures for balance exercises can be found in January–February 2005 issue of *Arthritis Self-Management* magazine. Tai chi and other exercises which improve balance and coordination are recommended by the Centers for Disease Control (CDC) as part of the program "What YOU Can Do to Prevent Falls." Physical therapy staff at many health and fitness centers can instruct people on fall-prevention exercises. Persons wanting to improve their balance and prevent falls should learn and practice balance exercises.

Starting to Exercise

How should a person start an exercise program? The experts suggest talking to a person's doctor for guidelines and following those guidelines. The doctor may recommend a period of rest when the patient deals with periods of flares and fatigue or just a temporary change in type of activities and amount of exercise during the flare. As the flare decreases, the doctor will probably recommend gradually increasing the exercise.

What should a person with osteoarthritis consider while planning exercise? Osteoarthritis affects joint cartilage and exercise should involve taking care of the cartilage. According to *The Arthritis Helpbook*,[11] cartilage inside joints can be compared to a sponge. When people walk and exercise, the fluid inside cartilage flows out into the knee joint. When at rest, the cartilage soaks up needed nutrients and fluids from the joint. These nutrient-rich fluids that soak back into the cartilage during rest contain necessary oxygen and nutrition used by the body to nourish and repair the cartilage. When arthritis changes occur, the cartilage becomes damaged, but it continues to need the nutrition obtained from movement. Osteoarthritic joints benefit from exercises with the caution of paying attention to the body's pain level. Start very slowly and build gradually. Basics such as good posture, strong muscles, and shock-absorbing shoes help protect joint cartilage. The three types of exercise advocated by the Arthritis Foundation for osteoarthritis includes flexibility, strengthening and aerobic exercises.

What should people dealing with rheumatoid arthritis consider while planning exercise? Flexibility and strengthening exercises help people with rheumatoid arthritis (RA). Aerobic exercises give over-all health benefits also. People dealing with RA often find morning stiffness to be a problem. Flexibility exercises even before they get out of bed and during a warm shower or bath can help loosen muscles. "Stretching like a cat" is recommended to help a person get moving and to stay flexible. Some people find flexibility exercises before bedtime increases their flexibility when they get up the next morning. Because RA may affect the neck, recommendations for exercising the neck include avoiding extreme neck movements or putting pressure on the back of the neck and head.

Healthcare professionals who help with exercise and rehabilitation include physical therapists and occupational therapists. Physical therapists "provide exercises designed to preserve the strength and use of your joints."[12] These experts teach the best, safest ways a person can move from one position to another. When a person finds that walking aids such as a cane, crutches or walker are needed, physical therapists teach how to use these aids. Occupational therapists teach how to "reduce strain on your joints during daily activities. They can show you how you can modify your home and workplace environments to reduce motions that may aggravate arthritis."[13] Occupational therapists provide splints to protect fragile joints. They know about gadgets and devices that simplify bathing, dressing, and other activities of daily living.

Making Exercise Fun

The Arthritis Foundation (AF) recommends, "Start slow and make it fun."[14] Each person should choose a fun exercise/activity. Many activities will fit into the low-impact, gentle-to-joints activities the AF recommends. Walking, water aerobics, tai chi and bicycling begin the list. Many gyms and fitness centers include arthritis exercise classes for people who enjoy group activities. Regional Arthritis Centers provide information on local arthritis exercise classes. People who like to exercise at home with videotapes may find PACE (People with Arthritis Can Exercise) and Pool Exercise Program valuable resources. Both these tapes can be purchased from the Arthritis Foundation.

The "most common risk of exercise is aggravating your arthritis by working your joints or muscles too much. This can happen if you exercise too long or too hard, especially when you are first beginning your exercise program."[15] Don't overdo it. A person should start slow, increase slowly, have fun and reap the benefits of regular exercise. Persons with and without arthritis who want to avoid damaging their joints should participate in gentle-to-the-joints exercises and sports.

Flexing Those Muscles

Flexibility exercises loosen a person's muscles. Flexibility can mean fingers that button a shirt. Also known as range-of-motion and stretching exercises, these exercises give better movement, especially for persons dealing with arthritis. Flexibility exercises should be done every day and are considered by the Arthritis Foundation to be "the most important of all your exercises. Flexibility exercises can help you protect your joints by reducing the risk of joint injury, help you warm-up for more strenuous exercise by getting your body moving and help you relax and release tension from your body."[16] Tai chi and gentle versions of yoga are considered good flexibility exercises. The Arthritis Foundation recommends, "Work up to 15 minutes of flexibility exercises a day. Once you can do 15 continuous minutes, you should be able to add strengthening and aerobic exercises to your routine."[17]

Strengthening Those Muscles

Strengthening exercises help build muscles. Muscles become weak when joint pain and stiffness make a person less active. Strong muscles protect joints and prevent injuries when individuals do activities such as climbing stairs, reaching, and lifting items. For the person with arthritis, strengthening exercises make muscles stronger by gently adding resistance in the form of a person's body weight, or extra hand-held weights or elastic bands. Two types of strengthening exercises are important for people with arthritis: isometric and isotonic. A group of teenage boys showing off their arm muscles illustrates isometric exercise. The muscles are tightened without any movement at joints. An elderly lady sipping a cup of tea involves isotonic exercises when she tightens her muscles and moves joints. The Arthritis Foundation recommends, "Strengthening exercises should be done every other day after warming up with some flexibility exercises."[18]

Exercising Heart and Lungs

Aerobic exercise, also known as cardiovascular or endurance exercise, makes a person's heart, lungs, blood vessels and muscles healthier and more efficient. A healthy heart doesn't have to beat as fast or hard to circulate needed blood. Benefits of aerobic exercises include improved coping with stress and anxiety, better sleep at night, more energy, and better weight control. Aerobic exercises also combat osteoporosis. During aerobic exercises, a person uses his large muscles to perform rhythmic, continuous motions such as walking, swimming, bicycling or dancing. Raking leaves and pushing the lawn mower qualifies as aerobic exercise. The Arthritis Foundation recommends including aerobic activity "three to four times each week, with a goal of working in your target heart rate for 30 minutes each session. You should work up to this goal slowly, starting with as little as 5 minutes and increasing as you get stronger."[19]

Tips for Success

Pay attention to pain. Exercising should not be painful. "Pain is actually your body's way of telling you that you might be getting injured."[20] People who haven't been exercising should start very slowly and use very light of weights for only a few minutes. Pain should not be endured and the exercise should not cause pain. A little soreness may be experienced; however, if a person is still sore two hours after the exercise, the recommendation is to cut back.[21]

Make it fun. People get bored with the same old exercises. Do something new. Join a class. Take up a gentle-to-the-joint exercise such as tai chi or bicycle riding. Find a buddy. Socializing during walking or exercise increases the fun. Equip yourself. Learn what equipment is needed for the exercise. For walking, proper shoes will prevent injury and increase the pleasure. Excellent suggestions on how to make exercise successful can be found in *The Arthritis Helpbook* by Kate Lorig and James J. Fries. This self-help book also includes illustrations and descriptions of different exercises.

Arthritis Foundation Approved Exercises/Activities

Bicycling

Bicycling enjoys renewed popularity and interest as bikers enjoy the beautiful scenery and get exercise. Borrow a helmet and bike from a buddy and hit the road, right? No.

Proper preparation and safe practices will enhance the benefits and protect the rider. Learning about the different features such as gears, brakes and handlebars can be done through visiting bike shops, talking to people and researching. After obtaining a bike, proper fitting needs to be done. The bike must fit the rider. The most common and easiest adjustment involves seat height. While someone holds the bike upright, the rider should sit on the seat. The rider's heel needs to be on the pedal and his leg out straight when the pedal is at extension (at its lowest point). Knee pain can occur if the seat is too low and the rider's knees are always bent. The exception to the rider's leg being at full extension when his heel is on the pedal involves people who have loose knees that bend backwards. These people need a little bend in the knee at full extension to prevent injury to their knees.[22]

Safety tips for outdoor bicycling include wearing a properly fitted helmet. Safety-approved helmets display a sticker showing one of the safety boards, Snell or ANSI. Other good advice includes following the rules of the road, pedaling with the ball of your foot and using bike gears to enhance comfort and safety.[23]

Some people would prefer to bicycle inside the comfort of their home or the nearest gym. For persons looking to purchase a stationary or recumbent bike for home usage, important features that vary with different bicycles involve the bike seat, handlebars and resistance. Many people will say a wider, flatter seat provides more comfort to the rider. The height of the seat should be adjusted similar to the outdoor bicycle: the seat should be at a height where the rider's knee is straight when the rider's heel is on the pedal at the pedal's lowest point. Handlebars vary also. Stationary handlebars provide balance and support while moveable handlebars enable the rider to exercise the upper body. The recommended fit involves being able to grip handlebars comfortably with the elbows slightly bent. The rider shouldn't have to bend or stretch to reach handlebars. Resistance involves the tension of the bike and dictates how hard the rider works while riding. Resistance can be adjusted on the bike. Persons who exercise at gyms and fitness centers should ask the staff to answer questions about safe usage of stationary and recumbent bikes.

Tips for success include starting out easy with no or very little resistance, pedaling comfortably, and building slowly.[24] Some people find stationary biking to be boring. If so, plan a diversion such as watching a favorite television show. One woman reads while biking; another enjoys her favorite music while she rides. Videotapes of exotic bike tours can be a welcome diversion.

"Walking Is a Man's Best Medicine"[25] (Hippocrates, 460 B.C.–357 B.C.)

An ideal exercise because it's gentle to joints, walking requires little money except to purchase good walking shoes and can be done almost anywhere. Walking requires little skill and almost anyone can participate. The heart and lungs become more efficient with walking while it lowers LDL (bad) cholesterol and raises HDL (good) cholesterol levels. As a gentle exercise, walking strengthens muscles. Another benefit of walking involves making bones stronger and reducing the risk for osteoporosis. The benefits of walking involve more than the physical: Walking decreases stress and depression when the body's natural pain-killing endorphins are released.

People who want to begin walking should wear comfortable shoes. According to Arthritis Today Walking Guide, people should consider the following features when testing new shoes: The sole of shoes should "grip the walking surface for good traction."[26] A person buying safe walking shoes should avoid slick-soled shoes and the opposite, sticky, non-skid shoes with a rubber lug over the toe, which can cause trips and falls. Walking shoes should fit comfortably. The toes should have room to spread out and a thumb's width between the end of the longest toe and the shoe. The fit should be snug enough that a person's heel doesn't slip. The shoes should be flexible enough to bend at the forefoot when stepping but remain rigid through the midsole. An angled heel gives a smoother walk and helps prevent injuries and pain. Cushioning and support at the heel and arch help protect the feet of walkers. Personal preference dictates whether the shoes have laces or Velcro closures. Breathability of the shoe will keep the feet drier and more comfortable. Remember to replace shoes that are worn a lot. "A walker who takes 30-minute walks three times a week might need replacements after about 9 to 12 months."[27]

A person need not purchase special clothing to wear while walking. Comfortable, loose-fitting clothing will meet the occasion. Cold winter weather creates the challenge of keeping dry and warm. The term layering of clothes means the practice of wearing multiple layers that can be removed or added to keep the walker a comfortable temperature. Three layers are recommended for persons wanting to keep warm while exercising in chilly weather. The innermost layer should be soft, lightweight, synthetic long underwear that dries easily. The middle layer should be the insulating layer made of fleece or wool. The outermost layer, a jacket, protects the walker from rain and wind. A water-resistant but venting material provides best protection. People should remember to wear a hat and gloves to preserve warmth. Socks made of fabric that wicks the moisture away keep feet dry and warm.[28]

People who prefer walking inside during the cold weather find that many malls welcome walkers. Many gym and fitness centers provide track facilities as well as treadmill-type machines.

The person who begins walking should start slowly, which warms muscles and allows the heart to respond gradually. After a few minutes of slow walking, do some stretches or flexibility exercises. Then resume walking at a quicker pace. "A good pace is one at which you can still hold a conversation without too much huffing and puffing."[29] Good posture and alignment help protect the joints. "Make sure your ears, shoulders, hips and knees are in alignment. Rather than tilt your head down to look at your feet, keep your chin parallel to the ground and keep your eyes focused ahead of you to see any potholes, curbs, or other obstacles that you might trip over."[30] The walker benefits from bending the arms at 90 degrees and swinging them. Beginning walkers should start out with a short walk and increase the speed and duration of walks gradually. A slowdown, or cooldown, during the last five minutes of the walk is recommended. If the person is exhausted upon finishing, that person overdid it and should decrease the distance walked or walk more slowly or do both.

Avoid pain while walking. Check into the source of pain and heed the body's warnings. The two-hour rule applies here also: If still sore after two hours, the person overdid the exercise and should decrease intensity and duration the next time and build slowly.

Walk safely. People walking on streets or roads need to watch traffic. The person walking where there's no sidewalk should walk facing the traffic. The person walking at dusk or after dark needs to wear reflective clothing to be safe and easily seen by drivers.[31]

Tai Chi

Tai chi, a 600-year-old Chinese practice, uses a combination of slow fluid movements and meditation aimed at balancing the vital life energy, called qi (pronounced chee and spelled "chi" by Westerners). Traditional Chinese medicine believes disease and illness occur when imbalances or blockages of the vital life energy, qi, occur. As people move through tai chi, "they are gently working muscles, focusing concentration and according to Chinese philosophy, improving the flow of qi, the vital life energy that sustains health and calms the mind."[32]

Embraced by Westerners, tai chi classes can often be found in gyms, fitness centers, and many healthcare facilities. Sun style tai chi is recommended by the Arthritis Foundation for arthritis sufferers. Its higher stances take the pressure off joints.[33] "Tai chi takes the joints gently through their range of motion while the emphasis on breathing and inner stillness relieves stress and anxiety." Often described as "meditation in motion," tai chi uses fluid, controlled motions in sequences with poetic names such as "waving hand in the cloud."[34] Tai chi provides flexibility exercises and should be combined with aerobic and strengthening exercises.

Experts believe tai chi improves the balance of participants. Researchers at the Emory School of Medicine in Atlanta found that "older people taking part in a 15-week Tai Chi program reduced their risk of falling by 47.5%."[35] The participants slowed their steps, made them more deliberate and were less fearful of falling. After the study, only 8 percent expressed fear of falling compared to 23 percent prior to the classes.

For best results, recommendations include talking to a person's doctor about tai chi, whether to participate during flares and whether to avoid any specific movements. Those interested in learning tai chi should find a teacher who is knowledgeable about arthritis. This teacher should ensure that tai chi movements are correctly done and are gentle to joints. Classes should begin with warm-up and end with cooldown. Other common sense suggestions involve not overdoing, stopping when it hurts and being consistent to practice tai chi daily.[36]

Aquatics or Water Exercise

Exercising in warm water soothes aching joints and increases mobility. The Arthritis Foundation recommends warm water (84 degrees Fahrenheit) with surrounding air temperature the same.[37] Water buoyancy supports a person's body and decreases the load on joints. Aquatic exercise classes can be found in many fitness centers and gyms. Local chapters of the Arthritis Foundation can recommend classes in the area. People who want to exercise on their own and have access to a pool can benefit from exercise videotapes available from the Arthritis Foundation.*

Suggestions for successful water exercise include protecting your feet from rough floors, keeping warm and wearing a floatation belt. To protect feet, a swimmer could use beach shoes with rubber sole and mesh top, one-size-smaller-than-feet terry cloth slippers with rubber soles or footgear designed for water exercise. Keeping warm while in and around the pool may require extra clothing like a T-shirt or full-leg Lycra exercise tights in addition to a person's swimwear. Persons with Raynaud's phenomenon may find that disposable surgical gloves help keep hands warm and fingers a normal pink color. Wearing a floatation belt or life vest lifts weight off a person's joints and may increase comfort. The beginning

---

*The brochure, "Water Exercise: Pools, Spas and Arthritis" can be obtained from the Arthritis Foundation at www.arthritis.org.

swimmer may notice being short of breath quickly. When that happens, the person can rest either in the water or out. Another way the person can decrease his effort is to move more slowly and turn his hands to meet less water resistance.

Yoga

The word yoga brings to mind a person performing gentle stretching exercises and meditation. Yoga, a part of the Indian holistic healing system called ayurveda, has been practiced for 5,000 years to improve flexibility and muscle tone while decreasing stress. Hatha yoga, the type of yoga most familiar to Westerners, uses gentle stretches and balancing exercises. Yoga's participants are "everyday people just like you who want to treat their bodies well. And what better way than through a low-impact exercise that induces relaxation, lowers stress and relieves tension? Even better, yoga also helps tone and strengthen your muscles and loosen your joints."[38]

The individual wanting to learn yoga would benefit from learning the moves in a class aimed at people with arthritis. This person should talk to a doctor about any moves to be avoided before starting class and also talk to the yoga instructor. Because there are different types of yoga and different levels of intensity in the workouts, a prospective student could watch a class to see if the class and instructor share the same goals as the prospective student.

Equipment recommended as potential aids during class include a non-slip mat or rug. Yoga blankets, foam blocks, yoga straps and bolster pillows are items a person might want to purchase if the person enjoys the yoga. Appropriate dress for yoga class includes loose-fitting tops, sweatpants and no shoes.

Too Much Fun to Be Called Exercise: Gardening

Munch on a scarlet red, plump, juicy tomato picked from one's own garden and share the satisfaction of many gardeners. Eighty-four million American households participate in gardening and lawn-care activities. Among all ages and sexes, gardening or yard work involves 29 percent of Americans.[39] Gardening improves people's health when it gets them moving. The Arthritis Foundation recognizes the health benefits of gardening for people with arthritis. Gardeners benefit from increased flexibility and stronger bones. Gardening helps people emotionally when it adds beauty to their lives. Many people with high-stress lives say digging in the dirt, plucking weeds, and watching flowers bloom decrease their stress level.

Gardening can cause injuries. Common injuries from gardening include repetitive-motion injuries such as carpal tunnel syndrome or tennis elbow, pinched nerves and strains or sprains. Experts recommend warming up by flexibility/stretch exercises followed by a five-minute walk. Weekend gardeners should pace themselves, take rest breaks, and avoid exhaustion. "Buy gardening tools with adaptive handles that are easy to grasp, or build up handles that are easy to grasp, or build up handles yourself by wrapping them with electrical tape, bubble wrap or foam padding."[40] These tools will decrease stresses on joints.

Golf

Fore! Try to explain the pleasure of the perfect drive and watching that little white ball flying straight at that flag on the distant green. Experience the satisfaction of winning that $5 bill from your friend; a tattered bill traded back and forth with the success of each day's game. Golfers understand these pleasures. When right hip pain interferes, the golfer can't finish his swing, the ball goes awry, and pleasure diminishes. Can people with arthritis continue playing golf? The Arthritis Foundation says, "Whether you've played golf for years or are interested in trying it for the first time, arthritis doesn't have to slow you down."[41]

Golf, like all activities and physical exercise, provides benefits to participants. Golfers benefit from increased flexibility, range of motion, and strength. Golf improves balance and coordination. Like any aerobic exercise, golf helps raise "good" (HDL) cholesterol levels and aids in weight loss.

"Adaptation is the key to playing golf if you have arthritis. Grips, shoes, balls, and clubs can all be adjusted to fit your specific needs and abilities."[42] The Arthritis Foundation suggests making some minor changes to avoid jarring one's joints. Hit a 90 compression ball instead of 100 because a softer ball "gives" more. Golfers may find clubs with shock-absorbing technology gentle to joints. This technology includes perimeter-weighted heads, lightweight graphite shafts, and shock-absorbing shaft inserts. Oversized, softer grips on clubs reduce stress and pain in fingers and arms. Golfers will find spikeless golf shoes more gentle to hip and knee joints.

As with other activities, warming up with stretching (flexibility) exercises and a short walk before those practice swings of the club will help get golfers ready to play. "Easy practice swings, trunk twists, hamstring (rear thighs) stretches, and walking are good warm-up exercises."[43] Start with practice swings using shorter clubs and partial swings and increase into full swings with long clubs. Other suggestions include, "Always brush through the grass so you will hit the ball solidly and carry your momentum out to the target, use tees whenever you hit the ball—even on the practice range—to avoid striking the ground and jarring your joints, and play from the 150-yard markers if you begin to get tired."[44]

People wanting to learn how to play golf should talk to their doctor or physical therapist. Neophyte golfers can hurt themselves if they swing improperly. Lessons from a local golf professional would be a good investment in developing a good swing and proper form.

Everyone agrees exercise done properly benefits people with arthritis. A person should choose an enjoyable activity or exercise, learn how to participate safely, and go have fun.*

*More information on golf and arthritis can be found at www.arthritis.org/golf.php

9

Drug Therapies

"Almost half of Americans use at least one prescription drug.... Prescription drug use is rising among people of all ages, and use increases with age. Five out of six persons 65 or older are taking at least one medication and almost half the elderly take three or more."[1]

Prescription drugs help people live longer and improve people's lives by controlling chronic health problems. However, people need to remember that almost every drug has potential side effects. Even the old familiar drugs, aspirin and acetaminophen (Tylenol), can cause problems in some patients and certainly when taken in too large dosages. For safe and effective drug therapy, individuals should consult with their doctor and pharmacist to learn about their medications, whether prescribed, over-the-counter (OTC), or herbal medicines.*

As the number of drugs a person takes increases, whether from prescriptions, OTC drugs, or herbal supplements, the risks of polypharmacy increase. Polypharmacy means "many drugs" and describes problems that occur when a person takes several drugs.[2] Polypharmacy can occur from drugs prescribed by doctors and nurse practitioners. Polypharmacy also occurs when people add OTC drugs such as laxatives, antacids, cold remedies, pain medications, and herbal supplements to their prescription drug medications.

Symptoms of polypharmacy can be rather vague. The Family Caregivers' Alliance describes polypharmacy, as including these symptoms: "excessive drowsiness, confusion, depression, delirium, insomnia, Parkinson's-like symptoms, incontinence, muscle weakness, loss of appetite, falls and fractures, changes in speech and memory."[3]

Persons can decrease the risk of polypharmacy by keeping all their doctors and pharmacists aware of what they're taking. This can be accomplished by carrying all medicines in a sack (called a brown-bag exam) or taking a written, up-to-date list to doctor visits for the doctors to read and check for problems. If

---

*The Arthritis Foundation provides detailed information about drugs used to treat arthritis at the website, http://www.arthritis.org/conditions/DrugGuide/index.asp. Information about herbal supplements can be accessed from the Arthritis Foundation at http://www.arthritis.org/conditions/supplementguide/.

	Medication	Dose	Frequency
Prescription			
Over-the-counter			
Vitamins			
Herbs, dietary supplements, homeopathic remedies			
Other (alcohol, drugs)			

Speak Up® is sponsored by the Joint Commission on Accreditation of Healthcare Organizations

My Medication List
A Speak Up™ safety initiative

Individuals can utilize My Medication List to keep an up-to-date list of medications for share with their physicians, nurse practitioners, and pharmacists (courtesy Joint Commission of Accreditation of healthcare Organizations, JCAHO at http://www.jointcommission.org/Patient Safety/SpeakUp/speak_up_med_mistakes.htm).

using a list, all medications should be listed, even medicines such as patches, creams, eardrops or eye drops, inhalers, sample medications, herbal and mineral supplements, and vitamins. This should be done at every doctor visit. This medication list (kept in a person's wallet/billfold) would also be valuable information in case of an emergency hospital visit.

Risks of polypharmacy can increase when a person forgets to take medications or has difficulty reading the label. A multi-dose, multi-day pill box aids remembering to take medicines. These inexpensive, easy-to-use organizers can be purchased at many pharmacies and stores. The person or responsible family member can fill the pill box on a regular basis to simplify taking medication. Pharmacies make large-print labels for medicine bottles upon request for people with vision problems.

Pharmacists can also examine a person's medications and look for adverse drug interactions to prevent polypharmacy problems. Pharmacists print out drug information with details such as side effects. This information will go home with the prescription and be readily available if the patient keeps it. The pharmacist can print drug information sheets in large print for people with vision problems. Using one pharmacy for all medications helps decrease risks of polypharmacy. Before buying a multi-symptom OTC cold formula, the individual should talk to a pharmacist and purchase a cold remedy to treat only his symptoms. Contrary to popular belief, a multi-symptom cold remedy may not be better. The additional ingredients in a multi-symptom cold remedy may cause polypharmacy problems and overmedicate a person.

When patients and family caregivers learn about the patient's medications, the risks of polypharmacy decrease. One elderly woman noticed she had gradually developed a dry cough weeks after her doctor started her on a high blood pressure medication. Despite her efforts to clear up this cough, it persisted. She read the product information from the pharmacy and found "a dry nonproductive cough" listed as a side effect. This lady talked to her doctor about the chronic cough that had developed, her doctor changed her blood pressure medication and the cough stopped. This lady used her resources wisely.

Arthritis Drugs

Several types of drugs provide help to persons dealing with osteoarthritis including analgesics, NSAIDs, corticosteroids and osteoporosis medications. People dealing with rheumatoid arthritis may use those drugs plus the disease-modifying antirheumatic drugs (DMARDs) and biologic response modifiers (BRM). Two FDA-approved non-drug therapies are protein-A immunoadsorption (Prosorba) therapy and viscosupplements. Both these therapies are administered by physicians.*

Analgesics

Acetaminophen (Tylenol, Datril, others) was first available in 1955 as an aspirin-free analgesic. "Because of its lowcost, effectiveness and safety, rheumatologists recommend acetaminophen as a first-line option against osteoarthritis (OA) pain."[4]

While doctors see definite benefit in people using acetaminophen, there's a danger when people take too much. The directions found on acetaminophen packaging recommend not taking more than 4,000 mg daily (8 extra-strength 500-mg tablets). Persons who have liver disease, including hepatitis, or who drink alcohol regularly should talk to their doctor about how much acetaminophen they can safely take. Research published in the December 2005 *Hepatology*, the official journal for the American Association for the Study of Liver Diseases, reported that acetaminophen overdosing causes liver failure. The percentage of acetaminophen-related acute liver failures has grown from 28 percent in 1998 to 51 percent in 2003. When they looked at 662 patients with acute liver failure over a six-year period, 48 percent of the causes (131) involved unintentional overdosing with acetaminophen. Of those patients, 38 percent of them took two or more acetaminophen preparations simultaneously, and 63 percent used narcotic-containing compounds.[5]

*A free drug guide updated yearly can be ordered from the Arthritis Foundation at 1-800-283-7800 or accessed at http://www.arthritis.org/conditions/DrugGuide/default.asp.

Individuals should be aware that acetaminophen is found in many pain relievers, both over-the-counter (OTC) and prescription. Many cold medicine formulas in both liquid and pill form contain acetaminophen. A conversation with a pharmacist or doctor will answer questions about contents of medications. Persons should discuss with their doctors the amount of acetaminophen each person can safely take. This study concludes that "acetaminophen hepatotoxicity (liver damage) far exceeds other causes of acute liver failure in the United States."[6]

Other analgesics prescribed by doctors include narcotic-based drugs that contain codeine, hydrocodone, morphine, etc. These narcotic-based pain medicines provide valuable pain relief for short-term situations such as post surgery. Sometimes physicians prescribe these drugs for people dealing with arthritis when pain is extreme and prolonged. Synthetic narcotics include pentazocine (Talwin-NX or Talace), nalbuphine (Nubrain), butorphanol (Stadol or Stadol NS) and buprenorphine (Buprenex).[7]

A February 26, 2007, *Archives of Internal Medicine* article reported that regular usage of acetaminophen, aspirin and ibuprofen appears to be associated with development of high blood pressure in men.[8] An earlier study involving women found similar findings. "The Arthritis Foundation recommends people considering or taking any pain reliever for arthritis work with their doctor to determine a treatment plan that is best for their individual situation."[9]

Non-Steroidal Anti-Inflammatory Drugs (NSAIDs)

The original anti-inflammatory, aspirin, was introduced in 1899. Over the past century, aspirin found its home in most medicine cabinets. Aspirin relieves pain, lowers fever and decreases inflammation. Researchers at Brigham and Women's Hospital demonstrated that low doses of aspirin (81 mg) "trigger the body to generate its own anti-inflammatory compounds that help fight unwanted inflammation."[10] This study, published in 2004, found that low-dosage aspirin raised levels of ATL (anti-inflammatory 15-epi-lipoxin A4), a known anti-inflammatory. Doctors and researchers will consider how best to use this information in treatment of heart disease, arthritis, and other inflammatory diseases.

The next anti-inflammatory drug came 50 years after aspirin when phenylbutazone was released in 1949. During the 1970s through 1980s a large number of NSAIDs came onto the pharmaceutical market. Today, "nonsteroidal anti-inflammatory drugs (NSAIDs) annually account for 70 million prescriptions and 30 billion over-the-counter (OTC) medications sold in the United States alone."[11]

NSAIDs have four benefits: pain relief, fever reduction, anti-inflammation action, and prolonged clotting of blood by affecting platelet function. NSAIDs are routinely used for osteoarthritis, rheumatoid arthritis, gout, fever and pain.

NSAIDs work by blocking an enzyme, cyclo-oxygenase or COX. When this enzyme is blocked, the body's ability to produce inflammatory proteins called prostaglandins diminishes and analgesia or pain relief occurs. Scientists recognize at least two COX enzymes. COX-1 inhibits the inflammatory proteins plus helps protect the lining of the stomach, regulate blood flow to kidneys, and helps blood to clot normally. The COX-2 enzyme involves the inflammatory response and pain but apparently doesn't affect the stomach lining, blood flow to kidneys or blood clotting. Early NSAIDs (also called traditional NSAIDs) blocked both kinds of COX enzymes, and persons who took those drugs noticed stomach upset and sometimes developed ulcers and bleeding. Scientists created COX-2 NSAIDs in an effort to avoid the side effects of traditional NSAIDs: stomach pain, ulcers and potential bleeding from ulcers. At first the COX-2 NSAIDs seemed to do well for many patients dealing with arthritis and other inflammatory diseases. Many people with arthritis tried the first COX-2 drug (refecoxib, commonly called Vioxx) and found their lives better and more enjoyable with less pain and fewer stomach problems. Over 91 million prescriptions of refecoxib had been written in the U.S. in the years between 1999 when Vioxx came available by prescription and 2004 when Merck pulled it off the market.[12] Two other COX-2 NSAIDs, celecoxib (Celebrex) and valdecoxib (Bextra) became available by prescription. The increased risks of heart attack and strokes associated with refecoxib came to light during a study in which researchers tested whether refecoxib would prevent colon polyps. Those people taking higher doses showed "significant increase in cardiovascular events at 18 months."[13] Refecoxib (Vioxx) was pulled from the market by the manufacturer. Later, Bextra was withdrawn from the market. Of the COX-2 NSAIDs, Celebrex is still marketed today. Confusion has reigned. Some patients and doctors question whether this single COX-2 NSAID and even the traditional NSAIDs are safe. Other patients still mourn the loss of refecoxib (Vioxx) because they felt it made life better.

Risks of NSAIDs involve gastrointestinal (GI) risks, and hematologic (blood), heart, and renal (kidney) effects. As a group of drugs, traditional NSAIDs can cause stomach symptoms of abdominal or stomach cramps, pain, diarrhea, heartburn or indigestion, nausea or vomiting, and stomach ulcers with bleeding. "In fact, NSAID use leads to more than 103,000 hospitalizations and 16,500 deaths each year in the United States. That's more deaths than from AIDS and more than four times as many deaths as those from cervical cancer."[14] As a group, NSAIDs are metabolized, broken down mainly in the liver, and excreted by the kidneys. Doctors may monitor liver function in patients at risk for liver problems.[15]

With the recall of two of the COX-2 NSAIDs, individuals may be wondering what they should be taking. Each person should talk to their doctor about health risks and the safest pain control. In particular, patients with heart, liver, and kidney disease and people who drink alcohol regularly should talk to their physician about NSAIDs, including over-the-counter NSAIDs, and safe dosages to avoid problems. Some medications that may be recommended to prevent stomach ulcers, discomfort, and bleeding include over-the-counter medicines such as omeprazole (Prilosec OTC),or famotidine (Pepcid) and prescription drugs such as omeprazole (Prilosec), pantoprazole (Protonix), esomeprazole (Nexium), lansoprazole (Prevacid), or rabeprazole (Aciphex). A drug called misoprostol (Cytotec) may be prescribed to promote healing of stomach ulcers by replacing prostaglandins in the stomach. According to the *Arthritis Today's Drug Guide 2005*, individuals can help avoid stomach problems from NSAIDs by doing the following:

"Skip alcohol." Taking NSAIDs and consuming alcohol increase the risk of gastric (stomach) bleeding.

"Take with food and water. Unless the product label or your doctor advises otherwise, always take medications with a full glass of water and some food— even if it's just a few crackers."

"List your medications." Talk to your doctor and pharmacist about all the drugs being taken, including over-the-counter and herbal supplements to avoid complications. Consider that some over-the-counter medicines, especially cold remedies, may contain NSAIDs or acetaminophen and don't overdose. Another potential medication problem involves the blood thinner warfarin (Coumadin) and NSAIDs, which could increase the risks for a gastrointestinal bleed. A third potential medication problem involves corticosteroids and NSAIDs, which could also contribute to gastrointestinal bleeding.

"Check the clock." Some people find taking a once-daily NSAID causes less stomach upset when taken later in the day. Talk to your doctor.

"Don't overdo it. Avoid the temptation to take more NSAIDs than prescribed or more often than prescribed."[16] The American Heart Association (AHA) suggests "this rule of thumb: use the safest drug first." The AHA recommends: "Medications like aspirin and acetaminophen (Tylenol) in recommended doses and durations have minimal toxicity, which makes them good first choices."[17] If pain control isn't obtained, the AHA recommends that patients talk to their doctors about stronger NSAIDs, whether over-the-counter such as naproxen (Aleve) or prescription NSAIDs.

A December 2005 press release announced a huge painkiller risk study to gain accurate data about NSAIDs and the risks involved. "The new trial will look at 20,000 arthritis patients with heart risks—people typically excluded from clinical trials—around the globe to determine the safety and effectiveness of Celebrex, ibuprofen and naproxen." While Pfizer, the manufacturer of Celebrex, will pay for the trial, researchers say safeguards will prevent any interference with results. "Pfizer will get a courtesy copy of study results but cannot change how it is reported in scientific journals. The federal government will store a copy of the entire completed trial database, ensuring public access."[18] This study, called the Precision (Prospective Randomized Evaluation of Celecoxib Integrated Safety vs. Ibuprofen vs. Naproxen) Trial, will be conducted by the Cleveland Clinic.

Efforts to bring the recalled Vioxx and Bextra back to the marketplace are under way. "The Arthritis Foundation urges the FDA and Merck to review their decisions on Vioxx and Bextra and to reconsider putting these drugs back on the market. We believe that selective Cox-2 inhibitors are an important and valuable class of drugs for many people with arthritis, that a very large number (of people) stand to benefit from these drugs, and will decide to use them and fully accept the risks."[19] The FDA Advisory Panel voted in February 2005 to allow Merck to bring rofecoxib (Vioxx) back to the American market. So far, the drug hasn't been made available. In the meantime, Bextra was removed from the market by its manufacturer in April 2005 because its usage for post-operative coronary bypass patients showed those patients had "two to three times the risk of heart attack, cardiac arrest, stroke or blood clots." [20] Another side effect of Bextra was a rare, but life-threatening skin reaction. The FDA, Health Canada (Canada's version of the FDA) and Merck are currently considering returning rofecoxib to the market. "Though the return of Bextra is not expected, its manufacturer, Pfizer, will work with the FDA to explore how the drug could be available on a compassionate use basis."[21]

Individuals and their doctors need to discuss each individual's risk factors and work together to achieve pain relief and minimize the risks of their drugs, whether prescription or over-the-counter.

Corticosteroids

Corticosteroid drugs, commonly called cortisone, are powerful medications. Corticosteroids used for arthritis are different from the androgen, or sex steroids, abused by some professional athletes. Cortisone is a hormone produced by the outer layer of the adrenal gland, a small gland located on top of the kidneys in the human body. The Nobel Prize for Physiology and Medicine in 1950 recognized three doctors who identified and duplicated cortisone. Considered a miracle drug, cortisone was used to suppress rheumatoid arthritis inflammation. Patients noticed they felt better and experienced decreased swelling and pain. However, over the years doctors recognized that side effects caused problems.

Currently, doctors balance the usage of steroids to gain the greatest benefits while minimizing the side effects. According to Lorig,

> Side effects of corticosteroids can be divided into categories, depending upon the length of time you have been taking the steroid and the dose prescribed. If you have been taking steroids for less than one week, side effects are quite rare, even if

the dose has been high. If you have been taking high doses for one week to one month, you are at risk for development of ulcers, mental changes including psychosis or depression, infection with bacterial germs, or acne. The side effects of steroid treatment become more apparent after one month to one year of medium to high dosage.[22]

Persons taking high-dosage steroid treatments for longer time frames experience side effects of increased body fat, including a buffalo hump over the shoulders and a round moon-face, increased facial hair growth, and increased risk of osteoporosis with fractures, development of cataracts, and high blood pressure.

Persons being treated with long-term steroids must consult with their doctor before changing dosages or stopping steroids. Medical dosages of steroids suppress the adrenal gland function and must be decreased slowly to allow the person's adrenal gland to resume normal functioning. "Adrenal gland crisis" can occur if a person stops taking the steroid abruptly and not enough cortisone is available. Weaning off steroids by decreasing the drug dosage is often recommended by doctors to avoid this problem.

Corticosteroids can be given in pill form, intravenous form by medical personnel, and in the form of injections such as "cortisone shots" by a doctor. The first two forms affect the entire body. A cortisone shot into a joint affects mainly that joint with only a small effect to the entire body. Cortisone shots result in decreased pain and inflammation. Doctors gauge the benefit of the steroid shots by the decreased pain symptoms a person experiences. A person who gets only a few days of relief isn't getting the desired result. The desired effect is weeks and months of relief or a permanent cessation of the pain and inflammation in that joint. Because some studies have indicated that ten cortisone shots into a joint can cause bone damage, doctors limit the number of steroid joint injections.[23]

Osteoporosis Drugs

Osteoporosis could be defined as "thinning of the bones, with reduction in bone mass, due to depletion of calcium and bone protein."[24] More details about osteoporosis can be found in Chapter 2. With improved screening and treatments, osteoporosis fractures should decrease. However, individuals must participate in prevention, screening and treatments to benefit from this technology. After a conversation with the doctor about personal health, persons can improve bone health by doing weight-bearing exercise, adding calcium and vitamin D to their diet or taking supplements. Other recommendations include limiting smoking and alcohol intake. What about bone necrosis in the jaw for some people taking biophosphonates? The Arthritis Foundation reported (January 2008) researchers at Harvard School of Dental Medicine included over

700,000 people in a study and found those taking oral biophonates were "slightly less likely to have adverse jaw outcomes than osteoporosis patients who were not taking the drugs."[25]

Other treatments for osteoporosis include estrogen, calcitonin, selective receptor molecules and bone formation agents.

DMARDs (Disease-Modifying Anti-Rheumatic Drugs)

DMARDs treat rheumatoid arthritis by controlling synovitis and preventing joint damage. Current thought involving DMARDs and biologic-response modifier drugs says early treatment of rheumatoid arthritis with these drugs slows the joint damage and improves the long-term results. Many of the new and aggressive drug therapies cost more. Patients and doctors may wonder whether they're worth it. Researchers in Japan evaluated this issue over a four-and-a-half-year period (2000–2004) and the results were announced at the 2005 American College of Rheumatology annual meeting: "While early, aggressive treatment of rheumatoid arthritis can result in increased costs for medications and short-term outpatient services, it substantially improves disease symptoms and, ultimately, reduces long-term medical expenditures for these patients."[26]

DMARDs include drugs such as gold salts, penicillamine (Cuprimine, Depen) and azathioprine (Imuran). Methotrexate (Rheumatrex, Trexall) is a DMARD that can be used alone or in combination with other drugs, such as TNF inhibitors, biologic-response modifier drugs, or corticosteroids to better control RA while decreasing side effects. A study cited in the January 2006 *Arthritis and Rheumatism* looked at methotrexate alone, methotrexate and adalimumab (Humira) together and adalimumab alone. Of the 799 patients enrolled in the study, 57 percent had RA for fewer than 6 months and the majority of participants were women. At year 1 and year 2 of the study, the patients receiving combination treatment had better results (decreased symptoms and less joint damage apparent on x-ray) than the other two groups who received only one drug, either methotrexate or adalimumab.[27] Individuals should get information regarding specific drugs from their physicians or pharmacists. Online drug information sources can be found at the end of this chapter.

Biologic-Response Modifier Drugs

Six drugs, etanercept (Enbrel), infliximab (Remicade), adalimumab (Humira), anakinra (Kineret), abatacept (Orencia) and rituximab (Rituxan), are classified as biologic-response modifier drugs. Three of those drugs, etanercept, infliximab and adalimumab, are tumor necrosis factor alpha (TNF alpha) inhibitors. These three block the inflammatory TNF proteins by binding with them and preventing the inflammatory response. Anakinra (Kineret) blocks the interleukin-1 (IL-1) cytokine. "Abatacept (Orencia) blocks T-cells, which play a key role in the development of RA."[28] Rituxan, originally used as a cancer drug, targets and blocks B-cells (B-lymphocytes).

All these drugs are expensive and cannot be taken by mouth, but require an injection either by the patient or a healthcare professional. "The BRMs, however, have given doctors a powerful new weapon with which to temper the destructive inflammation of RA."[29]

Prosorba Treatment

Prosorba (protein A immunoadsorption) therapy gives another option for patients with moderate to severe rheumatoid arthritis whose DMARD drug treatments haven't given relief. "Blood is withdrawn from one arm and passed through a cell separator machine that separates liquid (plasma) from the blood cells. The plasma is passed through a Prosorba column, where antibodies are removed. The treated plasma and blood cells are then recombined and returned to the patient through a vein in the other arm."[30] During the Prosorba treatment, the machine removes the antibodies the person's body produced during the auto-immune process of rheumatoid arthritis. The decreased antibodies will result in decreased damage to joints and organs. Prosorba involves a time commitment of 12 weekly sessions, each lasting two to three hours. Prosorba therapy costs approximately $1,500 per session.

Viscosupplements

Doctors recognize that knees affected by osteoarthritis are deficient in hyaluronic acid. Viscosupplement or hyaluronan injection (shot) replaces that lubricant. This treatment has been used in Europe and Asia for several years and in the U.S. since 1997. Some patients get relief while others do not. Routine treatment of hyaluronan consists of a series of three to five shots over several weeks. Patients accepting this treatment should not expect immediate results but can anticipate months of pain relief in the injected knees. Immediately after the injection, a local reaction such as pain, warmth and slight swelling may occur. This should subside fairly quickly. Hyaluronic acid does "seem to have anti-inflammatory and pain-relieving properties. The injections may also stimulate the body to produce more of its own hyaluronic acid."[31] The logic behind hyaluronic acid injections and glucosamine, chondroitin oral supplements is to make these compounds available for the joint cartilage to heal itself.

Glucosamine and Chondroitin

People with osteoarthritis have been trying glucosamine-chondroitin for several years. Some people swear by it while others think it's useless.

The human body produces both glucosamine and chondroitin. Glucosamine, a complex carbohydrate (sugar), is made within the body from glucose and the amino acid glutamine. Inside the cartilage cells glucosamine is a building block of the cartilage itself. "In normal cartilage production, the derivatives of glucose (glucosamine, galactose, and glucuronic acid) form chains called glycosaminoglycans (GAGs). Those formed by the derivatives of glucose include hyaluronic acid, chondroitin sulfate, and keratin sulfate. The latter two bind to protein cores within the cell and are excreted into the extracellular matrix; there they bind to the longer hyaluronic acid chains. When bound to the hyaluronic acid, these GAG-protein structures (proteoglycans), which resemble bottle brushes, constitute the hydrophilic, gel-like, cushioning portion of the cartilage."[32]

The European GUIDE (Glucosamine Unum In Die [once a day] Efficacy) study was reported at the American College of Rheumatology 2005 Annual meeting. This study compared glucosamine, acetaminophen (Tylenol) and placebo (sugar pills). The GUIDE study included 318 people with knee osteoarthritis. The participants during this random study took either oral glucosamine sulfate (1,500 mg once a day), acetaminophen (1,000 mg three times day), or placebo for a six-month period. "Results showed that both glucosamine sulfate and acetaminophen had greater efficacy (effect) than placebo use in reducing pain. However, patients taking glucosamine sulfate appeared to experience more relief than did those of acetaminophen."[33] Readers should note that the glucosamine sulfate in this study is slightly different from the glucosamine HCl commonly sold in the U.S.

The National Institutes of Health (NIH)-funded study, Glucosamine/Chondroitin Arthritis Intervention Trial (GAIT) was released in November 2005. One thousand five hundred eighty-three people participated in this 24-week study, which compared celecoxib (Celebrex), the supplement glucosamine HCl by itself, chondroitin sulfate by itself, and combination glucosamine HCl-chondroitin sulfate. "As expected, celecoxib improved knee pain in patients with osteoarthritis. For the study as a whole, the supplements were not shown to be effective; however, an exploratory analysis suggested that the combination of glucosamine and chondroitin sulfate might be effective in osteoarthritis patients who had moderate to severe knee pain."[34] The researchers noted the glucosamine and chondroitin alone or together did not provide relief from mild pain.

In April 2007, researchers analyzing 20 prior studies summarized their findings in the Annals of Internal Medicine: "Chondroitin probably does not prevent or reduce joint pain in people with osteoarthritis."[35] While these studies involved chondroitin only, not the combined chondroitin-glucosamine commonly used in the United States, this analysis questions the value of chondroitin-glucosamine for arthritis pain. Dr. David Felson, editor of the *Annals of Internal Medicine*, summarized his opinion. "The best current evidence is that chondroitin sulfate does not reduce joint pain in osteoarthritis.... Because no frequent or severe adverse effects have been reported, chondroitin sulfate should not be considered dangerous. If patients say that they benefit from chondroitin, I see no harm in encouraging them to continue taking it as long as they perceive a benefit."[36]

People who should avoid glucosamine include women who are pregnant or breastfeeding and children. Diabetics should talk to their doctor before taking glucosamine-chondroitin because it's an amino sugar that may affect blood sugar levels. Chondroitin chemically is similar to the blood thinner heparin and may increase the risk of bleeding for persons on blood thinners, so a doctor should be aware when such a person starts taking chondroitin. Persons with allergies to shellfish who want to try glucosamine should consult their doctor for an opinion and possible allergy testing. Most shellfish allergies involve the shellfish protein, not the carbohydrate chitin from which glucosamine is extracted. The most common side effects of glucosamine and chondroitin sulfate include intestinal symptoms such intestinal gas and softened stools.[37]

Many people buy the supplement recommended by friends or family and manage their own glucosamine and chondroitin supplement. People would be wise to consult with their doctor and get the optimal results. An important question to ask the doctor would involve which brand glucosamine/chondroitin to buy.* The Arthritis Foundation makes this recommendation: "Because dietary supplements are unregulated, the quality and content may vary widely. If you decide to take these supplements, choose products sold by large, well-established companies that can be held accountable. Read the product labels carefully to make sure the ingredient list makes sense to you. If you have trouble, ask your pharmacist for help."[38] Another key to quality is cost. Individuals should expect to pay $30 to $45/month for quality supplements. The Arthritis Foundation warns "beware of no-name bargains that may turn out to be substandard."[39]

Heat Wraps/Topical Creams

"Heat activates complex mechanisms that block or blunt the transmission of pain signals through nerves."[40] Wraps also can support and stabilize muscles,

*The January 2006 Arthritis Today article, "Good News for Knees," recommends a consumer lab website to evaluate glucosamine-chondroitin supplements at http://www.consumerlab.com/results/gluco.asp.

tendons and ligaments. For information about brands and their costs, the *Arthritis Today's Buyers' Guide* published annually gives specific information.

Topical pain relievers work as a counter-irritant or a distraction from the pain. The original topical pain relievers contain menthol and methylsalicylate (oil of wintergreen). When applied, these topical creams feel cool, followed by a feeling of warmth. Another topical cream contains capsaicin (Capzasin-P or Zostrix), a compound obtained from chili peppers. Capsaicin binds with receptors on peripheral nerves and inhibits activation of the pain pathway. Cetylated fatty acid topical cream (Celadrin) is a third type of cream. In a small study, the forty participants found better joint movement and range of motion during several activities, including walking, climbing stairs, rising and sitting down.[41]

Safety tips for these pain relievers include washing hands after using. Avoid getting these topical creams on mucous membranes, including the eyes. A heating pad should never be used with these topical creams to avoid burns.

Coping with the Prices of Prescription Drugs

Prescription drugs can cost a lot of money. Many people find the cost of drugs cutting into their budgets. News stories have highlighted the pharmaceutical companies as greedy. According to the book *Smart Buys, Drug Wise*, the pharmaceutical companies try to influence patients, doctors and pharmacists to utilize the latest, most expensive drugs. Patients are influenced by advertising that encourages patients to "ask your doctor if this drug is right for you." Surveys show that one in three patients will ask for an advertised drug and the doctor prescribes that drug about half the time.[42] Often, free samples of drugs help patients. But free samples provide a benefit to the drug companies if the sample packages don't contain enough doses for full treatment. The drug companies hope the physician will more likely prescribe their drug after becoming familiar with the new drug.

On the other hand, miracle drugs come from these same pharmaceutical companies. Prior to the discovery of antibiotics, an infection often killed. Many cancer treatments save lives. The average cost of developing and bringing a new drug to the consumer mounts to $800 million.

What can consumers do to decrease their drug costs? Several things. Consider generic drugs instead of brand-name drugs. The patient should ask whether a generic drug would be as good as the higher-priced brand-name drug. Often, the drug advertisements lead people to believe the newest drugs are the best. According to Food and Drug Administration (FDA) data, only 20 percent of new drugs "offer any significant improvement over those already in use."[43] Another reason to consider generic drugs is that their benefits and side effects are documented. The same side effects and benefits that occurred when people took the brand-name drugs will result from generic drugs because generic drugs are chemically equivalent (according to the FDA). New drugs can have unexpected side effects.

What is the difference between brand-name and generic drugs? When a new drug is developed, the pharmaceutical company obtains a patent that prohibits any other company from making that drug. During the time of patent protection, the patent-holding company sets the price for that drug. Research and development costs plus profits are earned during the years of patent protection. When the patent expires on the brand name drug, any pharmaceutical company can make that drug in generic form and compete with pricing. "Generic drugs are drugs the FDA (Food and Drug Administration) has determined to be equivalent to their name-brand counterparts."[44] Being chemical copies of the brand-name drugs, generic drugs almost always contain the same amounts of active ingredients and have the same actions. On the average generic drugs cost half the price of brand-name drugs. A few generic drugs will be considered less effective by doctors who will recommend the brand name, but generally, generic drugs are less expensive, safe and effective choices.

All consumers benefit financially from generic drugs. Patients with no drug coverage pay less because generic drugs cost less. People who have insurance coverage should review the details of their plan. Generic drugs probably will save them money also. Many insurance plans have different drug coverage levels (tiers). If so, the lowest co-pay (what the patient pays) tier includes generic drugs. Higher tiers include drugs such as brand-name or more expensive generic drugs and the co-pay costs more. Also, patients will get the best pricing on their prescription drugs at an "in-network" pharmacy. This pharmacy and insurance company have agreed to provide prescription drugs to the insurance company's clients. The clients/patients only pay the co-pay as listed in the plan.

Individuals can save money by comparing prices between pharmacies. All pharmacies do not charge the same prices for the same drugs. While many Americans compare prices for food and cars, they neglect to do this at the pharmacy. Persons calling to compare prices may save money. The person price shopping for his drugs will probably need a new prescription from the doctor to change pharmacies.

Another way to save money on prescription drugs is to buy in larger quantities. The patient should talk to his doctor and pharmacist about this option. If the prescribed dose is 10 mg and the same drug is available in a 20-mg scored, easy-to-divide tablet, the patient can divide a 20-mg tablet into two doses of 10 mg and save money. This does not work for capsules or timed release medications, which are impossible to divide equally. *Smart Buys Drug Wise* recommends patients "use a tablet cutter to split tablets evenly for medications. If your pharmacist doesn't normally sell them, he can easily order one for you. Unevenly cut tablets give you uneven, unknown amounts of the drugs."[45]

If the physician would order a 90-day instead of a 30-day supply, this saves money for some people. Patients should check with their prescription drug plan to determine if this suggestion will save money. This option will not be cost-effective for short-term medications such as antibiotics. Individuals starting on new medications should try the new drugs for a month or two before filling a 90-day supply because the individual may not continue taking that medication long-term.

Comparing prescription drugs to over-the-counter (OTC) drugs may save money also. Over the past years, 200 prescription drugs have been moved to OTC drugs by the FDA. Drugs such as Tagamet and Naprosyn, formerly available by prescription, can be purchased over the counter and may cost less. Doctors may still write prescriptions for those drugs and patients should compare prices between the two. If the doctor prescribes Tagamet 300 mg, the patient should take three of the OTC strength (Tagamet HB 100 mg) to equal the prescribed amount. Often, the OTC strength is a lower dosage and the patient should take the amount recommended by the physician.

Internet pharmacy (mail order) has become an option for some consumers. The written prescription is sent to a warehouse-type drugstore that sends the drugs through the mail to the patient. Many insurance prescription plans offer such a service. Consumers who utilize this service must plan ahead and order prescriptions at least two weeks before they need a delivery. Overnight deliveries are usually expensive, ranging from $9 to $25.[46] Internet pharmacy isn't recommended for short-term prescriptions such as antibiotics or new prescriptions.

The dangers of Internet pharmacy involve knowing whether or not you are dealing with a reputable company. If the Internet pharmacy is recommended by an insurance carrier, the insurer has probably already verified the reputable status of the internet pharmacy and can provide that information to consumers. The National Association of Boards of Pharmacy is a professional organization representing state boards of pharmacy in all 50 states in America, eight Canadian provinces, the District of Columbia, Guam, Puerto Rico, the Virgin Islands, South Africa and New Zealand. This organization oversees and verifies that internet pharmacies are reputable and in good standing. The designation of VIPPS Seal stands for Verified Internet Pharmacy Practice Site. This program began in 1999 when the NABP recognized the need to protect consumers. Several state pharmacy boards had received consumer complaints about illegal Internet pharmacies, and the NABP responded with the VIPPS program. The NABP recommends Internet pharmacies that have earned the VIPPS certification.*

The FDA warns consumers, "Don't buy from sites that offer to prescribe a prescription drug for the first time without a physical exam, sell a prescription

*Individuals without the insurance coverage can begin their research of an internet pharmacy at the National Association of Boards of Pharmacy website (www.NABP.net).

drug without a prescription, or sell drugs not approved by FDA."[47] Reputable Internet pharmacies have registered pharmacists available to answer patient questions. Another warning FDA makes: "Look for easy-to-find and understand privacy and security policies. Don't provide any personally identifiable information (social security number, credit card and health history) unless you are confident that the site will protect them. Make sure the site does not share your information with others without your permission."[48]

Other tips to consumers regarding Internet pharmacies include the following:

Wise consumers ask details such as costs of drugs, shipping charges, and times and conditions of delivery before ordering drugs. It's wise to know where the internet pharmacy is based. Look for a U.S. address and phone number to contact if there's a problem. While pharmacies outside the U.S. may be less expensive, the quality of those drugs will be questionable.

Drug companies offer patient assistance programs to those consumers who qualify and apply for their programs. To qualify for these programs, patients must "have no insurance coverage for prescription drugs ... meet income guidelines (usually tied to federal poverty guidelines), ... have your doctor contact the drug company."[49] Some of the drug companies provide free drugs. Other drug companies provide a limited supply such as 90 days. *Smart Buys Drug Wise* gives in-depth information, including phone numbers to research the patient assistance programs offered by pharmaceutical companies.*

News programs have documented Americans crossing the border into Canada or Mexico to buy their prescription drugs. Canadian drugs are considered to be high quality, safe drugs. Many of those drugs were manufactured in America and may carry the same labels. Also, some brand-name drugs in America have been made generic in Canada due to different patent laws. According to *Smart Buys Drug Wise*, efforts have been made by American lawmakers to legalize the purchase of prescription drugs in Canada. In 2000, Congress passed and President Clinton signed the law allowing individuals and pharmacies to re-import American-made drugs and pharmacies to sell these drugs at reduced prices. Unfortunately, the "Secretary of Health and Human Services, citing 'serious flaws and loopholes,' refused to enforce the measure. Congressional efforts to pass another, enforceable, measure continue."[50] In the meantime, Canada now requires a Canadian physician to write the prescription for drugs bought in Canada, which requires finding a Canadian doctor who will rewrite the prescriptions written by an American doctor. In practice, the FDA "doesn't interfere as Americans routinely cross the border with small quantities of

*RxAssist (http://www.rxassist.org) is recommended by the authors of Smart Buys Drug Wise as a free resource for consumers who need to apply for drug-manufacturer assistance programs. RxAssist is sponsored by the Robert Wood Johnson Foundation. The Arthritis Foundation recommends the Partnership for Prescription Assistance at 888-477-2669 or www.pparx.org.

Things You Can Do to Prevent Medication Mistakes

(Courtesy of Joint Commission of Accreditation of Healthcare Organizations)

Medication mistakes happen every day—at the doctor's office, hospital, even at home. Some mistakes are more serious than others, but all medication mistakes can be prevented. Here are some basic things you can do to help prevent a medication mistake from happening to you or your loved ones.

At the doctor's office and pharmacy
- Share with your doctor a list of your current medicines, including over-the-counter medicines, vitamins, herbs and supplements.
- Whenever you get a new medicine, remind your doctor about allergies you have, or negative reactions you have had to other medicines.
- If you are taking a lot of medicines, ask your doctor if it is safe to take those medicines together. Do the same thing with vitamins, herbs and other supplements.
- Understand that more medications may not always be better for you. Ask your doctor how a new medication will help.
- Make sure you can read the handwriting on prescriptions. If you can't read it, the pharmacist may not be able to either. You can ask to have the prescription printed.
- Read the label on your prescription medicine. Make sure it has your name on it and the correct medicine name. Some medicines have similar names that can be confused.
- If you are not sure whether you are supposed to swallow or chew your medicine, ask your doctor or pharmacist. Also, ask your doctor or pharmacist whether you can cut or crush a medicine.
- Ask your doctor or pharmacist if it's safe to drink alcohol with your medicine.
- Take your medicine as it is prescribed and do not stop taking it without asking your doctor.
- Whenever you are in doubt about a medicine, ask your doctor or pharmacist about it.

At the hospital and clinic
- Share with your doctor a list of your current medicines, vitamins, herbs and supplements.
- Make sure the doctor or nurse checks your wristband and asks your name before giving you medicine.
- Ask your doctor or nurse how a new medicine will help. Ask for written information about it, including its brand and generic names.
- Ask your doctor or nurse about the possible side effects of your medicines.
- Don't be afraid to tell the nurse or the doctor if you think you are about to get the wrong medicine.
- Know what time you normally get a medicine. If you don't get it then, tell your nurse or doctor.
- Tell your nurse or doctor if you don't feel well after receiving a medicine. If you

---

(Things You Can Do, *continued***)**

think you are having a reaction or experiencing side effects, ask for help
immediately.

- If you're not feeling well enough to ask questions about your medicines, ask a
relative of friend to ask questions for you and to help make sure you get and
take the right medicines.
- If you receive intravenous (IV) fluids, read the contents of the bags of IV fluids.
If you're not well enough to do this, ask a relative or friend to do it.
- If you are given an IV, ask the nurse how long it should take for the liquid to
run out. Tell the nurse if it seems to be dripping too fast or too slow.
- Ask for a copy of your medication administration record. This lists all the drugs
you should be taking. Check it for accuracy. If you're not well enough to do
this, ask a friend or relative to help.
- Before you leave the hospital or clinic, make sure that you understand all the
instructions for the medicines you will need to keep taking and ask any questions you may have about any of your medications.

American-made drugs purchased in Canada, and even order and receive prescriptions from Canadian pharmacies by mail-order or via the Internet."[51] However, Americans traveling to Canada for their drugs or ordering from Canadian
Internet pharmacies should recognize that purchasing and re-importing drugs
is still illegal and the FDA could change their practices and crack down with
tougher enforcement measures.

According to *Smart Buys Drug Wise*, "We recommend that you do not buy
drugs in Mexico.... Many drugs available in Mexico contain ingredients not
found in American versions with the same names, and some drugs are produced
in combinations that don't exist elsewhere."[52]

People dealing with pain face a lot of confusion. Conversations with doctors can help individuals choose the safest pain medications for their pain. Self-
management courses and lifestyle changes recommended by the Arthritis
Foundation can help people dealing with chronic pain to improve their lives.
"In addition to medications, the Arthritis Foundation stresses the importance
of weight control, exercise and physical activity, joint injections, the use of
orthotic and assistive devices and surgical options for the management of pain
and functional limitations caused by arthritis."[53]

10

Alternative Therapies

Worldwide, alternative medicine traditions account for 70 to 90 percent of health care.[1] Americans increasingly try alternative medicine, also known by the terms *holistic, unorthodox, integrative* and *complementary medicine.* A survey of 31,000 Americans published in 2004 showed that 36 percent of adults aged 18 or older used complementary and alternative medicine (CAM). When prayer for health reasons was added to CAM practices, the number of U.S. adults using CAM soared to 62 percent.[2] The results of this survey listed the 10 most frequently used CAM and percentage of Americans using each therapy:

Prayer for own health, 43 percent
Prayer by others for the respondent's health, 24 percent
Natural products (such as herbs, other botanicals and enzymes), 19 percent
Deep breathing exercises, 12 percent
Participation in prayer group for own health, 10 percent
Meditation, 8 percent
Chiropractic care, 8 percent
Yoga, 5 percent
Massage, 5 percent
Diet-based therapies, ... 4 percent[3]

CAM is defined as "a group of diverse medical and health care systems, practices, and products that are not presently considered to be part of conventional medicine."[4] "People use CAM therapies in a variety of ways. CAM therapies used alone are often referred to as 'alternative.' When used in addition to conventional medicine, they are called 'complementary.' The list of what is considered to be CAM changes continually, as those therapies that are proven to be safe and effective become adopted into conventional health care and as new approaches to health care emerge."[5]

A few of the alternative medicine practices include acupuncture and acupressure, hypnosis, bee venom and herbal supplements.* People contemplating

*http://www.nccam.nih.gov/.

a CAM should become knowledgeable about the CAM to protect their health and finances. According to the National Center for Complementary and Alternative Medicine (NCCAM),* "Take charge of your health by being an informed consumer. Find out what scientific studies have been done on the safety and effectiveness of the CAM treatment in which you are interested."[6] Secondly, the NCCAM recommends people discuss plans to use CAM with their physician or nurse practitioner. Because of the increasing popularity of CAM, more research is being done. Doctors and nurse practitioners read the research results, looking for effective treatments.

People without Internet access can obtain information at a public or medical library, either through publications or books. The *Arthritis Foundation's Guide to Alternative Therapies* by Judith Horstman provides valuable, balanced information about the different complementary and alternative therapies.

When considering CAM, a person should ask questions such as: Is this therapy safe or will it harm me? Will this CAM be effective, relieve pain or make me healthier? How much does this cost? Will my health insurance pay any of this expense?

"Americans visited alternative therapy practitioners 629 million times in 1997.... They spent approximately $27 billion out-of-pocket [not covered by insurance] on alternative therapies in 1997, which is about the same as estimated 1997 out-of-pocket spending for all U.S. physician services."[7] The American Medical Association recommends that a person "discuss any type of medical therapy with your doctor."[8]

Acupuncture

"More than 15 million Americans have used acupuncture, primarily for pain relief."[9] Acupuncture, an ancient Chinese philosophy, treats disharmony or imbalance within the human body, which causes illness, pain and disease. In this philosophy, the vital life force called qi (pronounced "chee") flows through meridians, invisible channels, which touch every organ. When blockages occur in the meridians, illness and disease can occur. Acupuncture relieves the blockages and restores the balance between yin and yang, the opposing male and female aspects of life. Practitioners of acupuncture believe it promotes wellness and health.

Acupuncture happens when the practitioner inserts tiny solid needles of 32 to 36 gauge into specific areas of the body.[10] Reputable practitioners will use disposable, new acupuncture needles and alcohol swabs to avoid risk of germ

*Alternative Treatments for Arthritis: an A to Z Guide *can be ordered from the Arthritis Foundation at www.arthritis.org.*

transmission. Sometimes a low-level electrical current is attached to the acupuncture needles for a more powerful effect (called electroacupuncture). Other treatments a practitioner may use include herbs (moxibustion) or heat, magnets, low-level laser, or bee stings. A practice called "cupping" involves placing warm glass cups on the skin. The vacuum that forms as the cups cools stimulates the skin area.

Acupuncture seemed unexplainable for many years to Westerners. One possible explanation for its effectiveness involves endorphin levels. "Needling affects cerebrospinal fluid levels of endorphin and enkephalin, and such effects can be blocked by the opiate antagonist naloxone."[11] Scientists recognize endorphin and enkephalin as "the body's own morphine," two substances the human body produces to decrease pain and enhance a person's sense of well-being.[12]

Another possible explanation was shown on January 2006 on the BBC TV series *Alternative Medicine*. This experiment indicates that acupuncture may deactivate part of the pain center in the human brain. Doctors and scientists compared the brain studies of subjects who received "deep needling" vs "superficial needling." Deep needling involved the scientist inserting the acupuncture needle one centimeter into an acupuncture point on the person's hand and rotating that needle until the subject felt a tingling sensation (called de chi). During superficial needling, the needle is inserted into the same area, but only about one millimeter deep. The brain scan showed "'superficial needling' results in activation of the motor areas of the cortex, a normal response to touch or pain. With 'deep needling' and *de chi* effect, a deeper part of the brain is affected."[13] This deeper brain area called the limbic system involves emotions from happy and joyful to sad and anxious. Pain involves a person's limbic system and emotions. This research supports the idea that acupuncture affects the limbic system. "Surprisingly, this part of the brain is deactivated with 'deep needling'; neuroscientists are more familiar with interventions causing activations."[14] Scientists continue to search for the answer to why acupuncture decreases pain.

The National Institutes of Health (NIH) determined in 1997 that acupuncture was effective for treatment of nausea due to chemotherapy, anesthesia and pregnancy. Also acupuncture was found to be valuable in treatment of headaches, carpal tunnel syndrome and fibromyalgia.[15]

"Acupuncture provides pain relief and improves function for people with osteoarthritis of the knee and serves as an effective complement to standard care."[16] The National Institutes of Health (NIH) research study on acupuncture as a pain-relieving treatment for knee osteoarthritis is complete and results have been made public. The study enrolled 570 persons age 50 years and older who deal with knee osteoarthritis. The groups were randomly assigned to one of three groups: acupuncture, sham acupuncture (in which the needles were taped to their skin) and control group. The control group participated in the Arthritis Self-Help Course, a proven success. All participants continued with their regular medical care, including anti-inflammatory drugs and pain relievers. This study was continued over 26 weeks and participants were assessed at 4, 8, 14 and 26 weeks. "By week 8, participants receiving acupuncture were showing a significant increase in function and by week 14 a significant decrease in pain, compared with the sham and control groups.... Those who received acupuncture had a 40 percent decrease in pain and a nearly 40 percent improvement in function compared to baseline assessment."[17]

A German study addressed the question, "will the pain relief persist after acupuncture treatments stop?" This study involving 294 participants agreed that persons receiving acupuncture reported less pain and improved knee function when compared to persons who received minimal or no acupuncture. When long-term (26- to 52-week) effects were evaluated, the scientists concluded, "The benefits did not persist after acupuncture was discontinued."[18]

"Acupuncture is considered safe if it's done by a licensed practitioner with sterilized, disposable needles."[19] The acupuncturist should know the person's complete medical history, including pregnancy, and should know all medications and supplements being taken. The patient should tell the acupuncturist about having a pacemaker or breast implants.

Acupressure

Acupressure technique involves the practitioner using hands and fingers to exert pressure on the same points of the body as acupuncture. Acupressure, like acupuncture, works to unblock and balance the energy flow. Needles are not involved in acupressure. Some people believe it may not be as powerful or specific as acupuncture, but few research studies have been done on acupressure. Shiatsu technique is the Japanese version of acupressure. Tuina (tway-nah), a Chinese acupressure and massage technique, is gaining popularity in America.

A practitioner of acupressure shouldn't apply pressure to open wounds, bruises or broken bones, varicose veins or any areas of fragile skin such as scars or swollen, reddened and sore areas of skin. A pregnant woman should tell the acupuncturist of her pregnancy so some pressure points will be avoided. According to *Alternative Treatments for Arthritis*, persons with heart, lung and kidney disorders as well as infectious illnesses should not undergo acupressure.[20]

Bee Venom

Some people dealing with arthritis pain endure bee stings in their quest for pain relief. The bee venom can be injected by a practitioner or by live bee stings. Studies done on rats and mice show that bee stings decreased the inflammation of arthritis. This ancient treatment contains anti-inflammatory substances called adolapin and melittin. These substances stimulate the body to produce a powerful anti-inflammatory steroid called cortisol (the body's version of cortisone).*

Persons interested in bee venom should talk to their family doctor. They should also heed the advice of the Arthritis Foundation: be prepared for allergic reactions to the bee venom by obtaining an emergency sting kit from a doctor and learning how to use it. A person should know the number and location of the nearest hospital emergency department in case of allergic reactions. Another suggestion is to "never sting yourself when alone"[21] and be sure anyone around the bees has been tested for bee venom allergies. Persons dealing with heart disease, high blood pressure problems, diabetes, and tuberculosis shouldn't use bee venom. Bee venom doesn't work for everyone. According to Alternative Treatment for Arthritis, bee venom treatments should be discontinued if no improvement is seen after eight sessions (or a total of 20 to 70 injections or bee stings).[22]

Chiropractic Care

Chiropractors manipulate or adjust the spine. Chiropractors graduate from four-year chiropractic colleges and are licensed practitioners. The chiropractic theory says misaligned or subluxed vertebrae cause almost all diseases and by correcting the misalignment, a cure can be achieved. Some chiropractors use additional treatments such as ultrasound, traction, and electrical stimulations to accomplish the corrections. Nutritional therapy, including herb and vitamins, may be included in chiropractic techniques.

Alternative Treatments for Arthritis recommends that patients talk with their physician before using a chiropractor.[23] Good communication with the chiropractor should include important details such as arthritic joints that may be fragile or osteoporotic. The chiropractor should know about all medications the person takes, including vitamins and supplements. A person taking blood thinners (anti-coagulants) should notify the chiropractor because blood thinners could contribute to bruising from the manipulation.[24]

Herbs and Supplements

Can Chinese Thunder God Vine give relief from rheumatoid arthritis? Is turmeric an antioxidant that will help with arthritis symptoms? Volumes of

*More information about bee venom treatment can be found through the American Apitherapy Society at www.apitherapy.org.

books have been written about herbs and supplements and the Internet is a useful resource as well.*

"The poison arrived in a plastic bottle from India bearing a simple label in English and Hindi. 'Useful in flu and body ache,' it read. 'Two tabs twice a day or as per physician's advice.' What it didn't say was that the herbal medicine, on sale at a store in Queens, New York, contains 2,190 times the amount of mercury considered safe by the Institute of Medicine of the National Academies."[25] This news story expressed the concerns of many Americans: Herbal medicines and supplements aren't tested or regulated by the Food and Drug Administration (FDA).

Under the Dietary Supplement Health and Education Act (DSHEA) of 1994, "dietary supplements" aren't required to pass tests to prove their safety and effectiveness. This lack of oversight leaves consumers on their own when it comes to safety in herbal supplements. In the case of the mercury-laced pills, the New York City health officials seized the pills and got them off the shelves as soon as they knew about them.

Persons wanting to try herbal supplements would be wise to heed these suggestions from the Arthritis Foundation: talk to your doctor about the supplements, their possible side effects and dosage to take, learn about the supplement before buying, avoid taking multiple supplements at the same time, continue with your regular medicines and stick with reputable herbal manufacturing companies.[26]

Magnets

George heard June say her magnet bracelet helps her arthritis. When asked for details, June said, "Since my son bought me this bracelet, I wear it all the time. I've noticed my arthritis doesn't hurt as much." George's wife Sherry said, "What do you have to lose? I'll buy you a magnet bracelet for your birthday." George started wearing the bracelet and thought maybe it helped but he wasn't sure. When he broke the bracelet and could not wear it, he noticed he had to take more NSAIDs to get through the day. George sent the broken bracelet back to the company under warranty. When the replacement magnet bracelet arrived, George put it on and routinely needs less NSAIDs. Placebo effect? No one knows.

The theory behind (static) magnet bracelets involves electrical charges in the human body. Putting magnets over the painful area may increase blood supply while helping decrease inflammation and pain. Scientific studies have been few

---

*The NCCAM website offers information about herbs and supplements at www.nccam.nih.gov/health/ supplements.htm. The Arthritis Foundation provides free online information about herbs and supplements at http://www.arthritis.org/conditions/supplementguide/herbs.asp.

Tell Your Doctor About ALL Supplements Before Surgery

Common Herbal Supplements	Uses	Possible problems from herbal drugs during surgery
Chamomile	Decrease gas & indigestion Relieve insomnia	Bleeding
Echinacea	Treat infections	Bleeding, cause allergic reaction, decreases effects of steroids
Ephedra (Ma huang)	Asthma, Increase energy Decrease appetite	High blood pressure, insomnia, irregular heart rates/beats, stroke Heart attack/death, seizures
Feverfew	Headaches, Fever Psoriasis	Bleeding (decreased platelet function) overreact with vasoactive anesthesia drugs
Garlic	Treat cholesterol Lower blood pressure Antibacterial, Bronchitis	Bleeding
Ginger	Nausea, indigestion, motion sickness	Bleeding
Gingko	Poor memory, diabetes, Poor circulation	Bleeding, Increased intra-cranial pressure
Ginseng	Anti-stress, fatigue, viral infections	Bleeding, Low blood sugar High blood pressure, Prolong blood thinner warfarin
Kava	Anxiety, Sedative	Strengthens anesthetic drugs, barbiturates/narcotics
Licorice	Arthritis, asthma, poor appetite, stomach ulcers, cough suppressant	High blood pressure Retain salt & water/edema
St. John's wort	Depression, anxiety	Prolong anesthesia drugs change drug metabolism
Valerian	Nerves, depression, insomnia	Strengthen anesthesia & central nervous system drugs & narcotics
Vohimbe	Impotence	Decrease anesthesia effects, Cause tremors, fast heart rate/high blood pressure

MacKichan, C., Ruthman, J. (2004). Herbal product use and perioperative patients. *AORN Journal* 79(5), 948–959.

DeLamar, L.M. (2005). Preparing Your Patient for Surgery. *Topics in Advanced Practice Nursing eJournal* 5(1). http://www.medscape.com/viewarticle/500887_print (accessed 03/29/2005).

Herbal Supplements. (2004) *Nursing 2004.* 34(12), 52–53.

and inconclusive. The NCCAM is sponsoring studies to investigate the value of static magnets for fibromyalgia pain and quality of life and their effects on networks of blood vessels involved in healing.[27]

Persons who have pacemakers or other implanted electronic devices should consult the doctor because magnets may interfere with the function of a pacemaker or other electronic devices. Any magnet-sensitive switch, such as electric blankets or electronic equipment may be affected by magnets and should be turned off. A magnetic mattress pad should not be slept on.[28] Pregnant women should not use magnet therapy. A person starting magnet therapy should be mindful of changes and report those to the doctor. If magnets increase a person's circulation, medications may be absorbed more quickly.

Mind-Body Aspect of Medicine

"Mind-body medicine focuses on the interactions among the brain, mind, body, and behavior and the powerful ways in which emotional, mental, social, spiritual, and behavioral factors can directly affect health."[29] Mind-body medicine recognizes that people can become aware of self and care for self by practicing wellness behaviors. Mind-body medicine involves techniques such as biofeedback, hypnosis, relaxation, visual imagery, meditation, yoga, tai chi, spirituality and group support. Meditation is discussed in chapter 6; details about yoga and tai chi can be found in chapter 8. Persons wanting to care for their spiritual aspect should look in chapter 4.

Biofeedback

Biofeedback uses modern-day technology to monitor certain body functions and enable a person to learn control over those functions. By wearing sensors, a person can either see squiggly lines or hear beeps that indicate body functions such as pulse, body temperature, muscle tension, or digestion. The person can learn to control the beeps or squiggles through relaxation techniques. "People have learned to control blood pressure, brain activity, bowel and bladder problems, digestion, muscle tension, nausea, heart rate, even sweat glands."[30] Several visits to the therapist's office will be needed to learn biofeedback techniques.

Biofeedback techniques have gained acceptance with people and have been approved by the National Institutes of Health (NIH) for complementary treatment of insomnia and pain.[31] Individuals interested in learning biofeedback should consult their doctor, especially if that individual has heart problems, a pacemaker or diabetes.

Hypnosis

"Don't worry; you won't lose consciousness. You won't do anything against your will."[32] Hypnosis helps a person voluntarily focus and relax. Hypnosis helps people dealing with pain, anxiety, and depression cope with less medication. A 2000 study by psychologists found that hypnosis could affect the experience of pain.[33] A 2003 review of multiple studies on hypnosis agreed. Hypnosis could accomplish "significant reductions in ratings of pain, need for analgesics (pain medicines) or sedation, nausea and vomiting, and length of stay in hospitals."[34]

Chronic indigestion and irritable bowel syndrome symptoms improve when people learn how to hypnotize themselves. People wanting to quit smoking find the American Cancer Society includes hypnosis as a stop-smoking technique. While hypnosis cannot cure the overweight problem, hypnosis can help reinforce lifestyle changes that people use to succeed in weight loss. Hypnosis works best when a person wants to change a behavior and thinking. This explains the success of hypnosis for people wanting to overcome addictions. Scientific studies find changes occur within the human brain under hypnosis, especially the area used when a person focuses attention.[35]

Hypnosis has gained acceptance as a medical treatment. A 1995 National Institutes of Health (NIH) recommendation for treatment of chronic pain includes hypnosis.[36] The person considering hypnosis should talk to the doctor when searching for a hypnotist.*

Relaxation Techniques

Scientists recognize this fact: When a person experiences pain, stress and other negative emotions, he breathes in shallow, quick breaths and may even hold his breath for short periods of time without realizing it. When a person experiences positive emotions such as love and pleasure, long and deep breaths happen automatically. Routinely, people only use the upper portion of their lungs and occasionally take deep breaths. Scientists and doctors recognize that deep-breathing techniques have great value. Persons can practice deep-breathing techniques to control pain better, lower blood pressure, turn off the body's fight-or-flight adrenalin response, calm feelings of panic, and relax.

Deep-breathing techniques involve focusing on deep breaths and feeling the chest rise and the belly suck in. These techniques can be learned from yoga, tai chi and qi gong classes or videotapes. These techniques can be used to deal with daytime stressors as well as relax for a good night's sleep.

*The National Guild of Hypnotists at www.ngh.net and the American Council of Hypnotist Examiners at www.hypnotistexaminers.org also give referrals to hypnosis practitioners.

Progressive muscle relaxation involves tensing and relaxing parts of the body, muscle by muscle. One woman starts her relaxation technique by tensing her toe and feet muscles followed by relaxing those muscles. She continues this tensing and relaxing routine up her legs into her body.

A third relaxation technique called body scan involves the person focusing on feeling the different parts of the body section by section.

Be safe. After practicing deep-breathing techniques, a person should be alert to possible dizziness and stand slowly to avoid the risks of falling. Also, persons experiencing a flare of rheumatoid arthritis, fibromyalgia, or pain should consult with the doctor and start slowly and gently to avoid muscle spasms.[37]

Visualization/Guided Imagery

Guided imagery/visualization techniques lessen headaches and pain. A person practicing guided imagery benefits from less stress, lowered blood pressure, and decreased pulse while the immune system gets a healthy boost. Some athletes improve performance by using these techniques.

· In guided imagery, a practitioner or a videotape can teach the person how to visualize a happy relaxing place or situation, and then use deep-breathing and relaxation techniques to achieve a restful state. Three principles of guided imagery include the mind-body connection, the altered state, and being in control.

The mind-body connection says, "To the body, images created in the mind can be almost as real as actual, external events." The mind cues and the body responds with senses and emotions. "These sensory images are the true language of the body, the only language it understands, immediately and without questions."[38]

The altered state says "we're capable of more rapid and intense healing, growth, learning and performance."[39] A person's ability to ignore pain or lift an extraordinarily heavy object expands due to need.

The control principle says "when we have a sense of being in control, that, in and of itself, can help us to feel better and do better."[40] Researchers have shown people respond negatively to feelings of helplessness. Conversely, people who feel in control of their lives experience more positive feelings and perform better.

Studies agree that guided imagery techniques decrease stress, boost the person's immune system, and increases that person's health. One small study involving 28 older women with osteoarthritis combined guided imagery and progressive relaxation techniques to judge their effectiveness. The treatment group listened to a 10–15 minute audiotape teaching guided imagery and progressive relaxation. "The treatment group reported a significant reduction in pain and mobility difficulties at week 12 compared to the control group." Members of the control group found their pain level and mobility did not change in that 12-week period.[41]

Guided imagery techniques can be learned and practiced by persons wanting to improve coping skills. Guided imagery may allow nightmares or bad memories to surface and the person dealing with these should get professional help. Guided imagery techniques will be taught through stress management programs as well as mental health programs.

Alternative and complementary therapies are gaining in popularity. Many alternative and complementary therapies decrease pain levels and improve life for people dealing with arthritis. Persons interested should educate themselves, talk with their doctor and wisely choose therapy to improve their lives while avoiding dangerous, expensive treatments.

11

Preparing for Surgery

"To be able to walk and not think about it is a gift."[1] *Hip Replacement or Hip Resurfacing* author Peggy Gabriel expresses the emotion of many dealing with hip and leg pain. When less-invasive treatments cease to bring pain relief, total joint surgery improves quality of life for many people.

Techniques to Restore Cartilage

When the smooth, shiny white articular cartilage wears off, bone rubs against bone and pain occurs. Surgeons looking to restore articular cartilage discuss new techniques called osteochondral grafting, autologous chondrocytes implantation and mesenchymal stem cell (MSC) regeneration.

According to the American Academy of Orthopaedic Surgeons, these new technologies look more useful for people suffering an acute injury to a knee, not an overall arthritic joint.[2] Readers can find information about research into stem cell technology and cartilage restoration in Chapter 17, "Researching Arthritis."

Arthroscopy, Osteotomy and Other Surgeries

The *New England Journal of Medicine* published a study in July of 2002 that questioned whether arthroscopy of the knee has value in treating arthritis. The newspaper headlines read, "arthroscopic surgery no better than placebo [sham surgery] in treating the pain and dysfunction of osteoarthritis of the knee." This finding was based on a study of 180 patients at a VA hospital who were either given arthroscopic debridement, arthroscopic lavage or placebo surgery. The arthroscopic debridement procedure used special instruments to remove unneeded tissue from the joint. The arthroscopic lavage procedure washed fluid through the knee joint without removing any tissue. The placebo surgery occurred when the incisions were made but no instruments entered the

knee joint. The same surgeon did all the cases and the patients and nurses did
not know which patient received which treatments. The researchers reported,
"At no point did either of the intervention groups report less pain or better
function than the placebo group."[3] Does this mean arthroscopy should never
be performed? No. According to the Arthritis Foundation, "surgeons use
arthroscopy to make a diagnosis, to assess joint damage, to remove or repair
damaged cartilage, and to smooth rough joint surfaces. Despite a recent study
suggesting arthroscopy is ineffective in treating knee OA, it is useful for cleaning up loose particles, torn cartilage, or ligament and tendon damage in some
patient's knees."[4] During arthroscopy, the surgeon inserts an arthroscopic tele-
scope attached to a camera into the joint to see internal structures. Instruments
commonly used include "a blunt hook to pull on various tissues, a shaver to
remove damaged or unwanted soft tissues, and a burr to remove bone. A heat
probe may also be used to remove inflammation (synovitis) in the joint."[5]

Arthroscopy is most commonly performed on knees and shoulders, but
other joints such as wrist, elbows, ankles and hips can be examined using
arthroscopy. Arthroscopy routinely means outpatient surgery; the individual
goes home the day of surgery. "While arthroscopy can ease pain by smoothing
the joint's surface or removing pieces of tissue that cause discomfort, it cannot
change the progression of arthritis."[6]

Osteotomy surgery straightens crooked joints by cutting the bone, reset-
ting the bone in better alignment and using implants to hold it while it heals.
Usually hips and knees are the joints doctors would straighten by performing
an osteotomy. This surgery could be done on a young person's crooked lower
leg in an effort to avoid damage from the unusual stresses.

Resection surgery removes part of or all the bone in an effort to ease pain
and improve movement. Bunionectomy is an example of this type of surgery.
Doctors also do resections on elbows, thumbs and wrists.

Synovectomy involves removal of the synovium. This inner lining of joints
secretes synovial fluid, which contains hyaluronic acid, the shock absorber and
lubricant of joints. In rheumatoid arthritis (RA), the synovium becomes
inflamed, painful, and overgrown while damaging the articular cartilage and
bone of the joint. In osteoarthritis, the synovium can become inflamed and cause
pain but doesn't become the damaging structure found in RA. Synovectomy can
often be done during arthroscopy surgery for knees, shoulders, wrists and ankles
but may require open surgery in some cases. For example, synovectomy of the
hand must be an open procedure.

Total joint replacements bring relief from pain and get many people going
again. Total joint replacement surgery, or arthroplasty, could be defined as repair
of a joint by replacing diseased/damaged parts with artificial joints.

For example, during total hip replacement or arthroplasty, surgeons remove
the arthritic surfaces of the acetabulum (hip socket) and femoral head (ball of

the thigh bone that lives inside the hip socket) and replace that joint with implants. During total knee replacement or arthroplasty, the walking surfaces of the femur (thighbone) and tibia (shinbone) and patella (kneecap) are replaced with implants. Similarly for shoulder, ankle, elbow, etc., the joint surfaces are replaced with implants. These surgically implanted new parts move smoothly on each other (articulate) and provide pain-free movement.

The Arthritis Foundation lists a third benefit to joint replacement surgery. It improves "alignment of deformed joints."[7]

According to the American Academy of Orthopaedic Surgeons, surgeons perform 300,000 total knee replacements and 193,000 total hip replacements each year in America.[8] Total knees and hips rank as the most frequently performed total joints, but other joints such as ankles, shoulders and wrists can be replaced.

Who Needs Total Joint Surgery?

Who's a candidate for total joint surgery? People whose arthritis pain and symptoms cannot be controlled by conservative treatment. Occasionally, a specific type of fracture injury (such as fractured femoral head) in a younger patient will cause a doctor to recommend a total hip or a partial total hip.

When should surgery be considered? The Arthritis Foundation gives these indicators that it may be time for surgery:

The pain keeps a person awake at night.

A series of different pain medications no longer relieve the pain.

Pain has caused a person to decrease or stop outings such as visiting friends, taking vacations or going shopping.

A person has difficulty getting up out of a chair, off the toilet, going up stairs or getting up off the floor.[9]

Choosing a Health Care Advocate

In the book *How to Survive Your Hospital Stay*, Kaneagan recommends having a family member or friend "who will look out for your interests during hospitalization."[10] This person does not have to be listed on the Power of Attorney for health care. This person functions as support and should be willing to speak for the patient who's physically not feeling well. The ideal health care advocate is "medically knowledgeable ... assertive but not aggressive ... trustworthy ... available ... familiar with any special fears or concerns, wishes, or instructions ... and organized."[11]

Finding a Surgeon

Total joint surgery requires an orthopaedic surgeon. A person looking in the telephone directory of a large city will find many orthopaedic surgeons listed. Which one would be best?

When the person checks with his insurance/medical plan for in-network surgeons, he will find information that gives the best financial protection. People whose insurance plan specifies in-network vs. out-of-network doctors will find themselves paying more money if they choose an out-of-network surgeon. Often a person can find a skilled surgeon within the network who will give excellent surgical care. However, if the out-of-network surgeon and hospital rank vastly superior, the patient has the choice to use that out-of-network surgeon and that hospital. However, the patient should check his coverage and know how much this decision will cost and be prepared to pay the difference in both doctor and hospital bills.

Patients with Medicare coverage may have more options in doctors. The patient should check with his coverage plan to make wise financial decisions regarding surgery.

Individuals contemplating surgery may want to talk to people who've had similar surgeries and get their opinions about doctors. Remember, this gives subjective information. Even the best doctor cannot please everyone. However, the doctors who receive positive comments from their patients rank high on the list of acceptable surgeons. This is the time to confer with a doctor, physical therapist or nurse, neighbor or friend. They have medical knowledge and can give an opinion to the question, "Which surgeon would you choose to perform a total joint replacement on yourself or your loved one?"*

A board-certified surgeon spends extra time, effort, and money to take his knowledge and expertise to the highest level. Board-certified surgeons are proud of their achievement and often display their certificates on waiting room walls or hallways. The certificate will list the surgeon by name as a Fellow of the American Board of Orthopaedic Surgeons (ABOS). To determine whether a doctor is board certified, ask the physician or his staff. Another way to learn whether a doctor is board certified is to look at the American Board of Medical Specialties (ABMS) website under "Who's Certified" or by calling toll-free 1-866-ASK-ABMS (275-2267).[12] A physician who has studied and passed his specialized training, but not yet taken and passed the board, is called "board-eligible." According to *Dr. David Sherer's Hospital Survival Guide*, "Find out if the surgeon is in practice with others who are already board certified. That tells you that other, more experienced hands are happy to have this surgeon on their team."[13]

*The American Academy of Orthopaedic Surgeons at http://www6.aaos.org/about/public/members.cfm features a database listing of surgeons trained to perform total joint surgeries. A local medical society will provide a list of surgeons available locally but won't make recommendations.

Healthgrades, a private healthcare quality service, provides information regarding doctors' and hospitals' performance for a small fee.[14]

Lastly, an individual's family doctor or primary care physician will be a resource for finding a specialist surgeon. The primary care doctor continues to take care of the whole patient and will coordinate the patient's care through surgery. The person contemplating surgery could ask his doctor about a surgeon. Again, the question to ask is, "Which orthopaedic surgeon would perform a total joint on yourself or your loved one?" The patient's primary care doctor helps the patient be in optimal health for surgery. For example, patients who routinely take medications such as blood thinners and non-steroidal anti-inflammatory (NSAIDs) will need to stop taking these medications a specific time frame before surgery. Both these medications interfere with normal blood clotting and dosage may be adjusted to avoid bleeding during and after surgery.

How to Survive Your Hospital Stay author and nurse practitioner Gail Van Kaneagan states, "Surgery is as much art as science. Surgeons must know not only what to do; they must also have the ability to perform the procedure flawlessly. Like an athlete's, a surgeon's talent is part of a physical skill and part a mental one."[15]

Finding a Hospital

Everyone wants to receive the highest quality care while in the hospital. Aren't all hospitals comparable? Apparently not. Quality improvement organizations such as the American Healthcare Quality Association (AHQA) work with hospitals to assist them in their efforts to improve the care given. For example, to improve surgical care given in the nation's hospitals, a cooperative effort focuses on four areas of post-surgical complications: infections, blood clots, heart problems, and pneumonia. The major doctors', nurses', hospitals' and government organizations working cooperatively aim to decrease surgical complications by 25 percent by 2010.[16]*

Phrases like "National Quality Standards" reflect the emphasis of Joint Commission of Accreditation of Hospitals (JCAHO). Hospitals who care for patients with Medicare and most insurance coverage deal with JCAHO. JCAHO does on-site visits of each hospital facility at least every three years.[†] JCAHO's

---

*The U.S. Department of Health and Human Services presently makes a report card for America's hospitals available to consumers at http://www.hospitalcompare.hhs.gov/. Called Hospital Compare, the report card results are determined by patients who grade the care they received. They currently access routine care for acute heart attack, congestive heart failure, pneumonia and prevention of surgical wound infections.
†People researching JCAHO ratings for specific hospitals can do so at http://www.qualitycheck.org/consumer/searchQCR.aspx

standards relate to patient safety concerns such as medication use, infection control, fire safety, prevention of patient falls, and communication of patient information when a patient is moved to another facility.[17]

While the patient researches the hospital, he should contact his insurance carrier to identify in-network hospitals and may need to get approval for surgery. Often, staff in the surgeon's office will get the pre-procedure approval.

"How many total joint procedures are done at this hospital?" Research shows that numbers bring experience and that counts.[18] Surgeons who perform large volumes of specific procedures and the hospitals where these procedures are performed find their patients do better. In other words, high-volume hospitals have lower mortality rates for certain conditions, specifically, elective vascular surgeries such as coronary artery bypass (CABG or open heart surgery), elective aortic aneurysm repair and carotid endarterectomy. Patients undergoing surgeries for rare types of cancers such as pancreatic cancer and esophageal cancer also do better when their surgery is performed at a high-volume hospital.[19]

High-volume total joint hospitals often dedicate an area to total joint patients, and staff members know how to care for total joint patients. They quickly spot potential problems, take appropriate nursing actions, and work with the surgeon for the patient's best outcome. The physical therapists have experience with total joint patients. The physicians and nursing staff are adept at dealing with the chronic health problems found among total joint patients.

With today's competition for the healthcare dollar, hospitals who achieve awards for high quality will publicize those distinctions. Distinctions for "Best in Missouri for Total Joint Surgery" or "Magnet Status for Nursing" are awards that hospital personnel and surgeons work to achieve. They will want the public to know of their honors.

Visit the hospital and look around. Do the nurses smile and speak in a friendly manner? Does the hospital look clean and comfortable? Does it smell good? Ask for a tour of the total joint floor to see a patient room for issues such as privacy. Do the patient rooms include a private bathroom? Is there room for visitors?

Considering the Personnel

When researching the hospital, consider the nursing staff and support staff. Nurses "top Gallup's annual list of occupations rated for their honesty and ethical standards, earning high marks from more than four in five Americans."[20] Economic pressures and shortages of staff can cause nurses to be overworked, overstressed and tense. Do staff members smile and act friendly? Do they come promptly? Sometimes delays will happen due to emergencies or admissions, but "if nurses are constantly running late with medications and other tasks, it probably means they're spread too thin."[21] Hospitals with adequate numbers of registered nurse (RN) staff are committed to quality care. Patients should see the RNs assigned to them several times per shift. "Good hospitals give nurses enough flexibility to do a good job and don't impose a lot of needless rules and restrictions."[22] That's called empowerment. Nurses possess knowledge and want to educate their patients. The best hospitals consider patient teaching an integral part of nursing functions.

Patients should consider RNs to be a valuable resource. The RNs work at the bedside around the clock, often recognizing complications in the patient's condition, giving nursing treatments, and alerting the physician before a crisis occurs. Nurses can act as advocates for the patient who needs more pain medication or even a laxative. Even simple things like room temperature and the noise level at night are within the nurse's or nursing assistant's domain. The nurse and her staff are the ones who know "how to deal with the day-to-day problems of hospital life."[23]

Working with the registered nurse (RN) will be support people such as licensed vocational or practical nurses (LVNs or LPNs) and unlicensed assistive personnel (UAP). LPNs and LVNs both graduate from a practical nursing program and are licensed by the state they're working in. Unlicensed assistive personnel (UAP), formerly known as "nurse's aides," have no license and work with the nurses to give quality patient care. The UAPs may have on-the-job training or a shorter-term formal nursing or medical education. Nursing or medical students working during their college journey to become registered nurses or doctors often work as UAPs. Many LPNs and UAPs are hard-working, caring individuals who assist the nurses in providing for the patient's needs.

During hospital stays, dietitians/nutritionists teach and provide information about nutrition and diet to patients. Patients benefit from learning a healthier diet.

Physical therapists (PTs) teach patients "how to use a walker or crutches and which movements to avoid because of dislocation risk [e.g., leg crossing]."[24] Exercises to strengthen the leg muscles will be included. The PT will have the patient practice these exercises and learn proper walker and crutch use.

Occupational Therapists (OTs) "address activities of daily living, such as bathtub or shower transfers, dressing, housekeeping and meal preparation. Occupational therapists also teach and reinforce behaviors that protect patients' hips from dislocation."[25] OT staff recommend gadgets and assistive devices such as dressing sticks, long-handled shoe horns, sponge brushes, reachers, and grabber tools. During a pre-operative visit to the PT/OT department, therapists introduce the patient to exercises and equipment needed after the total joint surgery.

Advanced practice nurses (APNs) are registered nurses with additional education and skills. Most APNs have completed a master's degree in nursing and function in their specialty, whether as nurse practitioner (NP), certified nurse anesthetist (CRNA), or other specialties. A certified nurse anesthetist (CRNA) completes a master's level nursing degree with anesthesia specialty. Depending on the laws of the state where they practice, they may function without oversight of anesthesiologists (specialty doctors with training in anesthesia).

The surgeon's physician assistant (PA) and certified registered nurse first assistant (CRNFA) will assist the surgeon in surgery by providing knowledgeable assistance. Total joint surgery calls for teamwork because the surgeon's two hands cannot handle all the needed equipment and positioning of the patient for optimal, timely surgery.

A typical total joint surgical team includes a minimum of five people: the surgeon, his PA or CRNFA, a scrub nurse or technologist, circulating nurse, and an anesthesia care provider, either an MDA or CRNA. A well-trained surgical team who work together often and know the needed equipment and supplies give the best quality care to patients.

Physician Specialties Related to Surgery

After the patient chooses his surgeon, he may not think of other physician services he will need during hospitalization. Several physician services will be provided by the hospital such as anesthesiologists, radiologists, pathologists, and hospitalists.

Anesthesiologists are specialty doctors trained to give anesthesia and pain control to patients under their care. Medical doctor anesthesiologists (MDAs) do more than give anesthesia; they look at the entire person's health in efforts to make anesthesia safe. In the preoperative phase, they listen to the patient's lungs and heart, and check on lab tests and electrocardiogram results to ensure optimal results. The MDA would want the elective total joint patient in optimal health with no signs and symptoms of acute infection, heart, or lung problems.

Radiologists read x-rays and perform radiological tests. These specialty doctors read pre-operative chest x-rays to validate the absence of infection and post-operative x-rays. Radiologists oversee the radiology department and deal with CT scans, MRI and a variety of x-ray procedures.

Pathologists are specialist doctors who examine tissue specimens and give a diagnosis that often determines the medical and surgical treatments. Pathologists often oversee laboratories.

The patient may notice a hospitalist visiting him and caring for his general health while in the hospital. Hospitalists are specialty doctors who work only in the hospital and see patients at the request of the patient's primary care physician or family doctor. They will make rounds and coordinate the

Help Avoid Mistakes in Your Surgery: Speak UP Initiative

Courtesy of Joint Commission of Accreditation of Healthcare Organizations (JCAHO)

Preparing for your surgery

Ask your doctor

- Are there any prescription or over-the-counter medicines that you should not take before your surgery?
- Can you eat or drink before your surgery?
- If you have other questions, write them down. Take your list of questions with you when you see the doctor.

Ask someone you trust to

- Take you to and from the surgery facility.
- Be with you at the hospital. This person can make sure you get the care you need to feel comfortable and safe.

Before you leave home

- Shower, wash your hair, and remove any nail polish from your fingers and toes. Do not wear make-up. Your caregivers need to see your skin and nails to check your blood circulation.
- Leave your jewelry, money or other valuables at home.

At the surgery facility

The staff will ask you to sign an informed consent form. Read it carefully. It lists:

- Your name
- The kind of surgery you will have
- The risks of your surgery
- That you talked to your doctor about the surgery and asked questions
- Your agreement to have the surgery

Make sure everything on the form is correct. Make sure all your questions have been answered. If you do not understand something on the form—speak up.

For your safety, the staff may ask you the same question many times. They will ask:

- Who you are
- What kind of surgery you are having
- The part of your body to be operated on

They will also double-check the records from your doctor's office.

Before your surgery

- A healthcare worker will mark the spot on your body to be operated on. Make sure they mark only the correct part and nowhere else. This helps avoid mistakes.
- Marking usually happens when you are awake. Sometimes you cannot be awake for the marking. If this happens, a family member or friend or another healthcare worker can watch the marking. They can make sure that your correct body part is marked.

(continued on next page)

(Avoid Mistakes in Your Surgery, *continued***)**

- Your neck, upper back or lower back will be marked if you are having spine surgery. The surgeon will check the exact place on your spine in the operating room after you are asleep.
- Ask your surgeon if they will take a "time out" just before your surgery. This is done to make sure they are doing the right surgery on the right body part on the right person.

After your surgery
- Tell your doctor or nurse about your pain. Hospitals and other surgical facilities that are accredited by the Joint Commission must help relieve your pain.
- Ask questions about medicines that are given to you, especially new medicines. What is it? What is it for? Are there any side effects? Tell your caregivers about any allergies you have to medicines. If you have more questions about a medicine, talk to your doctor or nurse before taking it.
- Find out about any IV (intravenous) fluids that you are given. These are liquids that drip from a bag into your vein. Ask how long the liquid should take to "run out." Tell the nurse if it seems to be dripping too fast or too slow.
- Ask your doctor if you will need therapy or medicines after you leave the hospital.
- Ask when you can resume activities like work, exercise and travel.

---

patient's care while in the hospital. "Outcomes of critical illness improve because of the consistency of care and the level of expertise of the hospitalist."[26] When discharged, the patient will return to the care of his primary care physician.

The patient does not have to find the anesthesiologist, radiologist, pathologist and hospitalist; they will work at the hospital the patient chooses.

Researching Total Joint Surgery

The Internet functions as a source of information, including health-related subjects. Not all those sites will give unbiased information. A study presented at the 2005 American Academy of Orthopaedic Surgeons (AAOS) looked at Internet information. When "Minimally Invasive Hip Replacement" was typed in three Web search engines, the top sites were analyzed. "Many of the sites made claims about benefits to minimally invasive hip replacement surgery that are not currently supported by existing peer-reviewed medical literature: 44% stated that the procedure results in less blood loss; 47% said it leaves a smaller scar; 61% claimed that it results in shorter hospital stays; 68% said it was less painful than traditional hip replacement and more than 91% of the sites claimed that the recovery time was faster."[27]

Consumers researching total joint surgery can find accurate information on the Web by using unbiased sources. Three sources of unbiased, quality information include the Arthritis Foundation,* the American Academy of Orthopaedic Surgeons (AAOS)† and the Association of Hip and Knee Surgeons (AAHKS).‡

Meeting the Surgeon

The patient and patient advocate and/or a caretaker member of the family should be included in this visit. The American Association of the Hip and Knee Surgeons (AAHKS) Office Visit Tips[28] recommends that patients bring insurance information, including insurance cards for the doctor's office staff and hospital staff. Other items to bring to the doctor's office include:

a list of medications, including over-the counter medication, vitamins, minerals and herbal supplements

a list of allergies, including latex, or adverse reactions to drugs or anesthesia

a written medical history including past surgeries, past and present medical conditions. Include all the doctors currently being used and their phone numbers

a copy of advanced directive/living will

any x-rays or other film copies from a patient's primary care doctor

results of lab tests done recently

a list of questions for the surgeon to answer

Since a first visit to the doctor's office usually means paperwork must be filled out, go early for the appointment. When the patient meets the physician, he should be honest and complete when answering questions. Don't worry about being embarrassed, but share concerns about incontinence, memory loss, or sex. Surgeons want their patients to do well and need to know about the person's health and priorities. Some patients will want to take notes or ask for brochures/handouts that can be studied at home. The patient should use his

---

*The Arthritis Foundation offers excellent information about total joint surgery at http://www.arthri tis.org/conditions/surgerycenter/default.asp. Brochures and pamphlets can be obtained from the Arthritis Foundation online, by phone at 1–800–568–4045 or by mail at: Arthritis Foundation, P.O. Box 7669, Atlanta, GA 30357–0669. One hundred fifty chapters of the Arthritis Foundation nationwide provide information and can be accessed through their website at www.arthritis.org.

†The American Academy of Orthopaedic Surgeons (AAOS) welcomes patient/public visits to their patient education library site at http://www.orthoinfo.aaos.org/. Click on Arthritis or Joint Replacement to reach pertinent information on total joint surgeries.

‡Another website is offered by the American Association of Hip and Knee Surgeons (AAHKS). This organization's web-based resources for hip and knee replacement patients and families can be accessed at http://www.aahks.org/index.asp/fuseaction/patients.main.

question list to get answers from the busy doctor. Good questions a patient may want to ask regarding total joint surgeries include:

"Why is this procedure being recommended? Are there alternatives?

What are the benefits of this procedure in terms of pain relief and improvements of function and mobility?

How long will the benefits last?

What are the risks involved?

What is the procedure called? How is it done?

What percentages of patients improve following the procedure?

If I want a second opinion, whom can I consult?"[29]

If the patient has questions written on a paper, he will more likely get all his questions asked and receive valuable answers about the surgeon's plan for surgery. The surgeon and the office staff will have information brochures and pamphlets to share. The patient can ask the surgeon's nurse permission to call for more information if questions come up.

The surgeon recommends surgery and the patient agrees. The patient needs to know the surgeon's plan for the type of anesthesia, what type of implant, and how long the patient can expect to stay in the hospital. The surgeon and staff will probably give explanations of what the patient can expect to happen before, during and after surgery.

The surgeon will probably tell you to stop taking certain medications such as aspirin, NSAIDs, any blood thinner medications, and some herbal medicines that may interfere with anesthesia, surgery, and healing.

If the patient does not want a blood transfusion if needed, this topic should be discussed. Autologous blood donation whereby the patient donates his own blood and can receive it later during the hospital stay if needed may be available. The process for autologous blood begins at the hospital's blood bank and needs to begin approximately six weeks prior to surgery date. Another technology allows the surgeon to collect the patient's blood during surgery, using a cell-saver system and giving the patient's own blood back in the immediate post-operative phase. This cell-saver technology maintains a sterile connection to the patient at all times, including when the blood is reinfused or given back to the patient. Blood donation from a family member or friend is an option that needs to be discussed at the office appointment. The surgeon's office staff can also answer any questions regarding hospital admission.

Individuals planning on future travel should discuss dealing with airport security after total joint replacements. The American Academy of Orthopaedic Surgeons (AAOS) 2004 meeting news release discusses possible security concerns. Airport security varies in different countries, but detection of metal has increased. The researchers suggested introducing an "internationally recognized joint replacement card linked to a joint registry database."[30] Until that card becomes reality, the AAOS suggests physicians offer a letter or card as proof of implant surgery. However, this card or letter may not be sufficient. "If a security alarm sounds, the Federal Aviation Administration requires a resolution: a hand-held screener is used, and, if needed, the implant patient must consent to a noninvasive body search in order to board the plane."[31]

Preparing Your Home

Making the home environment safe for the post-operative patient's return home involves many commonsense tasks.[32] Some modifications require little money and time to improve safety:

Make the home slip-proof and fall-proof. Put away or anchor throw rugs or carpeting that can slip. Make pathways/walkways wide enough for a walker or cane. Keep electrical extension cords and phone wires out of walkways, but do not put wires under rugs and create a fire hazard. Ensure that adequate lighting, including nightlights, illuminate the patient's environment. Handrails should be located at all stairways.

Consider making the bathroom safer by adding a shower chair, grip bars and a raised toilet. Adding a shower hose to the shower will help the patient put the water where he wants it. Women who may not want to get their hair wet during every shower will find a shower hose handy. A long-handled sponge facilitates bathing. Aids for getting dressed include a dressing stick, a sock aid, and a long-handled shoe horn for putting on and taking off shoes and socks without excessively bending your new hip.[33] A "reacher" gadget can be used by the patient to grab objects and avoid excessive bending at the hip.

The surgeon may have instructed the patient to keep the dressing dry for the first week to 10 days post-operatively. During this time, bathing will be a challenge. After her left hand surgery, one woman laid her left hand through the opening over the shower door to keep her dressing dry. Her husband assisted her in her shower. Another woman had her husband help her sit on a shower chair with her post-operative leg hanging outside the shower doors and she used a hand-held shower head to get the job done. Others may feel a sponge bath will be adequate. However bathing is accomplished, it's important for the patient to follow instructions regarding keeping the dressing dry.

Organize items used frequently so the patient can reach them easily. According to the American Academy of Orthopaedic Surgeons (AAOS), "get a chair, one that is firm, and has a higher than average seat. This type of chair is safer and more comfortable than a low, soft-cushioned chair."[34] The remote control should be handy. Medications and reading materials/hobby items can be stored in accessible locations.

Arrange the kitchen so frequently used utensils, pans and supplies can be

Planning Your Recovery: A Speak Up Safety Initiative

Courtesy of Joint Commission of Accreditation of Health Care Organizations (JCAHO)

Find out about your condition.

- Ask about your condition and how soon you should feel better.
- Find out about your ability to do everyday activities like walk, climb stairs, go to the bathroom, prepare meals, drive, return to work, and other activities that are important to you.
- Find out about any special instructions for daily activities. For example, most patients should use the shower instead of the bathtub.
- Find out how much help you will need during your recovery. For example, if someone should be with you 24 hours a day.
- Ask about any signs and symptoms that you should watch for. Find out what you should do if you have these signs or symptoms.
- Make sure your home is set up to help with any physical limitations you may have. Make sure any equipment you need is set up before you return home. The hospital can provide information about where to get equipment.
- Write down any questions you have and ask them before you leave the hospital. It's helpful to keep a notebook for your questions, the answers and who answered your questions, in case you need to get more information. If needed, ask a family member or friend to help.
- Ask a family member or friend to be with you when discharge plans are being made, or to go through the discharge process with you. He or she can help get written instructions and ask questions.
- Ask for the phone number of a person to call at the hospital for any problems you may have after leaving the hospital, or call your doctor's office.
- Ask a family member, friend or neighbor to stay with you when you first get home and then to check on you at your home for a few days.
- If you are not confident about how to care for yourself after leaving the hospital, or if you have any doubts about getting the care you need at home, speak up. Ask to speak to the nurse in charge, or ask your nurse, social worker or discharge planner if you could be referred to a home health agency that could come to your home to make sure your needs are being met.

Find out about your new medicines.

- Ask for a list of all the medicines you will be taking at home. The list should include all your medicines, not just new ones started in the hospital. Check the list for accuracy. You or your doctor should also share the list with anyone providing you with follow-up care.
- Ask for written directions about your medicines. Read the directions and make sure you understand them. Ask any questions you have before leaving the hospital.
- Tell your doctors, nurses and pharmacists about all the medicines, vitamins and herbs you usually take. Ask if there are any of these that you should not take with your new medicines.

(continued on next page)

(Planning Your Recovery, *continued*)

- Ask if there are any foods and drinks—including alcohol—that you should avoid.
- Ask about the side effects of your new medicines. Find out what you should do if you experience any of them.
- Find out if your new medicines can make you sleepy or forgetful, which could make it difficult for you to take your medicines on time.
- Find out if your new medicines can make you dizzy or confused, which could cause you to fall.

Find out about your follow-up care.

- Ask for directions about physical exercises you may need to do. Ask your doctor, nurse, or physical therapist to write down the directions.
- If you have a wound, ask for directions on how you should take care of it.
- If you need special equipment, make sure you know how to use it, where you can get it, and if it's covered by your insurance, Medicare, or other health plan.
- Ask about any tests that need to be followed up on after you leave the hospital and who you should follow up with to get the results.
- Find out about any follow-up visits with your doctor or other caregiver. Make sure you have transportation to get there. Many cities provide transportation for the elderly or disabled.
- Review your insurance to find out what costs are covered and not covered after you are discharged (like medicines and equipment).
- If you need to receive home care services or you need to be sent to a nursing home or assisted living center for follow-up care, make sure that the facility or service is covered by your insurance, Medicare or other health plan; and that it is licensed or accredited. Joint Commission organizations and programs are listed at www.quality-check.org.

---

reached without bending. Planning ahead for meals can be accomplished by cooking double and freezing half or stocking the kitchen with ready-made foods the patient likes.

A temporary parking permit for a disabled person may simplify finding a parking place. The application form can be gotten from the Department of Motor Vehicles or possibly the surgeon's office.[35] Firm pillows in the vehicle may be needed to help the recuperating total hip patient sit with knees lower than hips.[36]

Patients who live alone need a plan for return home. A trusted friend or family member can stay with them for a short while. Another option is a specialized rehabilitation facility where the patient can recover from surgery and continue therapy.

Reasonable Expectations of the Patient

The patient should ask the surgeon what to expect after surgery. According to "A Caregiver's Guide for the Joint Replacement Patient At Home,"[37] the total joint replacement patient should not be alarmed if he experiences less energy, decreased appetite, and difficulty sleeping after surgery. For decreased energy and difficulty sleeping, the patient should recognize it's probably a temporary problem. Staying awake during the day will help with nighttime sleep and the energy level will return to more normal levels after several weeks. For decreased appetite, the patient should drink plenty of fluids to avoid dehydration and expect the appetite to return to normal. When the appetite returns, a healthy diet including vegetables and protein will give the body building blocks to heal.

A well-informed individual can prepare for total joint surgery. By preparing, this individual will know what to expect and can avoid potential problems. Total joint surgery brings pain relief to many patients every year.

12

Total Hip Replacement

John C. Fisher, a hard-working Missouri farmer, faced right total hip surgery at age 50. Over the past several years, John had tried conservative treatments and pain medications to cope with his arthritis. When he first noticed his leg feeling tired, John was farming 500 acres, driving tractors, and walking miles to check his fields. The tired feeling became hip pain and eventually kept him awake at night. John returned to Campbell Clinic in Memphis where he had had surgery on that hip at age 12.

John and his teacher wife Carol researched and learned about hip arthritis and all the options available. John saw the surgeon over a period of three years and they discussed options of surgery and how surgery would affect John's work. John says the doctor "never said I would have to give up farming. He said I should never lift more than 50 pounds. All the feed sacks routinely weigh 50 pounds. We often picked up hydraulic cylinders and machinery parts that weigh over 50 pounds. I knew there was a good chance I would do some damage to the new hip, so it was a good time to make that choice. By that time, the pain had gotten so bad that I knew it was time to have something done."[1]

Several months' preparation for John's total hip surgery included renovating their home. They turned the main floor guest room and bathroom into a master suite. They took "the tub out of that bathroom and put in a walk-in shower so it was in place before the surgery."[2] John also lost some weight and made his body as healthy as possible.

John's porous total hip replacement was performed in December 1999 and has done very well. Being a motivated patient, John shares this advice: "One of the toughest things is making yourself do the exercise. You have to be determined to get your muscles built back up. That's the only way you have to get back on your feet. I was very diligent about doing my exercises."[3]

When the arthritic hip pain interferes with life and the activities people love, many start to consider surgery. Total hip replacements (THR) enable persons with painful arthritis to walk on a pain-free hip after recovery. Instead of limping and enduring the pain, that individual walks comfortably.

Pain-Free Healthy Hip

The hip joint has been described as a "ball and socket." The ball (head of the femur or thighbone) sits inside the socket (acetabulum) of the pelvis. The bony surfaces of a healthy hip joint are covered by a smooth durable covering called articular cartilage. This cartilage reduces the friction during movement. Synovial tissue, a thin tissue lining of the joint, produces a lubricating synovial fluid that could be called the body's joint oil. Soft tissue muscles and ligaments give strength and stability to the hip joint.[4] Normal healthy hips do not hurt. However, not all hip pain means arthritis and surgery. The person with hip pain needs to see a doctor for diagnosis and treatment.

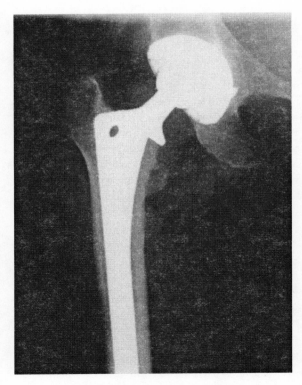

The total hip implants shown in this x-ray picture consist of a metal cup inside the hip joint, a liner inside that metal cup, and a metal stem in the intramedullary canal of the femur (thighbone) with a metal head atop the stem (courtesy DePuy Orthopaedics).

Causes of Hip Pain

Three common forms of arthritis cause hip pain: osteoarthritis, rheumatoid arthritis, and traumatic arthritis. Osteoarthritis, which affects 27 million Americans, occurs when the articular cartilage of the hip joint wears off and pain occurs.[5] Rheumatoid arthritis, an autoimmune disease affecting 1.3 million Americans, does damage when the normal synovial membrane of the joint goes awry and starts a process that damages the articular cartilage.[6] Traumatic arthritis results from injury or fracture and causes arthritic changes.

Two other hip conditions may require total hip surgery, avascular necrosis and hip dysplasia. Avascular necrosis occurs when the blood supply to the femoral head (ball of the femur or thighbone) fails or is damaged. Without adequate blood supply, the articular cartilage of the femoral head becomes damaged and pain results. Avascular necrosis occurs in approximately 10,000 to 20,000 Americans. Besides dislocations and fractures of the hip, other causes for avascular necrosis include long-term steroid usage, some glandular diseases and alcoholism.[7]

Hip dysplasia, a malformation of the hip joint, is recognized and treated in infancy currently. However, before the newborn screening and treatments began, people born with hip dysplasia had fewer options. Some people still deal with their misshapen and arthritic hip joints.

Symptoms of Hip Arthritis

Symptoms of arthritis in the hip socket include pain in the groin, inner thigh and buttock. This pain may be felt more in the knee or side of thigh rather than the hip. Doctors call this referred pain, meaning the pain is felt somewhere other than where it originates. A diagnosis of hip arthritis will be made by a doctor and x-rays may be done to help differentiate the hip arthritis from other problems such as knee or back problems. Also, people with arthritis in the hip may limp when walking.[8] Getting in and out of a chair often causes pain.

Conservative Treatments First

Before total hip surgery becomes the topic of conversation with a surgeon, the patient should be trying non-surgical treatments. Early treatments recommended by the American Academy of Orthopaedic Surgeons for hip arthritis include: "resting your hip from overuse, follow a physical therapy program of gentle, regular exercise like swimming, water aerobics or cycling to keep your joint functioning and improve its strength and range of motion, use nonsteroidal anti-inflammatory medications like ibuprofen for pain, and get enough sleep each night."[9] Because of concerns with NSAIDs causing higher risk of stroke and heart attack, people should talk to their doctors periodically about the best pain management.

Total Hip Procedures

Total hip procedures replace the painful hip joint with implants. The surgeon makes the acetabulum smooth by removing the irregular bone of the acetabulum and inserting acetabular implants. The surgeon then removes the arthritic femoral head and fits an implant stem down the shaft of the femur (thighbone) and puts a smooth round implant head on top of the stem. The goal of the new joint is to provide pain-free movement of the hip.*

Historical information about total hip surgeries can be found in chapter 3. A huge step forward occurred in 1962 when a British orthopaedic surgeon, John Charnley, performed the Charnley total hip replacement. Sir John Charnley, who was knighted in 1977 for his work, "glued" the implants into that joint. For years, the plastic cup (socket joint implant) and femoral stem (thighbone implant) were glued in using polymethylmacrylate (PMMA) bone cement. The glued components provide immediate fixation as the "glue" sets up during the surgical procedure. "The chance of a hip replacement lasting 20 years is about 80%."[10] Cemented THR procedures are still recommended for patients of all ages whose poor bone quality and density (osteoporosis) require the bone-cement-implant interface that becomes strong quickly.

Porous implants were implanted first in the 1980s. Because these implants have a rough texture, bone cells grow into the metal and hold the implant secure. During the several months of the healing process, the patient may be instructed to use a cane or walker. Some patients with porous implants implanted during early years complained of thigh pain in the operative leg for weeks or months after surgery. Surgeons speculated that the reason for the thigh pain was micromotion of the implant inside the bone during the healing process. Efforts by implant companies improved the irregular surface of porous implants. Efforts by surgeons to "press-fit" the implant inside the bone also decreased the pain. Patients must have good bone quality and strength for successful bony ingrowth, the healing process whereby bone cells attach to the implant and hold it secure.

Since the porous implants are newer, the time frame of studies is shorter. A study published in the *Journal of Bone and Joint Surgery* in 2001 reported a ten-year survival rate of 96.4 percent (plus or minus 2.1 percent) for the entire prosthesis.[11] This means that 96.4 percent of those implants were doing well without signs of loosening at ten years post-surgery. Porous THR implants are used on people of all ages but especially in younger, active people.

A third type of total hip replacement involves a combination of glued and porous implants and surgeons call this a "hybrid" hip. Usually a porous acetabular component is combined with a glued femoral stem in a hybrid hip. This technique was introduced in the early 1980s.

A hip procedure being performed in Europe called metal surface arthroplasty or "resurfacing" catches the attention of doctors and patients. According to *Hip Replacement or Hip Resurfacing* author Peggy Gabriel, she suffered excruciating hip pain at age 51. Because she regularly taught yoga and Pilates, Peggy

---

*The Arthritis Foundation animation for total hip procedure can be accessed at ww2.arthritis.org/con ditions/SurgeryCenter/surgerycenterflash/totalhip.html.

did not want to lose the ability to continue those activities. A total hip surgeon recommended that Peggy give up teaching Pilates classes after total hip surgery. "Bringing the knees to the chest, crossing the legs, and various movements that were required of me as a Pilates teacher could cause a dislocation."[12] Finding this option unacceptable, Peggy began research on total hip replacement vs. hip resurfacing. Her medical insurance approved a total hip replacement but denied coverage for a total hip resurfacing as "experimental and investigational." This procedure and implants have been used in Europe since 1991 but is under FDA investigation in America. Peggy decided to pay for the hip resurfacing surgery herself and traveled to Belgium to have the procedure performed. At 21 months post-surgery, Peggy regularly does yoga and Pilates. When asked if she can do all she wants to, Peggy replies, "Yes, and more than I anticipated."[13] Peggy recommends that people facing arthritis treatments and surgery do research and learn of the options available. "When it comes to your own health, do not let anyone else hold the reins to your life. Talk to people who've had the surgery done and learn all you can."[14]

The hip re-surfacing procedure puts a short stemmed metal cap on the femoral head and metal cup in the acetabulum (hip socket). Earlier attempts at this procedure weren't successful, but improved metals and techniques have some surgeons watching to see if this procedure will be successful. A study published in the *Journal of Bone and Joint Surgery* reported early results of 94.4 percent implants doing well at four years.[15] With the promising results of the European doctors, several implant companies are working on developing similar implants for use in America after FDA approval happens. Time will tell the long-term results of hip resurfacing procedures.

Revision total hip surgery occurs when a patient's total hip implants loosen and cause pain. If the patient falls and breaks his leg at the area of hip implants, a revision surgery will be necessary. The goal of revision RHA is to "restore the patient's hip function by repairing the biomechanical kinetics."[16] In other words, the surgeon removes the pain-producing, loosened total hip prosthesis and while preserving all healthy bone, reconstructs the hip joint with new implants, possibly with bone graft products and glue (methylmethacrylate).

Efforts to Improve Total Hip Implants

Total hip replacements historically have brought pain relief to many people. Sir John Charnley's original implant consisted of two pieces, a plastic cup and femoral stem with attached head. Today's implants usually include at least four pieces: a metal cup; plastic, ceramic or metal liner that fits inside the cup; the stem; and a femoral head made of metal or ceramic. Many sizes of each component will be available to fit each patient. A 5'3" 100 pound grandmother

Ceramic head and liners for total hip implants are some of the innovations offered in the search for a "joint that will last the patient's lifetime" (courtesy Wright Medical Technologies).

Metal-on-metal acetabular cup and head promise to be more stable with less risk of dislocating (courtesy Wright Medical Technologies).

would need a much smaller size implant than a 6'1" tall 200 pound executive who played football in college.

In efforts to make total hip replacements that will last a lifetime, doctors and implant manufacturing companies continue to improve implants. When the acetabular plastic (polyethylene) cups wear, tiny slivers of plastic became loose particles inside the joint and doctors believe they caused loosening of the implants. Over the years, implant companies worked to improve the polyethylene used in the cups. One company has patented a process called "crosslinking" to strengthen the plastic. Another company believes ceramic heads for the femoral implant and/or liners of ceramic will provide the toughness needed to prolong implant life. Yet another company believes a metal head for the femoral implant and metal acetabular liner will be the answer to longevity for implants. The search for better implants brought into medicine metals such as tivanium and tantalum, ceramic implants and improved polyethylene. Physicians watch these changes with interest because they want long-lasting implants for their patients.

In the early decades of total joint replacement, doctors refused to do total joint surgery on young persons. Doctors wanted the patients to be old enough that their total joint would survive their life. Many of the cemented total hip implants lasted for a very long time as mentioned earlier (86.5 percent lasted 25 years or more.) However, no surgeon wanted to put that 25-year hip in a 40-year-old patient knowing the patient would face revision surgery at least once.

Doctors looking back over the past 25 years find that for every decade earlier in life that the patient was at time of surgery, the survivorship of total implants decreased.[17] In other words, younger people work and play harder and put more strain on a total hip. A young professional basketball player puts more stress on his total hip than an elderly grandmother whose main exercise is swimming. As patients live longer and younger patients need total joint replacements, the potential for revision surgery remains a concern for both surgeons and patients. With the new improved technology, implants tested in lab settings have a longer lifespan. Everyone hopes those predictions prove true when the implants are inserted into people. Surgeons and implant manufacturing companies continue their efforts to refine the surgical techniques and improve the implants.

Total hip surgery is an almost always elective procedure. The only emergency total hip would involve a fractured hip. For certain types of fractures, the surgeon might recommend a total hip replacement or partial hip replacement (unipolar or bipolar hemiarthroplasty). A partial hip replacement differs from the total hip in that the hip socket (acetabulum) is not changed. No implants are attached to that area. Instead, the femoral stem and hip sits inside the socket and articulates within it.

Efforts to Improve Surgical Techniques

This discussion begins and ends with advice: Accept the surgeon's proposed plan of surgery or find another doctor. After the patient finds a surgeon and develops a doctor-patient relationship, the patient should trust the surgeon's opinion. This doctor will consider the patient's overall health as well as hip anatomy and bone strength. Whether a patient's bone is strong or suffers from osteoporosis will be a factor in determining the procedure. A knowledgeable patient should listen to the surgeon, ask questions, and even get a second opinion if the patient wants to. According to *Dr. David Sherer's Hospital Survival Guide,* "Good doctors don't feel threatened by the thought that others are reviewing their cases."[18] Before surgery is scheduled, the patient should "feel comfortable" with the surgeon's proposed plan for surgical procedure.

Debate continues on what procedure is best: Traditional hip procedure vs. minimally invasive vs. two-incision minimally invasive. The traditional total hip incision measures 10 to 12 inches. The surgeon can easily visualize the bone and anatomy of the hip. Through this size incision surgeons can place the total hip implants in any patient and position the implants for stability. Any type of implant can be implanted through the traditional incision, whether porous, glued. hybrid, or even revision. The recovery and rehabilitation is pretty standard, several weeks, and maybe months to heal.

Surgeons caught the "minimally invasive" concept and began to shorten the traditional incision. They found they could accomplish the same excellent results through a smaller incision, either lateral (on the side) or posteriorlateral (on the side farther posterior). When the implant/instrument companies and doctors designed instruments that would enable the surgeons to accomplish the procedure through a smaller incision, progress was made. Many surgeons make their incisions shorter and accomplish the procedure through a smaller incision. The minimally invasive total hip procedures aim for an incision fewer than 10 cm (four inches), but the incision can easily be enlarged if needed. All three types of implants: porous, glued and hybrid can be accomplished through the smaller incision.

The "minimally invasive" procedures account for two procedures. During both these procedures, surgeons divide the muscles and work between the muscle fibers. They cut as few structures in the hip as possible. This accomplishes a stable hip, with a smaller incision and less noticeable scar. The minimally invasive procedures also tout the advantages of shorter recovery time, shorter hospital stay and less post-operative pain.[19] Surgeons debate which procedures are best for which patients.

The two-incision procedure developed in the last few years changed the way operating room staff think of total hip surgery. Through a small incision over the groin, the acetabulum portion of the joint is prepared and acetabular socket implants are put into place. Through a second small incision at the cheek of the hip, the femoral canal is prepared and the femoral stem is put into place. This innovative procedure was a radical change from the standard total hip procedure. Patients with healthy bone (not osteoporotic) and normal size (not carrying excess weight in their hip area) are two criteria in patient selection for the two-incision procedure. Early results of the two-incision procedure looked promising. However, surgeons began to report complications they've found with the two-incision procedure and concerns were raised. Some surgeons will continue to perform and improve the two-incision technique. Others will watch and see the results of their colleagues. Many surgeons would agree the two-incision procedure is challenging, even for surgeons specialized in total hip surgery.

Because these minimally invasive hip procedures are new, doctors are looking carefully at their patients' outcomes and the results of other surgeons also. Debate among surgeons continues as to whether the smaller incision actually accomplishes the quicker recovery or whether the patients do better because they expect to do better. One study presented at the 2005 American Academy of Orthopedic Surgery (AAOS) annual meeting involved 50 patients. These patients were divided into groups who received a traditional incision, a minimally invasive incision and a third group of patients requesting a minimally invasive incision. The third group of patients knew they received the minimally invasive incision. The first two groups of patients, their therapists and nurses did not know who received the small or large incision for the first 10 days post-operatively. There were no statistically significant differences in patient groups when comparing surgery time, estimated blood loss, necessary pain medications, time spent in the hospital before discharge and post-operative function. "The group who requested the small incision ambulated greater distances on post-operative days 2 and 3, and used significantly less narcotics than the other two groups." The conclusion reached was "patients who request and are aware that they have received a small incision recover quickly and require less narcotics." Patient expectation seems to be a factor in how quickly and easily they recover.[20]

Another study presented at the 2005 American Academy of Orthopedic Surgery (AAOS) annual meeting compared two groups of 60 patients. One group received the traditional procedure and the other group of 60 patients received the single-incision minimally invasive procedure. The results showed that there was no detectable difference in outcomes between the two groups with regard to blood loss, narcotic requirement, functional recovery and length of stay."[21]

. The debate continues over details such as incision size and which implants will prove to be best. For the present, many patients find their lives enhanced when a total hip replacement accomplishes pain-free movement.

John Fisher comments, "I've had several people talk to me who are thinking about having total hip surgery. I've told them, you'll know when you are ready to do it. After you do have it, you won't regret it because I haven't regretted it for a moment. Now I do basically anything I want to and have had no problems whatsoever."[22]

13

Total Knee Replacement

Knee osteoarthritis is one of the five top causes of disability among elders.[1] Whether the cartilage destruction and pain is caused by osteoarthritis, rheumatoid arthritis or post-traumatic (after an injury) arthritis, many people deal with knee pain. When conservative treatments fail, "more than 300,000 knee replacements" are performed in the United States annually.[2]*

Pain-Free Healthy Knees

The largest joint in the body is the knee. The lower end of the femur (thighbone) and the upper end of the tibia (shinbone) meet in the knee. The patella (kneecap) rides in a groove of the femur called the trochlea. The knee joint is bathed in a lubricant called synovial fluid, which decreases friction. Large ligaments give the knee stability and large thigh muscles give strength.[3] This weight-bearing joint gets lots of wear and tear. Articular cartilage, which is white, shiny and very smooth, covers the ends of these three bones (femur, tibia and patella) where they meet and move. When injury or disease causes damage to the articular cartilage, pain and decreased function can occur.

Causes of Knee Pain

As with hip arthritis, the pain comes when articular cartilage wears thin and raw bones rub together. Whether caused by injury (post-traumatic arthritis), osteoarthritis or rheumatoid arthritis, the damaged cartilage can no longer provide the smooth, pain-free movement.

---

*The Arthritis Foundation provides an animation showing the total knee replacement at http://ww2. arthritis.org/conditions/SurgeryCenter/surgerycenterflash/totalknee.html. Arthritis Foundation animation on unicompartmental total knee replacement can be accessed at http://ww2.arthritis.org/conditions/SurgeryCenter/surgerycenterflash/uni.html.

Symptoms of Knee Arthritis

According to the American Academy of Orthopaedic Surgeons (AAOS), usually arthritis pain develops gradually, although sudden onset can occur. "The joint may become stiff and swollen, making it difficult to bend or straighten the knee. Pain and swelling are worse in the morning or after a period of inactivity. Pain may also increase after activities such as walking, stair climbing or kneeling. The pain may often cause a feeling of weakness in the knee, resulting in a 'locking' or 'buckling.' Many people report that changes in the weather also affect the degree of pain from arthritis."[4]

Conservative Treatments First

Before total knee surgery becomes the topic of conversation with a surgeon, the patient should be trying non-surgical treatments. Early treatments recommended by the American Academy of Orthopaedic Surgeons for knee arthritis include: "activity modification, a program of regular exercise and weight loss. The muscles around the knee protect it during activity. Every step puts several times your body weight through your knee. Improved strength and decreased body weight will prolong the life of your knee. Soft knee braces and modifications of your shoe can sometimes help." Acetaminophen (Tylenol) or anti-inflammatories (NSAIDs) are usually the first medications recommended for arthritis. Some dietary supplements might also help. You may need to use a cane or walker. This can help you walk and improve your mobility.

The next step is injections. Steroids may be used to decrease inflammation. "A lubricant (hyaluronic injection) may be used to improve the function of the knee. These can offer some relief. They can be repeated from time to time if they help."[5]

Activity modifications means substituting low-impact activities such as swimming, walking and cycling for strenuous activities such as running or jumping. Minimizing activities that aggravate the arthritis pain such as stair climbing can help decrease pain.

Regular flexibility, strengthening, and aerobic exercises benefit people with arthritis. Exercises recommended by the Arthritis Foundation (AF) can be learned by attending AF-approved classes. Some persons will want to learn from a physical therapist/trainer or through the Arthritis Foundation PACE (People with Arthritis Can Exercise) videos. Excellent diagrams on exercise can be found in the book *The Arthritis Helpbook* by Kate Loring and James F. Fries. During flares (times of increased pain and disease activity), "it's important to rest more and to protect the inflamed joints. But continuing to be inactive after the flare is over can be bad for your health and actually increase some arthritis problems."[6]

People, especially those with RA, should discuss how to handle exercise during a flare with the rheumatologist or other doctor.

Because of concerns with NSAIDs causing higher risk of stroke and heart attack, people should talk to their doctor periodically about the best pain management.

Hyaluronic Acid Injections

Lubricant injections involve hyaluronic acid (HA) or visco-supplement. Not all patients experience relief from the HA injections, but many do. Several studies show that hyaluronic acid injections "significantly decreased pain and stiffness experienced" when compared to a placebo (saline) injection.[7] A 2004 study published in the *Journal of Rheumatology* and involving 240 patients at 17 centers found "intraarticular [into the joint] HA treatment was significantly more effective than saline" in mild to moderate osteoarthritis for the 13 weeks of the study.[8]

Hyaluronic acid (HA) injections replace the natural joint lubricant that decreases in osteoarthritis. The body produces HA, a part of synovial fluid acting as a shock absorber and lubricant inside joints. When osteoarthritis occurs, the concentration of HA decreases and it doesn't function efficiently. When the doctor injects hyaluronic acid directly into the knee joint once a week for three to five weeks depending on the brand, the concentration of HA is returned to more normal levels. HA injections should not be considered a cure, but another treatment option for "people with OA of the knee who have not responded well to exercise, physical therapy and simple over-the-counter (OTC) analgesics, such as acetaminophen and ibuprofen."[9] Doctors may recommend an HA injection for individuals at risk for stomach ulcers or kidney problems.

"Supplemental hyaluronic acid is a purified extract made from the combs of roosters."[10] Persons allergic to eggs and other bird products should tell their doctor about this allergy. "Allergic reactions have been rare."[11] Post-injection side effects are usually mild and include pain, rash and itching at the injection site and knee swelling. Injections of HA cost several hundred dollars but are covered by some insurance and Medicare. The person should check on whether his insurance/Medicare coverage will help pay for the injections to avoid a surprise at bill time.

Total Knee Procedures

Modern-design total knee replacements were developed in the 1970s. These implants consisted of a metal femoral component, an all-plastic tibial component

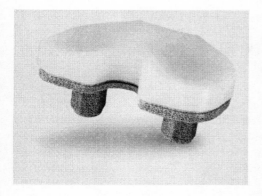

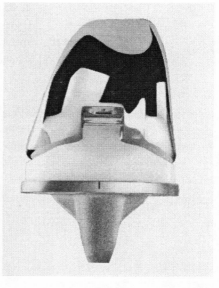

Above—Trabecular metal total knee tibial implant. In their efforts to increase the longevity of implants, implant companies offer new metals such as trabecular metal made out of tantalum. The porous design of this metal encourages bone to grow into its surface (courtesy Zimmer, Inc.). *Right*—Total knee implants of various designs account for over 300,000 joints annually (courtesy DePuy Orthopaedics).

and a plastic patella button and were held in place by methylmethacrylate (bone cement). Over the years, the femoral component has remained metal. The tibial and patella components have been manufactured from metals and plastics. Current models can be secured to the bone by the methylmethacrylate or bony ingrowth as the bone grows into and attaches to the porous components.

Efforts to Improve Total Knee Implants

Efforts to improve knee implants have continued since the first implants. Modern metals commonly used are titanium or cobalt-chrome alloy. Ultra-high-density polyethylene is used for the plastic components. Components weigh approximately 15 to 20 ounces, depending on size. Surgeons and implant companies have agreed that implants must meet certain criteria:

1. Biocompatibility, which means the implants don't cause a "local or a systemic rejection response."[12] The rejection response refers to the reaction people who receive organ transplants can develop and must be treated to avoid. The implants pose no danger of rejection by the body.

2. Implants must duplicate structures they're replacing. "They are strong enough to take weightbearing loads, flexible enough to bear stress without breaking and able to move smoothly against each other as required."[13]

3. Implants must "retain their strength and shape for a long time. The chance of a knee replacement lasting 15 to 20 years is 95%."[14] Implant companies and doctors hope the new implants last longer, and out-of-body (in vitro) testing promises longer life for implants, but no one knows for sure.

Efforts continue to improve upon the results and lengthen the life span of total knee implants. "To date, man-made joints have not solved the problem of wear. Every time bone rubs against bone, or metal rubs against plastic, the friction creates microscopic particulate debris. Just as wear in the natural joint contributed to the need for a replacement joint, wear in the prostheses may eventually require a second (revision) surgery."[15]

Over 150 designs of total knee replacement offer many options. Surgeons will have an opinion of which implant is best for each patient. Factors the surgeon will consider include "the patient's age, weight, activity level and health, the surgeon's experience and familiarity with the device, and the cost and performance record of the implant."[16]

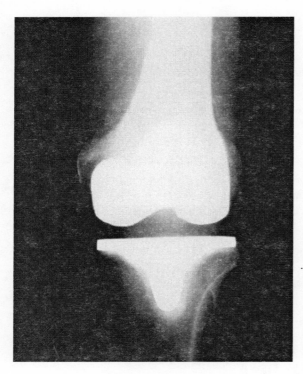

This x-ray shows total knee implants. The femoral component covers the walking surface of the femur (thighbone). The tibial component consists of a metal tray and its plastic articular surface, which shows as the gap between metal pieces. The patellar implant (kneecap) if inserted is often plastic, depending on company design (courtesy DePuy Orthopaedics)

Efforts to Improve Surgical Techniques— Traditional vs. Minimally Invasive Surgery

Total knee replacements relieve pain and restore function to people with painful arthritic knees. During the surgical procedure, the surgeon uses surgical saws and drills to remove the damaged ends of the femur (thighbone), tibia (shinbone) and maybe the patella (kneecap). A minimal amount of articular cartilage and bone are removed and new implants sized to the patient's knee are fitted onto the ends of bone. Some surgeons routinely replace the patella (kneecap) while others assess the condition of the patella and decide during surgery whether or not to resurface the patella (kneecap.) The implants are either press-fit with porous surface, which the bone grows into and holds firm, or glued in place using methylmethacrylate (a surgical putty-like glue or cement). The surgeon's goal is to restore the knee joint to anatomic alignment and function so the patient has a pain-free, stable joint.

Using the minimally invasive total knee procedures, surgeons work to perform the same surgery through a smaller incision that affects skin, quadriceps muscle and tendon. The patient sees a smaller healing scar. More important is what the doctor does to the inside structures during surgery. Proponents of the minimally invasive procedures say recovery is quicker. Potential benefits of minimally invasive technique include "increased range of motion sooner after surgery, less blood loss during surgery, faster recovery and a shorter hospital stay."[17]

The traditional total knee replacement incision measures 8 to 12 inches long and cuts the quadriceps muscle and tendon. The skin heals quickly, but healing and rehabilitation of the muscles and tendon require more time and care. "It typically takes the muscle and tendon months to heal, and it's this healing process that causes much of the pain of recovery."[18]

Several years ago, doctors began to consider the possibility of accomplishing the same surgery through a smaller incision. Could they do the same total knee surgery through a smaller incision? Pioneer doctors and implant companies began to work on this idea. By miniaturizing the instruments, surgeons could make the necessary cuts in the bone and fit the new prosthesis. But what results would their patient have when he began to walk on the new prosthesis? Without comparable good results, no one would want this new procedure. Several different surgical approaches have been considered, some rejected and some kept for improvements. Computer-generated navigation systems came into total joint replacements to assist surgeons in getting excellent results. Navigation systems, or global positioning devices for surgeons, enable precise shaping of bones and positioning of implants. Some minimally invasive approaches need the navigation to get quality results, while navigation isn't necessary for other procedures. Surgeons utilizing the other surgical approaches find navigation an option reserved for very deformed knee joints. Navigation system equipment costs hospitals many thousands of dollars and patients bills reflect the additional costs.

The minimally invasive total joint is still controversial among surgeons. Some surgeons see the benefit of "out-patient" total joints, in which the patient's recovery is shortened. Other surgeons worry about the long-term effects and feel that a shorter recovery is not worth the long-term risks. Will the results be as good when the smaller incision procedure is done? If the surgical cuts in the bone aren't right, the patient's new joint may not last as long. "Several early studies of MIS knee surgery have shown some benefits such as less blood loss, shorter hospital stays and better motion, while others have shown a higher rate of complications, suboptimal positioning of the knee implants and no real difference in the recovery."[19] Surgeons proficient in minimally invasive procedures have dedicated time and effort to become good at the new procedure. "This procedure is more technically demanding than a standard knee replacement, and the learning curve is fairly steep. Initially, it may take up to twice as long as a standard procedure; surgical time becomes shorter as the surgeon becomes more experienced."[20] Time will tell whether the new procedures are truly better. Surgeons weigh the benefits of new techniques against possible problems as they work to improve patient outcomes. They want each patient's knee replacement to last that person's lifetime.

Unicompartmental vs. Total Knee Replacement

When only the medial or lateral portion of femur and tibia are arthritic, a unicompartmental (meaning one compartment) total knee implant (shown here) can be inserted into the joint (courtesy Smith & Nephew, Inc.).

The knee could be described as having three compartments: medial (inside half of femur and tibia), lateral (outside half of femur and tibia) and patella-femoral (kneecap rides inside a groove of the femur. A unicompartmental knee involves either the medial or lateral compartments and does nothing to the patellar femoral joint. For the person who deals with arthritis in only the medial or lateral area of the knee, unicompartmental knee replacement may be a good option. Because the area to be operated upon is only half, the incision made is smaller than the traditional total knee replacement. Using surgical instruments, saw and drill, the surgeon removes the damaged articular cartilage on femur (thighbone) and tibia (shinbone) and replaces them with implants that are cemented into place using methyl-methacrylate (bone cement).

"1955 knee procedure gets new life."[21] A surgical procedure performed in the 1950s involved replacing the patella-femoral joint (where the kneecap rides inside a groove of the femur.) This procedure was called patello-femoral arthroplasty. Early efforts were unsuccessful due to inadequate instrumentation and implants and surgeons stopped performing this procedure. Renewed interest has developed among surgeons recently. This procedure may be considered for people whose arthritis involves the patella-femoral compartment only. Patello-femoral arthritis can be caused from a patella that's misaligned from birth or from wear and tear. Individuals suffering traumatic damage to the patella in a car accident might develop arthritis in that area. Patello femoral arthroplasty provides one more option in types of total knee procedures.[22]

One Knee or Two?

Patients may wonder whether it's better to have both arthritic knees operated on at the same time and should discuss this option with the surgeon. Some patients may feel passionately the need to "get it over with." Occasionally, both knees are deformed and painful. Some surgeons may prefer to do both (called bilateral) knees at the same operative session or a week apart, which they call a staged total knee procedure.[23] Other surgeons prefer that the patient have several weeks of recovery time before the second surgery.

Sex-Specific Total Knee

Sex-specific or gender-specific implants advertised recently involve changes built into the implants themselves. Researchers used computerized tomography (CT) technology to measure and compare female vs. male femurs and found that female anatomy of the femur (thigh-

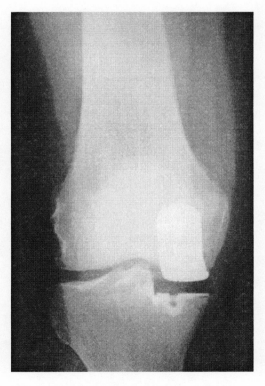

Xray showing a unicompartmental knee implant in the medial aspect of a knee. The plastic tibial portion shows as the gap under the metal femoral component (courtesy DePuy Orthopaedics).

bone) is smaller in certain dimensions, such as anterior/posterior, medial/lateral measurements and the anterior portion of the femur. Also, doctors recognized the Q-angle of the femur is larger for females than male. The Q-angle involves the hip-to-knee-to-ankle angle; the path of the kneecap (patella) when it slides over the femur. Based on these findings, implant companies offer more choices in sizes, some specifically addressing the smaller dimensions of females.

The new total knee replacement should give pain-free comfortable knee movement for many years. Patients enhance the good care they've received from their surgeon and hospital staff when they become a member of the team caring for the new joint.

14

Elbows, Shoulders, Fingers and Toes

After working as a nurse for many years, Ms. Jones had worn out her thumb joints. After years of starting IVs, checking blood pressures, giving medications and performing other nursing duties, she faced retirement with arthritic thumbs. Her thumbs appeared deformed, had decreased strength, and hurt. What could she do? Ms. Jones made the trek to an orthopedic surgeon who performed a procedure called ligamentous tendon reconstruction interposition (LTRI) Arthroplasty, which restored function to her thumbs and got rid of her pain.

Surgeons perform joint replacements on hips and knees to reduce arthritic pain and improve mobility for their patients.[1] The smaller joints of the arms and legs can also become painful and disfigured from osteoarthritis and rheumatoid arthritis. Surgery can correct deformity and replace arthritic joints to restore pain-free joint movement for many people. Surgery in the smaller joints may require less surgery time but should be considered seriously.

Conservative Treatments First

"Conservative management of arthritis may include medicines, rest, exercise, hot or cold treatments, activity modification, and the use of splints."[2] When conservative treatments no longer give relief, surgical options may be the answer.

Upper Extremity (Arm) Joints

Shoulders

Healthy shoulders enable baseball pitchers to throw a no-hit game. Pain-free shoulders allow a grandfather to pick up his four-year-old blonde-haired

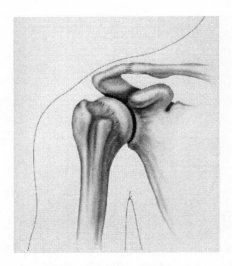

This illustration demonstrates a healthy shoulder. The articular surface of the humerus (upper arm) moves smoothly and easily inside the joint (courtesy Zimmer, Inc.)

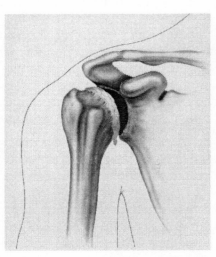

When one compares this illustration to the healthy shoulder, one should notice the irregular, rough-appearing articular cartilage of the humerus (courtesy Zimmer, Inc.).

granddaughter. In 2003, over 13 million Americans with shoulder problems sought medical care.[3]

The shoulder joint, called a ball and socket joint, allows a huge range of motion, including circular rotation. Three bones make up the shoulder joint: the clavicle (collarbone), scapula (shoulder blade) and humerus (upper arm bone). The ball of the humerus rests inside the socket (glenoid). Soft tissues called the capsule help hold the ball inside the socket and muscles, and tendons and ligaments help the arm move, while providing stability.

Because the shoulder has such a large range of motion, it's an unstable joint and susceptible to injuries. Signs of shoulder arthritis include pain, especially over the acromioclavicular (AC) joint (where the scapula joins the collarbone), and decreased shoulder motion.

The total shoulder procedure for arthritis replaces the worn ends of the bone. The upper ball of the humerus is replaced with an implant stem and head (similar in design to a total hip ball and stem but smaller). The socket implant of a total shoulder is a cap (glenoid) that fits inside the socket. The implants are secured in place and the patient begins recovery which includes physical therapy to regain strength and mobility in the affected shoulder.

Elbow

Elbows involve three bones: the humerus (upper arm bone) and two bones of the forearm (radius and ulna), which join together. Described as a "hinge joint," the elbow is "second in dislocations only to the shoulder joint."[4] The strong liga-

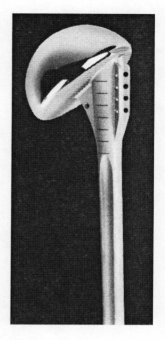

Shoulder implants can replace the arthritic shoulder joint. The stem fits down the upper arm long bone (humerus) and the head fits into the shoulder socket. The shoulder socket portion can be resurfaced by a plastic glenoid component, which is usually glued into the socket (courtesy Smith & Nephew, Inc.).

ments, muscles and tendons that surround the elbow help protect it from injury.

When arthritis affects the elbow, pain and decreased range of motion cause problems. Surgical procedures to resurface the elbow with a total joint can be performed. According to the American Academy of Orthopaedic Surgeons, "if the joint surface has been worn away completely, it is unlikely that anything other than a joint replacement would bring about relief. There are several different types of joint replacements available."[5] Depending on the design of the implant, the total elbow would likely be two implant stems. One stem would be inserted into the upper arm bone (humerus), while the second stem would sit inside the forearm bone (ulna) and the two stems would hinge together to provide painless, smooth motion.

Normal Wrists

The wrist joint involves the eight carpal bones (two rows of four bones each) and the two forearm bones (radius and ulna), which meet. The wrist also contains all the tendons, ligaments, blood vessels and nerves that allow humans to use their wrists and hands with dexterity. The wrist has movements in two planes.[6] A healthy wrist moves without pain.

When osteoarthritis affects the synovial joints of hands and wrists, the cartilage covering the end of the bones wears thin, causing pain. Bone spurs may form and pain increases. When rheumatoid arthritis affects the synovial joints, the tissue lining the joints (called synovial tissue) overgrows and becomes inflamed. Chemicals released by this inflamed synovial tissue damages bone, cartilage, ligaments, tendons and muscles. When the damage occurs, the joints become unstable. The person's grip or pinch becomes painful and weak. Other possible symptoms include swelling and decreased motion. Joint swelling may cause pressure on the nerves in the wrist joint and lead to carpal tunnel syndrome or a compression neuropathy (nerve symptoms due to the nerve being squeezed).[7]

Conservative treatments include splinting the wrist for a short time and a steroid shot into the joint to decrease inflammation and swelling. An individual may find relief by changing activities and work habits that cause wrist pain.

Surgical treatments for arthritic wrists include arthrodesis (fusion) and arthroplasty (replacement). During fusion, the arthritic cartilage is removed and the bones are held together while healing occurs. Motion at that joint is no longer possible, but the wrist no longer hurts. Wrist arthroplasty involves two implants made from the same metals and high-quality plastic (polyethylene) as total hip and knee implants. The surgeon removes the arthritic part of the wrist bones and inserts the new implants, securing them possibly with methylmethacrylate (bone cement).

Normal Hands and Fingers

> Early this morning, even before you were out of bed, your hands and arms came to life, goading your weak and helpless body into the new day. Perhaps your day began with a lunge at the snooze bar on the bedside radio, or a roundhouse swing at the alarm clock.... Where would we be without our hands? Our lives are so full of commonplace experience in which the hands are so skillfully and silently involved that we rarely consider how dependent upon them we actually are. We notice our hands when we are washing them, when our fingernails need to be trimmed, or when little brown spots and wrinkles crop up and begin to annoy us. We also pay attention to a hand that hurts or has been injured.[8]

The human hand consists of four fingers, one thumb and a palm connecting them to the wrist. Scientists might describe the hand as 27 bones that make up the hand and fingers. Fourteen of those bone are located in the fingers and five bones called metacarpals make up the palm. An additional eight bones, called carpals, meet the two forearm bones (radius and ulna) at the wrist joint. Fingers are described as "hinge joints," referring to the back-and-forth movements of hinges on a door.*

Normal healthy movements of the fingers and hands do not cause pain. When arthritis injures the hand, most commonly it affects the thumb and fingers. Early arthritis symptoms may be a dull or burning pain that happens after overuse of the joints. Morning pain and stiffness happens. A person may notice the pain improves with rest and gets worse with overuse. Weather changes may be felt in arthritic joints. People often try to compensate by adapting their grip to utilize neighboring joints.

Conservative measures for arthritic fingers and hands include many of those mentioned plus steroid shots and splinting. Some of the surgical procedures

*The American Society for Surgery of the Hand provides pictures of hand anatomy and terms surgeons may use to describe hand movements at www.assh.org/AM/Template.cfm?Section=Hand_Anatomy.

done on the hand involve fusions (arthrodesis) and arthroplasty (surgical repair and replacement of joints with implants).

As with other joints, arthrodesis or surgical fusion involves removing the cartilage of the bones and holding those bones together while healing occurs. After the fusion heals, no movement happens at that joint and no pain occurs. The surgeon's goal for a fusion is to get better function or better cosmetic position of a deformed joint.

Arthroplasty involves implants that replace deformed joints and improve function. Both the large knuckles and middle knuckles can be replaced with implants made from silicone, carbon or plastic. The most distal knuckle would more likely be fused instead of using implants.[9]

The hand without a thumb is at worst nothing but an animated fish-slice, and at best a pair of forceps whose points don't meet properly. Without the thumb, the hand is put back 60 million years in evolutionary terms to a stage when the thumb had no independent movement and was just another digit. One cannot emphasize enough the importance of finger-thumb opposition for human emergence from a relatively undistinguished primate background.[10]

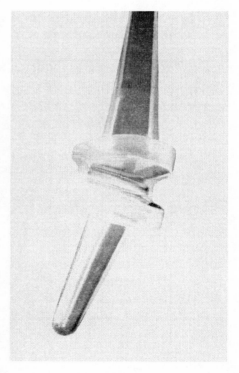

When osteoarthritis involves the base of the thumb called the carpometacarpal (CMC) joint, pinching and gripping may be painful and the ability to grip may be poor. Arthroplasty of the thumb may involve implants or using ligamentous tissue from the forearm in a procedure called ligamentous tendon reconstruction interposition (LTRI).

A thumb implant (trapezium) fills the joint after arthritic, articular cartilage is removed and the implant stem fits into the middle of the bony canal. During an LTRI procedure, the surgeon replaces the arthritic joint with a nonessential tendon from the person's forearm or wrist. The trapezium bone is partially or fully removed, and the tendon is used to reinforce the joint and placed inside the space where the trapezium was located. A cast or splint will hold the joint immobile during healing

Finger prosthesis of varying designs can be used to relieve pain and straighten crooked, arthritic fingers (courtesy DePuy Orthopaedics).

time. Physical therapy after healing may be recommended by the surgeon to regain strength and improve movement in the thumb joint. Two successful surgical procedures for thumb arthritis involve the arthroplasty with implants and the LTRI procedure.

Lower Extremity (Leg) Joints—Below the Hip and Knee

Healthy, Pain-Free Ankles

In 2003, people visited their doctors more than 11 million times because of foot and ankle problems.[11] The three bones of the ankle include the talus (anklebone), tibia (shinbone) and fibula (small support bone of the lower leg). Three groups of ligament make the ankle joint strong, while tendons and muscles provide movement and enable walking. A healthy ankle doesn't cause pain. As with other joints, arthritis of the ankle happens when the articular cartilage wears thin and the raw bones rubbing together results in pain. Arthritis of the ankle can be caused by injuries, osteoarthritis and rheumatoid arthritis.

Conservative measures specific to ankle arthritis include braces and supports, which reduce motion and stress. "Exercises to strengthen the muscles, especially when the osteoarthritis occurs in the ankle, may give the patient greater stability and help avoid injury that will worsen the condition."[12]

When conservative measures no longer relieve the pain, surgery may be the answer. Arthrodesis (fusion) of the three ankle bones and ankle replacement surgery are two surgical procedures performed. Fusion or arthrodesis happens when the surgeon removes the articular cartilage and fits the bones together. During healing, the bones are held together and immobile by screws,

Total ankle implants may be options for some patients with arthritis in their ankles (courtesy DePuy Orthopaedics).

external fixator or other surgical hardware. As with other joint fusions, after healing no motion occurs in the ankle joint and the patient should expect no pain.

Early ankle arthroplasty (replacement) procedures done in the 1970s were problematic and gave the procedure a bad reputation. "Second generation total ankle replacements have shown impressive results. For many patients, the new ankle lasts 10 years.... Nevertheless, complications do still occur, such as loosening of the joint."[13] While watching for the improvements of ankle arthroplasty, many surgeons will recommend an ankle fusion at present.

Normal Feet and Toes

"Walking puts up to 1.5 times your bodyweight on your foot. Your feet log approximately 1,000 miles per year. As shock absorbers, feet cushion up to one million pounds of pressure during one hour of strenuous exercise."[14]

Each foot consists of 26 bones that meet at 33 joints and more than 100 ligaments, tendons and muscles.[15] The foot is a hinge joint that permits flexion and extension.

As people age, so do their feet. Feet lose their cushion and become less flexible. Improperly fitting shoes cause problems such as bunions, hammertoes and neuromas. A bunion affects the big toe with painful bony overgrowth, which contributes to misalignment. Hammertoes are toes that are buckled and can't straighten. Neuromas happen when the nerve between the toes, often between the third and fourth toes, becomes irritated and painful. If arthritis affects the feet, bone spurs can form, causing pain and decreased motion.

The Arthritis Foundation recommends preventing these painful problems. An individual should buy comfortable, properly fitting shoes. A person should be able to stick his finger between his heel and the back of the shoe to ensure proper fit. Rubber soles add cushion and comfort to shoes. When comparing three-inch high heel shoes to one-inch shoes, the three-inch heel shoes exert seven times the pressure and stress on the wearer's foot. A well-fitting, comfortable shoe with low heel (less than 1½ inch heel) helps prevent foot problems and arthritis.[16]

As with other joints, conservative treatments for feet certainly should be utilized before surgery. For arthritic feet, orthotics adds value to conservative treatments. "Orthotic devices are intended to make the feet more comfortable, minimize stress on the foot or improve an abnormal or irregular walking pattern."[17] Commonly used orthotics includes arch supports, heel inserts and bunion shield pads. People with flat feet may find arch supports take the stress off. Heel inserts can aid people dealing with plantar fasciitis. These orthotic devices can be purchased over the counter or custom made by podiatrists, physical therapists and orthotic companies.

Considering Surgery

Surgery for the smaller joints involves both fusions and arthroplasty (implants). Patients need to discuss with the surgeon and understand what this surgery will accomplish.*

Tips for finding a surgeon and hospital can be found in chapter 11, "Preparing for Surgery." During both fusion and arthroplasty, the pre-operative state of the patient matters a great deal. Any infection on the patient's body should be treated successfully before surgery.

Many small joint surgeries are performed on the patient as an out-patient. That means the patient will go home after surgery or within 24 hours. Most patients need help getting home and caring for self for days to weeks. The patient should ask the surgeon how long help will be needed. Having a hand in a cast or splint will complicate chores such as cooking a meal. Tasks taken for granted such as getting dressed and daily hygiene present a challenge during recuperation. The patient who has a foot in a walking cast boot or splint will find maneuvering around the house a challenge. Pre-operative planning with family members and friends can simplify this situation.

During the preoperative visit, the surgeon may give instructions regarding this patient's regular medicines during the pre-operative time frame. For example, the surgeon may tell the patient not to take his blood thinner for a week prior to the surgery.

The patient needs to know "how long before I can walk on my foot?" or "when can I use my right hand to cook again?" With proper information and expectations, the patient can cooperate better with the rehabilitation phase of recovering.

People contemplating surgery need to consider that recovery time will be needed afterwards. Exercises and rehabilitation require a commitment from the patient to getting well. The benefits people get from joint surgery include pain-free movement and increased mobility.

Complication and Prevention Strategies

Modern-day joint surgery is amazingly safe. However, complications such as infection, loosening of implants, excessive wear or breakage of implants and nerve damage can occur. Complications after fusion (arthrodesis) include failure to heal, infection and nerve damage.

Many surgeries on other joints are done on an out-patient basis and the

---

*A list of pertinent questions can be found at the Arthritis Foundation website at www.arthritis.org/con ditions/SurgeryCenter/questions.asp.

patient will go home the same day of surgery or within 23 hours. For out-patient dismissal from the hospital, the patient will be ready for discharge to home when he scores high on the Modified Aldrete Phase I Post Anesthetic Recovery Score. The nurses will use this tool to determine when the patient is ready to be discharged. The Aldrete Recovery Score rates the patient's level of consciousness (awakeness), the ability of the patient to move all arms and legs, the patient's ability to breathe deeply and cough, and the patient's vital signs (specifically the patient's blood pressure and oxygen level).[18]

After Surgery and Returning Home

When the patient is dismissed from the hospital, the road to recovery begins. Someone other than the patient should drive home because of the medications the patient received during the surgery. With proper pre-operative planning with family and friends, details such as meals and personal care will be organized.

Pain control during the first few days after surgery makes recuperation easier. The surgeon usually writes a prescription for pain pills with details such as how often to take the pain pills and whether to take with food or not. Instructions from the hospital or surgery center for post-operative care should be discussed with the patient and caregiver before they leave the hospital. Elevating the limb on pillows (above the level of the heart) may aid in pain relief. The surgeon may include instructions for heat or cold applications and elevating the arm or leg to assist in controlling pain.

The surgeon or his staff will give instructions regarding weight bearing after leg and foot surgery. For best results, the patient should abide by those recommendations. The patient who tries to walk prematurely may cause damage that could result in complications.

The surgeon should give instructions about care of the surgical site. Surgeons often want the dressing kept clean and dry and not removed or changed until the patient returns for an office visit.

A list of possible complications the patient or caregiver needs to report to the surgeon and how to contact the doctor should be given to the patient before leaving the hospital or surgery center. The post-operative instructions will include instructions to "notify the surgeon's office" for symptoms such as fever greater than 101°F, reddened surgical site or draining from site, bleeding from surgical site, persistent nausea and vomiting, uncontrolled pain or urinary retention (patient can't urinate). The patient should know when to resume his regular daily medications and what to eat.

For best results, follow the surgeon's instructions. "In a multicenter British study, up to 25% of patients did not comply with post-operative instructions."[19]

By working with their surgeons, patients cooperate with his plan and get the best results from surgery on their joints.

Arm and lower leg joints can suffer from arthritic changes and cause pain. Orthopaedic surgeons perform surgery upon these smaller joints and bring welcome relief from symptoms for many people. Patients who learn about the surgery, prepare self for the procedure and cooperate in the recovery phase become team members in their own health.

15

Before, During and After Surgery

Mrs. Jones' left total hip replacement was scheduled for Tuesday morning and on Friday before, she noticed her right big toe looked red and felt sore. She wondered what she should do but didn't want to bother her surgeon. "He's a busy man you know." The day of surgery, she arrived at the hospital with her family accompanying her. When she mentioned her great toe problem, the pre-operative nurse became concerned and said, "Your surgeon needs to see this." Because of infection in her sore, reddened toe, Mrs. Jones' surgery was cancelled and she went home to take antibiotics.

Surgeons want their total joint patients to be at optimal health. Patients should report problems such as infection, flu or respiratory problems and cardiovascular (heart attack or stroke) symptoms. These problems need to be treated prior to surgery so the operation brings the very best results. The pre-operative assessment that surgeons do involves the overall health condition of each patient.

Signs and symptoms of infection include fever, tenderness, reddened, hot areas of the body, or any obviously reddened sores or skin areas. The presence of pus (white/yellow or green drainage from a sore or any area of the body) should be investigated by a doctor and treated appropriately. Rheumatoid arthritis patients may experience reddened, warm joints often as a part of their illness. According to *The Arthritis Helpbook*, "suspect infection if a single joint, usually a knee, becomes suddenly and severely worse."[1] People on routine corticosteroid medication should recognize that steroids increase the risk of infection. It's better to notify the doctor and let him decide whether there's an infection problem. Any signs of infection on the body should be treated and resolved before surgery.

Signs and symptoms of flu or any new respiratory problems should be reported to the surgeon and anesthesia doctor. Signs such as fever, cough, sore throat, or nasal drainage that is thickened, yellow or green should be reported. Even chronic conditions such as being short of breath or wheezing should be discussed with the doctors. Again, the doctors want the best outcome for each patient undergoing surgery.

Kidney infection signs and symptoms include pain, frequency and burning on urination, blood in the urine, and possibly fever. The patient who develops these symptoms should call the surgeon and notify him for appropriate treatment.

Heart disease ranks as America's number 1 killer. Many people undergoing total joint surgery are mature adults in a population group that may have cardiovascular (heart attack or stroke) problems. Patients experiencing acute symptoms of a heart attack or stroke should "call 9-1-1 or the emergency medical services (EMS) number so an ambulance can be sent for you."[2]

Classic heart attack symptoms include chest pressure or "discomfort in the center of the chest that lasts more than a few minutes or that goes away and comes back. It can feel like uncomfortable pressure, squeezing, fullness or pain."[3] This pain can also occur in one of both arms, the neck, jaw, back or stomach. Other more subtle symptoms include being short of breath with or without discomfort in the chest, nausea, feeling lightheaded, and breaking out in a cold sweat.

Mrs. Jones' infection was cleared and her total hip surgery rescheduled. She did not recognize that her fatigue, shortness of breath, and nausea were symptoms of a heart attack. When she went to the hospital the day of surgery, she mentioned her symptoms to the nurse in the pre-operative holding room. Thanks to good nursing and anesthesiologist assessments, she received the care she needed. Mrs. Jones' total hip surgery was again postponed and an emergency angioplasty was performed. Mrs. Jones lived to thank the staff for taking good care of her.

Classic heart attack symptoms often are dramatic and hard to ignore. People can ignore the less obvious symptoms of heart attack, which include shortness of breath, fatigue and nausea. When these subtle symptoms occur in women, researchers say, women often ignore their symptoms. In one study, doctors found that "women and minorities may have atypical symptoms when suffering a heart attack or angina." The patients with subtle symptoms tended to be "women under the age of 55 or minorities who reported shortness of breath as their main symptom instead of chest pain."[4] Both men and women can experience the classic or more subtle symptoms. Good advice for anyone is to seek help for either classic or subtle symptoms of heart attack.

Symptoms of stroke include "sudden weakness/numbness of face, arm or leg, especially on one side of the body, sudden confusion, trouble speaking or understanding, sudden trouble seeing in one or both eyes, sudden trouble walking, dizziness, loss of balance or coordination, sudden, severe headache with no known cause."[5] Patients who experience either heart attack or stroke problems should get help immediately. After that person receives medical care, notify the total joint surgeon and postpone the elective total joint procedure.

Complications and Prevention Strategies

According to the American Academy of Orthopaedic Surgeons, the complication rate following total joint surgery is low. "Serious complications, such as joint infection, occur in less than 2 percent of patients. Major medical complications, such as heart attack or stroke, occur even less frequently."[6] The most common complication to joint surgery is blood clots. One preventive measure recommended includes early ambulation. Getting out of bed and walking as the doctor and nurses recommend help prevent blood clots. Usually this happens the first day after surgery or maybe later in the surgery day in some cases. Support hose, blood thinner medications and usage of anti-embolism boots on feet and legs are commonly used prevention methods. Symptoms of blood clots include pain in calf and leg, tenderness and redness of the calf, and swelling of thigh, calf, ankle or foot. Notify your doctor immediately if you develop any of these signs.[7] Warning signs of a blood clot having traveled to lungs include shortness of breath and chest pain, particularly with breathing. This life-threatening complication requires a quick response of calling for emergency transport to the nearest hospital emergency room. (Call 9-1-1 or an appropriate number.)

Surgeons want infection-free surgery for their joint patients. One infection is too many. But they can happen either while in the hospital or at home. Infection-free surgery begins with a patient in optimal health. A malnourished and dehydrated patient has increased risk of infection.[8] Low hospital infection rates indicate quality patient care and are included in the JCAHO's 2005 National Patient Safety Goals. Operating room (OR) practices to prevent infection include routines such as sterilization practices of instruments, cleaning the operating rooms between surgery procedures, hand washing by surgeons and OR staff and sterile technique practices.

Efforts to prevent infection continue post-operatively in the patient's room. According to the Centers for Disease Control (CDC), the best prevention for infection happens when everyone washes their hands. "Improved adherence to hand hygiene [i.e., hand washing or use of alcohol-based hand rubs] has been shown to terminate outbreaks in healthcare facilities, to reduce transmission of antimicrobial resistant organisms [e.g., methicillin resistant staphylococcus aureus] and reduce overall infection rates."[9] Doctors and nurses should wash their hands when visibly soiled. When the hands aren't visibly soiled, either hand washing or an alcohol-based hand rub meets CDC recommendations of hand hygiene between patients. Often, an alcohol-based product dispenser will be mounted on the wall inside patient rooms. The patient who sees the doctor and nurses walk into the room and put their hands to a dispenser on the wall and then rub their hands together should ask what that product is. If the answer comes back, "It's alcohol-based hand cleanser," then the patient can rest assured the staff is following CDC recommendations for quality practice.

Forever after the total joint surgery, the patient should consider that joint a valuable part of his body and follow the surgeon's recommendations to keep that joint infection free. Many surgeons want their total joint patients to take an antibiotic before having dental work, even routine teeth cleaning, especially for the first two years after the joint surgery. The patient should consult with the surgeon's recommendations for infection prevention.[10] Any blood-borne infection in a person's body can travel to the bloodstream and lodge on the total joint (which the body considers a foreign body in this situation.) Even years after the total joint surgery, the patient must take infections seriously and see the primary care doctor who may refer the patient to his surgeon.

Dislocation of the total joint is rarely a problem for total knees or other joints. Total hip replacements pose a dislocation risk. Dislocation occurs when the prosthesis femoral head (ball) dislocates out of the socket. The patient can avoid dislocation problems by practicing what the physical and occupational therapists teach. Movements to avoid include crossing the legs, bending at the hip past 90 degrees and twisting side-to-side.[11]

Complications that can occur later include loosening of implants, excessive wear or breakage of implants. Surgeons and implant companies continue efforts to accomplish the goal of making implants to last the patient's life.

People contemplating surgery need to consider that recovery time will be needed afterwards. Exercises and rehabilitation require a commitment from the patient to getting well. The benefits people get from total joint surgery include pain-free movement and increased mobility.

Preparing Self for Surgery

The patient's teeth and gums should be healthy. The patient whose gums are reddened, sore and bleed easily may have gingivitis (gum disease and infection). Other symptoms of gingivitis include mouth sores, swollen gums, and gums that appear shiny and bright red or red-purple.[12] The patient needs to see a dentist for treatment. Quite likely the teeth need to be cleaned, plaque removed and infection cleared before any total joint surgery is performed. This needs to be "well in advance of surgery. Do not schedule any dental work, including routine cleanings, for several weeks after surgery."[12]

The American Academy of Orthopaedic Surgeons (AAOS) recommends:
Patients who smoke should cut back or quit if possible. Smoking "changes blood flow patterns, delays healing and slows recovery."[13]

Patients anticipating surgery should eat well-balanced meals for the weeks and months prior to surgery. Being nutritionally healthy promotes optimal healing. A person who knows he is not eating well pre-operatively should discuss with the surgeon whether to use a nutritional liquid supplement to attain optimal healing. The body needs a healthy balance of carbohydrates, fats, proteins and vitamins to heal after surgery. Unless the patient is on a restricted fluid intake because of a chronic health problem such as heart or kidney failure, a person should drink adequate fluids in the days prior to surgery.

Persons dealing with depression and anxiety should recognize that both weaken the body's immune system and increase the risk of infection or complications. A study presented at the American Academy of Orthopaedic Surgeon's 2004 annual meeting suggested that "a patient's mental status prior to surgery appears to be an excellent predictor of the surgical outcome. The overall study findings show that depressed patients not only scored lower on standardized quality of life testing prior to surgery, but also experienced less improvement in pain, function and stiffness postoperatively."[14] The patient dealing with depression should discuss this concern with the surgeon and consider treatment before surgery.

Patients should practice the exercises learned in the Pre-Admission Testing and Teaching (PATT) visit. Incorporating these movements into the patient's lifestyle will bring the reward of quicker recovery. Because dislocation can occur after total hip surgery more than other procedures, total hip patients need to learn the safe movements from the physical and occupational therapists. Practicing the safe movements and exercises will build strength and protect the hip from dislocation. Patients learn how to maneuver using crutches and/or a walker from the therapists. Tools such as a long-handled shoe horn and reacher/grabber will enable the person to dress self and pick up items easily.

Pre-Admission Testing and Teaching (PATT)

Often the hospital staff wants the patient to come for pre-admission testing and teaching (PATT) within the week or two prior to surgery. This PATT time gives the patient opportunity to ask questions of nurses knowledgeable about total joint surgeries. During this visit, the PATT nurse will ask pertinent questions about the patient's medications, including herbal supplements, allergies, previous surgeries, and medical conditions.

During the PATT process, blood work requested by the surgeon and anesthesiologist will be drawn. Individual labs may vary in the calibration of their equipment, so their "normal" lab values may vary slightly. However, any significant deviations from normal lab values will be evaluated by the patient's physician and nursing staff.

A complete blood count (CBC) will show that the patient has a normal (or abnormal) amount of specific blood cells. White blood cells (WBC, also called leukocytes) show the body's immune function and ability to fight infection. A WBC count below normal, called leucopenia, indicates possible bone marrow problems. Red blood cells (RBCs also called erythrocytes) count the number of this type of blood cell and describe it as RBCs or hematocrit. The oxygen-carrying ability of RBCs is called hemoglobin (Hgb). A low number would indicate anemia. The surgeon would want to know about significant anemia problems and might need to pre-treat the patient with iron. Chronic anemia problems accompany some chronic health problems. The platelet number of a CBC (also called thrombocytes) indicates the body's ability to clot blood. Additional CBC values involve details about the individual cells. A normal CBC (complete blood count) involves several numbers.[15]

Normal adult WBC value is 4,500 to 10,000/mcL^3
Normal platelet count is 150,000 to 400,000mm^3.[16]

Normal lab values for an adult male: RBC value 4.7 to 6.1 million/mcL^3
Hgb 13.8 to 17.2 gm/dL (often rounded 14 to 18gm/dL)
Hct 40.7 to 50.3% (often rounded to 42 to 52%)

Normal lab values for adult female: RBC value 4.2 to 5.4 million/mcL^3
Hgb 12.1 to 15.1 gm/dL (often rounded 12 to 16 gm/dL)
Hct 36.1 to 44.3% (often rounded 37 to 47%)

In a Chem-7 test, several health indicators are checked including the patient's glucose (blood sugar). Elevated blood sugars interfere with the body's healing after surgery and a normal blood sugar is desirable. K$^+$ (potassium, which some high blood pressure medications lower and kidney failure raises) is necessary for muscle cell function. Basic kidney and liver function tests are included in the Chem-7 test.

Normal Chem-7 lab results include:[17]
BUN (blood urea nitrogen) 7 to 20 mg/dL
Chloride 101 to 111 mmol/L
CO^2 (carbon dioxide) 20 to 29 mmol/L
Creatinine 0.8 to 1.4 mg/dL
Glucose 64 to 128 mg/dL
Serum potassium 3.7 to 5.2 mEq/L
Serum sodium 136 to 144 mEq/L

Clotting times include prothrombin time (PT), INR and PTT (partial thromboplastic time), which show the body's ability to clot blood. Anti-clotting medications affect these lab values.

Normal PT[18] values 11 to 13.5 seconds
Normal PTT[19] values 25 to 35 seconds

A clean-catch mid-stream urine test would show kidney infection. Surgeons want their patients to be infection free.

Any additional tests that the surgeon orders for individual patients will be done.

Chest x-rays and electrocardiogram (ECG) may be ordered for patients older than 40 years, depending on patient's health, the hospital and anesthesia department's policy.

For younger female patients who could be pregnant, a blood or urine test will be done to determine pregnancy. Doctors want to avoid any danger to the baby from anesthesia and surgery. Elective surgical procedures will probably be delayed until after the baby is born.

A patient with rheumatoid arthritis of more than five years may find the surgeon or anesthesia care giver wanting to see the patient's cervical neck x-rays. Because RA can affect the cervical spine, the patient's neck may be more fragile than normal.

Blood type and screen may be ordered in case a blood transfusion is needed.

Anesthesia Options

During PATT, the patient consults with the medical doctor anesthesiologist (MDA). The MDA looks at the entire patient but especially focuses on essentials like heart and lung function. Patients who suffer from post-operative nausea will find the MDA equipped with drugs that prevent and treat nausea. MDAs are experts in pain control during and after surgery. This specialist of anesthesia will give information about the type of anesthesia appropriate for the joint surgery.

Anesthesia safety for patients has dramatically improved over the years. "Patient deaths attributable to anesthesia have dropped from 1 in 10,000 cases in 1980 to less than 1 in 250,000 cases in the year 2000."[20] During the PATT visit with the anesthesiologist (MDA), the patient and MDA will decide the type of anesthesia. Choices of anesthesia for lower extremity (from the hip down) surgery include general anesthesia and spinal or epidural blocks.

General anesthesia involves giving intravenous medications and anesthetic gases to accomplish unconsciousness. The patient is unaware during the anesthesia. Risks of anesthesia, while extremely rare, do exist. Risks include "death, brain damage from lack of oxygen, dental injury, nerve injury, corneal abrasions, aspiration, pneumonia, awareness during procedure."[21] Side effects from general anesthesia include "nausea, vomiting, lingering drowsiness, sore throat and muscle aches."[22]

Spinal and epidural block anesthesia occurs when numbing medication is injected into specific areas of the spine. Benefits of both spinal and epidural block include numbness for the time period that the medication numbs the nerves, less nausea and vomiting than general anesthesia and that the patient's ability to choose whether to stay awake or be sedated. Risks of both blocks include "backache, nerve injury, spinal headache, infection or bleeding."[23] Side effects include temporary decrease in blood pressure, possible headache or shortness of breath. Occasionally, a patient's poor health causes the MDA to recommend a block. Some surgeons will want a combination of general and epidural anesthesia. The epidural anesthesia given pre-operatively gives hours of pain control afterwards, while general anesthesia is given for the surgery procedure.

During shoulder surgery, general anesthesia is most commonly given by a medical doctor anesthesiologist (MDA) or certified registered nurse anesthetist (CRNA). A shoulder block (interscalene block) can be used as additional pain control. During the shoulder block, a long-acting local anesthetic drug numbs the nerves to the arm for several hours and decreases the post-operative pain the patient experiences. During elbow surgery, general anesthesia is given and the shoulder block may be utilized to decrease post-operative pain. During wrist and hand surgery, general anesthesia can be used during the surgery. For this extremity, a regional block (called bier block) provides a safe alternative. During bier block, a tourniquet around the upper arm keeps all the local anesthetic injected into the vein of the operative arm. Bier block can be used for wrist and hand surgery provided the procedure doesn't take long (approximately an hour). After that time frame, the patient may find that the tourniquet pressure on the upper arm becomes uncomfortable.

During lower extremity (knee, ankle and foot) surgeries, anesthesia options include general anesthesia or regional anesthetics (spinal or epidural). A nerve block may be recommended by the anesthesiologist for lower arm (elbow, wrist and hand) and lower leg (ankle and foot) procedures. According to Dr. Sherer, "other compelling reasons to have local or regional anesthesia are that these forms of anesthesia often give pain relief that lasts longer than the surgery and so you need less of other pain drugs afterward. Also, you tend to have less bleeding."[24]

During the PATT visit, the MDA will instruct the patient about which of his usual medications to take the day of surgery. He may say something like this: "The morning of your surgery, you should take your blood pressure medicine with a sip of water and take one half of your usual insulin dose."

Pre-Operative Therapy Teaching

A physical therapist meets with the patient to teach post-operative exercises, which will help the patient gain strength and increased range of motion. The patient may learn to use crutches or a walker if the expected surgery requires not putting weight on the foot or ankle for a time period post-operatively. Occupational therapists often meet with patients to help equip the patient's home with needed equipment. These therapists offer gadgets and suggestions that help the patient get dressed without using his right hand after his hand surgery. Gadgets that will simplify dressing for the total hip patient practicing safe movements include a dressing stick to help put on underwear and slacks, a sock aid for putting socks on the operative leg, and a long shoe horn for putting on shoes.

Last Minute Preparations

After the PATT session, the time before surgery can be stressful for patient and family. Feeling nervous before surgery is completely normal. Thoughts such as "Am I doing the right thing? Maybe I should cancel this surgery and just go home" are experienced by most patients contemplating surgery. Relaxation methods such as meditation or distraction by using music, etc., can be used by the patient to improve coping with stress.

The patient should follow the instructions received from the surgeon and hospital. Patients should not drink alcohol for a minimum of 48 hours before surgery.

AAOS's "Preparing for Joint Replacement Surgery" suggests using a checklist for the last 24 hours prior to surgery:

"Take a shower or bath the night before your surgery. This will help reduce the risk of infection.

Do not shave the area of surgery. If this is necessary, the doctor will take care of it.

Do not wear any make-up, lipstick or nail polish.

Do not eat or drink anything after midnight the night before surgery. This will help prevent nausea from the anesthesia."[25]

If the surgery time is planned for afternoon or evening, the time to stop eating/drinking may be different. Consult the hospital PATT staff for the appropriate time.

Do pack a bag containing comfortable, non-skid house shoes, a knee-length gown or pajamas and robe, a book to read, personal care items such as hair brush, cases for dentures, eyeglasses or contact lenses. A person can bring a camisole or cotton shirt to wear it under the hospital gown. Pack comfortable clothes and shoes to wear home.

Do bring copies of insurance cards, living will, and medical history, including medications, and give these to the hospital staff.

Do leave valuables like cash, credit cards and jewelry at home.

Day of Surgery

The patient and family arrive at the hospital a few hours prior to surgery. The patient should expect to give his name (and possibly birth date) to staff members repeatedly at the hospital. This identification may feel cumbersome at times, but the purpose is patient safety. In a large, busy hospital, it's possible to have patients with the same last names on the surgery schedule the same day. The hospital staff will often ask for the patient's full name and birth date as an identifier. As the nurses talk to the patient, they will identify themselves: "Nice to meet you John Smith. I'm Sara Jones, a registered nurse and I will be getting you ready for surgery today." As a part of registration, a name bracelet will be secured to the patient, usually at the wrist. The patient will change into a hospital gown, lie on a cart and use a paper hat to cover the hair. The nurse will ask whether the patient has dentures in his mouth, any jewelry or any hearing aids in place. Any of those items will be given to family members for safekeeping. The patient signs consent papers for the surgery, the recommended anesthesia, and blood transfusion if needed.

After taking and recording vital signs such as blood pressure, heart rate and respirations, the nurse will attach a pulse oxymetry "finger clip" to the patient's finger. The pulse oxymetry machine ensures that the patient is breathing adequately and getting enough oxygen. As the patient receives pre-operative sedation medication and becomes sleepy, pulse oxymetry continues measuring the patient's oxygenation levels and alerts the staff if oxygenation levels drop.

If the patient donated blood for his surgery, a small amount of blood will be drawn and sent to the lab to check Hgb and Hct (hemoglobin and hematocrit to test that the patient's not too anemic for surgery). The nurses may call this an "H & H." The IV (intravenous) line is started and pre-operative medications will be given by the nurse. These medications were ordered by the anesthesiologist at the time of the PATT visit. Routinely, this medicine includes a relaxing medication such as midazolam hydrochloride (Versed), an anti-ulcer medication such as famotide (Pepcid), and anti-nausea medicine such as ondansetron hydrochloride (Zofran).

One of the Patient Safety Goals procedures involves identifying the patient by name and birth date, plus the surgeon or his designee marking the surgeon's initials on the correct site (and side if a limb) with indelible marker. For example, Dr. C. would mark his initials on the patient's operative hip.[26] Depending on surgeon practice and hospital policy, this may be done in the pre-operative holding room.

After the medications are given in the pre-operative holding room area, the patient will be easily aroused by the staff. The patient may nap and not remember much. If the patient feels cool, he should ask for warm blankets. The doctors and nurses don't want any patient to be cold because it contributes to increased risk of complications, including infection. At this point, the patient should relax and let the surgeon, nurses and other staff members do their jobs and take care of him.

Operating Room Personnel

The patient will meet his operating room (OR) registered nurse who will take him into the OR, help him move onto the bed and attach the monitors. The circulating nurse serves as "the patient advocate while the patient is least able to care for him or herself. The circulator is responsible for managing the nursing care of the patient within the OR and coordinating the needs of the surgical team with other care providers necessary for completion of surgery."[27]

Surgeons will tell you that the circulating nurse and scrub nurse are valuable team members. These two staff members prepare the OR room and bed for safe patient positioning. They gather needed instruments and equipment, which the surgeon will use during surgery. They check the inventory of implants to have all sizes available. Scrub nurses prepare needed instruments prior to the surgery and work "directly with the surgeon within the sterile field, passing instruments, sponges and other items needed during the procedure."[28] These staff members are the eyes above the surgical mask that the patient sees but may not remember.

A physician assistant (PA) or registered nurse first assistant (RNFA) works with the surgeon and provides a second pair of hands. Many PAs and RNFAs function in surgeons' offices as well as assist so they will be a familiar face to the patient.

The nurse and anesthesia care provider will tell the patient what's happening to him to allay concerns. When the surgeon, all needed staff members and equipment are ready, the patient will hear words similar to this: "It's time to go to sleep now. Pick out a nice dream. We'll be here with you all the time."

Immediately After Surgery

After surgery, the patient will wake up from anesthesia in the post anesthesia care unit (PACU) or "recovery room." The patient will be closely monitored in this area for approximately an hour. The nurses will stay close by, monitor vital signs and talk to the patient frequently. The patient should voice any complaints of discomfort, nausea and being chilly so the nurse can fix these problems.

After this time in the PACU, the patient will be taken to a room on the orthopaedic floor or the total joint area of the hospital. Family and the health-care advocate can stay with the patient in this area. The nursing staff will check closely on the patient, monitoring vital signs and asking questions such as, "How do you feel? On a scale of one to ten, tell me what your pain feels like." During this time, the patient will sleep a lot but can be easily aroused.

Depending on what time of day the surgery was completed, the patient will start getting up the next day or maybe sooner. At first the patient will sit on the side of the bed, then progress to sitting in a chair, and then walking. Physical therapists work with the patients and reinforce the pre-operative teaching regarding safe movements.

"You will be happy to know that pain control has become a major priority."[29] Patients will find the nurse asking about the pain level often. Each time the nurse will ask the patient to "rate" his pain. The nurse will say something like this: "We use a pain scale of one to ten. One means no pain and ten means the worst imaginable pain. Tell me where your pain ranks on this scale." Different hospitals will use different pain scales and the nurses will explain which pain scale they use. The point to this conversation is to promote comfort and pain control. However, if the patient needs medication anytime, he should call the nurse. The patient should ask for pain medication "as soon as you think you may need it."[30]

Depending on what the surgeon ordered, pain medication can be given in the following routes: by IV (intravenous through the IV by the nurse or a patient-controlled unit called a PCA), IM (intramuscular or a shot in the muscle), or PO (a pill by mouth). Usually, the PCA or IV pain medication given by the nurse is used for most acute post-operative pain. As the healing occurs and pain decreases, the medication route changes until the patient takes pain pill(s) as needed at home. Other options in pain control include immediate post-operative epidural block for hip and knee pain and shoulder blocks for shoulder pain given by the MDA to provide pain relief after surgery. Narcotic skin patches may also be utilized for pain relief.

Some post-operative joint patients will find a foley catheter in their bladder and a drain in their surgical incision. Some will not have those at the surgeon's discretion. If the foley and drain are in place, they'll probably be removed on the first or second post-operative day.

Because of the danger of dislocation after a total hip, the surgeon may want an abduction pillow (a wedge or A-shaped pillow) put between the legs or a knee immobilizer (leg brace) put on the operative leg. Both these devices prevent the dislocation movements and may be used until the patient is awake and able to cooperate.

Blood clot preventions used post-operatively may include exercises such as calf pumps and ankle pumps. "Even as you lie in bed, you can 'pedal' your feet and 'pump' your ankles on a regular basis to promote blood flow in your legs."[31] Other preventions for blood clots include blood thinner drugs, anti-embolism stockings such as TEDs and pneumatic anti-embolism foot wraps or leg sleeves.

The surgeon may utilize a machine called continuous passive motion (CPM) to begin restoring movement in the early post-operative time for total knee patients. This machine slowly moves the operative knee while the individual is in bed. The CPM machine decreases swelling by elevating the operative leg and improves venous circulation by moving the leg.[32]

Post-total knee exercises "restore your knee mobility and strength and a gradual return to everyday activities are important for your full recovery."[33] The patient should follow the instructions of the surgeon and physical therapist. Recommended exercises from the American Academy of Orthopaedic Surgeons (AAOS) include quad sets, straight leg raises, ankle pumps, knee-straightening exercises, bed-supported knee bends, sitting-supported knee bends and sitting-unsupported knee bends.*

This pre-operative physical therapy teaching should also include instructions for walking, stair climbing and descending as well as safe usage of crutches and/walker. The wise patient follows these instructions.

Returning Home

The patient should remember he has come through a big surgery and must be patient with himself. Expect good days and bad days, as the patient will begin to notice gradual improvement over time.

Prevent infection at home. All the recommendations mentioned previously regarding prevention of infection apply. Hand washing is recommended by the CDC as the best prevention of infections. Whoever cares for the patient's wound post-operatively needs to wash his hands before and after touching the skin and follow the post-operative instructions for wound care and dressing changes. General guidelines include: keeping the wound clean and dry and changing the dressing as directed. The surgeon wants to know if the patient experiences "shaking chills, increasing redness, tenderness or swelling of the knee wound, drainage from the knee wound, or increasing knee pain with both activity and rest."[34] Notify the surgeon if the patient's oral temperature goes above 100.5°F.

"Eat well. I didn't say eat a lot. I said eat *well*. You want a healthy mix of foods."[35] Patients with poor appetite might consult with the doctor or pharmacist for milk-shake-like products with adequate calories, vitamins and minerals to supplement the diet. Patients taking blood thinners when they return home should avoid foods containing vitamin K, because vitamin K will decrease the blood thinner's effectiveness. Vitamin K-rich foods include green vegetables such as broccoli, cauliflower, spinach, kale, lettuce, cabbage, onions, and several

---

*Specific instructions and pictures of these exercises can be found at http://orthoinfo.aaos.org/topic. cfm?topic=A00301&return_link=0

types of beans, including green beans, garbanzo beans, lentils and soybeans. The surgeon may recommend an iron supplement be taken to overcome anemia from the surgery.

For total hip patients, safe movements prevent dislocation. Physical and occupational therapy teaching both pre- and post-operatively ensure that patients know the safe movements. Safe movements include: "Avoid crossing your legs or ankles even when sitting, standing or lying. When sitting, keep your feet about 6 inches apart. When sitting, keep your knees below the level of your hips. Avoid chairs that are too low. You may sit on a pillow to keep your hips higher than your knees. When getting up from a chair, slide toward the edge of the chair and then use your walker or crutches for support. Avoid bending over at the waist.... When lying in bed, place a pillow between your legs to keep the joint in proper alignment. A special abduction pillow or splint may be used to keep the hip in correct alignment. An elevated toilet seat may be necessary to keep the knees lower than the hips when sitting on the toilet."[36] With repetition and practice, the patient becomes adept at safe movements that prevent dislocation. With healing, the chances of dislocation decrease, but safe movements are important and should be practiced forever after the surgery.

The person wanting optimal results from the total joint will follow the exercise program taught by the therapists. General guidelines from the American Academy of Orthopaedic Surgeons (AAOS) include a "graduated walking program to slowly increase your mobility, initially in your home and then outside, resuming other normal household activities, such as sitting and standing and climbing stairs, and specific exercises several times a day to restore movement and strengthen your knee."[37] The person should discuss with the surgeon what to expect and when to resume activities including driving.

Occupational therapy tips make it easier to get household chores done: "Carry hot liquids in covered containers, slide objects along the counter rather than lifting them, sit on a high stool when working at the counter, use a reacher to pick up objects from the floor, use a basket or bag attached to your walker to free your hands, and remove scatter rugs to prevent tripping."[38]

Post-Operative Long-Term Care

Patients with total joints in place should take care of their teeth to prevent a blood-borne (bacteremia) infection. The germs that cause teeth and gum infections can travel through the bloodstream and settle around a total joint. Regular home care of teeth and gums, combined with care by his dentist, helps keep a person's total joint infection free.[39] The patient should talk to the surgeon regarding routine care of teeth and recommendations for antibiotics before dental checkups or procedures.

Any time the patient develops an infection anywhere in the body, the patient should consult his family care physician. While mild respiratory infections may not require antibiotics, it's wise to consult the doctor.

The new total joint should give pain-free, comfortable movement for many years. Patients enhance the good care they've received from their surgeon and hospital staff when they become a member of the team caring for the new joint.

16

Caregivers Need Care, Too

"I can't sleep at night and I'm so tired." Two days earlier, Rebecca had passed out at work. When she came to, she saw the worried expressions on her co-workers' faces. The dizziness that overwhelmed her made the world spin and pulled all color from her face. Rebecca was coping with the terminal illness of her 91-year-old father, a recent diagnosis of Alzheimer's for her mother-in-law and a big, stressful project at work. This woman went to see her doctor, who recommended several days of rest, stress-management counseling and the possibility of anti-depressants. During counseling, this woman recognized she had failed to care for herself. Her overwhelming stress had affected her physical health. She started changing and simplifying her hectic life. She accepted help for her aging family members and used that free time for herself. She made time to exercise. She worked with her doctor to take an anti-depressant during her father's terminal illness. Afterwards she said, "When you find yourself saying 'it's too much,' an individual should recognize the danger of being overwhelmed. Get help, make changes and take care of yourself."   ·

"More than fifty million people provide care for a chronically ill, disabled or aged family member or friend during any given year."[1] By providing care to their family member, caregivers provide an "estimated $306 billion a year" in caregiving, double the amount spent on nursing home services and home care.[2] Some people say women provide all the caregiving, but not so. Men account for 44 percent of the caregivers. Both men and women adjust their work schedules to care for family members. "Both have modified their schedules (men 54%, women 56%). Both have come in late and/or leave early (men 78%, women 84%) and both have altered their work-related travel (men 38%, women 27%)."[3]

Learning About Stress

As a result of caregiving, the caregivers deal with additional stresses. A report from the National Academy of Sciences said caregivers of a person with dementia find their own immune system adversely affected for up to three years after caregiving ends. This increases their risk of illness. The National Family Caregivers Association finds "family caregivers report having a chronic condition at more than twice the rate of non-caregivers."[4] While many caregivers want to help their family member and feel good about doing so, juggling all the responsibilities can be wearing. Who's caring for the caregivers? Nobody, unless they do it themselves. Can caregivers balance all the demands on their time and energy? Can they cope with all the stress?

Webster's New World Dictionary defines stress as "mental or physical tension." Stressed out, a description that is heard frequently means "tired, nervous, etc., as from overwork, mental pressure, etc."[5] People describe themselves as stressed out when they feel "angry, afraid, excited or helpless."[6] Individuals perceive whether a situation is stressful or not. A person afraid to ride in an airplane will find an eight-hour flight to Hawaii stressful while another person enjoys the trip. The American Heart Association says, "Stress is your body's response to change.... Speaking to a group or watching a close football game can be stressful, but they can be fun too. Life would be dull without some stress. The key is to manage stress properly because unhealthy responses to it may lead to health problems in some people."[7]

Responding to Stress

Pre-historic man stumbled onto a tiger or bear and recognized the danger. His physical body responded with the "fight or flight" response. This response releases two types of chemicals called catecholamines (dopamine, norepinephrine, and epinephrine also called adrenalin) and steroid hormones. These chemicals cause strong emotions such as fear and prepare the body to run away or fight. Catecholamine released during stress acts in the same way as when a person suffers acute pain. The chemicals divert the body's blood supply to vital organs (away from non-vital organs). This causes the heart, lungs, and skeletal muscles to receive increased blood circulation. The person's breathing rate and heart rate increase and muscle tension increases. The person is primed for action. This response to stress still occurs in modern man. However, few people deal with tigers or bears. This response to acute stress happens today when things go awry, such as an auto accident, a lost job or contract, or a child's problem that demands a parent to leave work to solve. Often, there's no physical outlet for all the chemicals flooding through a person's system. However, people usually deal with acute stress satisfactorily.

When acute stress happens too often or becomes chronic, it grinds on people. Scientists believe the chemicals and hormones that enable people to fight or run away become harmful in chronic stress. Stress wears people down physically, mentally and emotionally. According to the National Institutes of Health, cortisol, the major steroid hormone, suppresses "the immune system and tones down inflammation within the body."[8] Studies show people dealing with high levels of acute stress or chronic stress "show a prolonged healing time, a decreased ability of their immune systems to respond to vaccination, and an increased susceptibility to viral infections like the common cold."[9]

Caregiving can be "physically demanding, emotionally draining and cause stress and conflict when combined with other major responsibilities."[10] According to the *Journal of the American Medical Association*, a four-year study compared 392 caregivers with 427 non-caregivers aged 66 to 96 years and found caregivers feeling stressed had mortality risks of 63 percent higher than non-caregivers.[11]

A person's perception of life events affects whether life events are bad stress or not. Life events considered stressful include "being laid off from your job, your child leaving or returning home, the death of your spouse, divorce or marriage, an illness, an injury, a job promotion, money problems, moving, or having a baby."[12] Caregivers would add to that list: caring for parents or family members and grieving their decline. Practical issues such as leaving work to drive Mom to a doctor's appointment can add tension to a busy day. Even the most loving adult child can become overwhelmed by all the demands.

"Control is a very important part of whether or not we feel stressed."[13] When dealing with aging and ill family, people find lots of things outside their control. While the parents' health may be failing and require increasing amounts of help, the parents do not want to give up their control, even when they may want and need help carrying out those decisions. How can the caregiver better deal with situations beyond his control? As with raising children, an adult caregiver of aging parents may find "pick your battles" to be valuable advice. If the aging parent has his mental faculties, the decisions he makes are legal and his to make. The caregiver may not agree with some decisions but must honor them. The caregiver can calmly voice why he disagrees but then forget it. The caregiver will decrease his stress if he decides to not worry about things outside his control.

Caring for Self First

The Family Caregiver Alliance says, "First, care for yourself.... When your needs are taken care of, the person you care for will benefit too."[14] When caregivers do not care for self, their own needs are ignored until they are exhausted, a crisis occurs and they want to just drop it all and run away. Caregivers must recognize their own needs have to be met. The caregiver should learn to recognize when he's feeling stressed. Early warning signs of stress include tension in your shoulders and your neck, or clenching your hands into fists." Other signs and symptoms of stress include "anxiety, back pain, constipation or diarrhea, depression, fatigue, headaches, high blood pressure, insomnia, problems with relationships, shortness of breath, stiff neck, upset stomach, weight gain or loss."[15]

The caregiver who feels overwhelmed should call for help. Recognize this clue to caregiver burnout: "You become numb to your loved one's needs and feelings and you just don't care."[16] This serious situation requires immediate attention. Make arrangements for everyone else to be cared for and take a break. Set aside a block of time for self. This time should be dedicated to resting and de-stressing. After the caregiver has caught his breath, rest some more and consider how to manage things better. Remember, events and situations are most harmful when we perceive them as bad stress.

Many caregivers neglect their own health. Healthful things caregivers can do include meditation and caring for physical needs by eating healthy, getting enough rest, and exercising. Caregivers should care for mental, emotional and spiritual needs. Adding laughter and fun to life will decrease stress and add health to a caregiver.

Meditation techniques provide valuable relaxing qualities. The American Heart Association recommends "taking 15 to 20 minutes a day to sit quietly, breathe deeply, and think of a peaceful picture."[17]

Stress often impairs a person's diet. Many people find themselves turning to comfort foods. For some people, comfort foods involve salty chips, while other persons indulge in sugary sweets. A healthy diet includes grains, vegetables, fruits, meat and dairy products. A newly released program from the U.S. Department of Agriculture called MyPyramid Plan can be used to personalize suggested caloric intake for each individual (see chapter 7).

Exercise relieves stress. According to the American Heart Association, "do what you enjoy in exercising—walk, swim, ride a bike or jog to get your big muscles going. Letting go of the tension in your body will help you feel a lot better."[18] The Arthritis Foundation recommends low-impact activities such as walking, swimming and riding a bike to people with arthritis.

Many people find that when they've managed their stress and gotten exercise, their sleep habits improve. Tips for better sleep from the National Sleep Foundation can be found in chapter 6, "Dealing with Pain."

The caregiver should consider how to bring some joy and pleasure back into life. One woman began a part-time writing career and brought positive feedback and pleasure into her stressful life. Another woman pulled out her long-neglected sewing skills and began to sew beautiful pillows that she gave to her grandchildren. Another woman joined a bike-riding club. As she rode all over the country, she benefited from the exercise.

Laughter helps keep people healthy. Dealing with chronic illness and/or being a caregiver can quickly take the laughter out of a person's life. Researchers at Loma Linda University found that laughing "lowers blood pressure, reduces

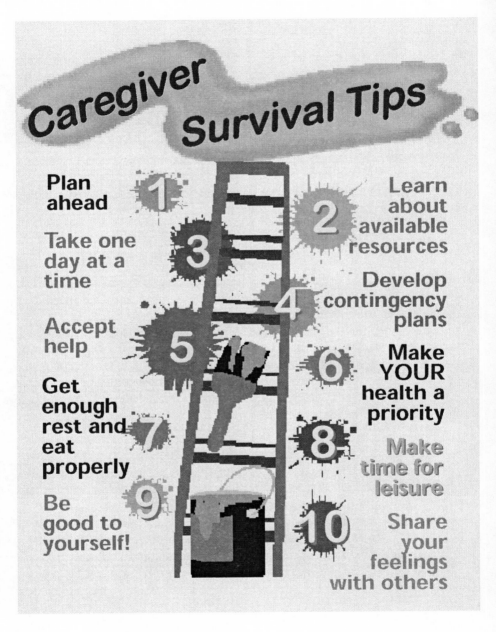

Caregivers must care for self or the caregiving responsibilities could become overwhelming (courtesy US Department of Health and Human Services, Administration of Aging).

stress hormones, increases muscle flexion, and boosts immune function by raising levels of infection-fighting T-cells, disease fighting proteins called Gamma-
interferon and B-cells, which produce disease-destroying antibodies. Laughter
also triggers the release of endorphins, the body's natural painkiller, and produces a general sense of well-being."[19] A good belly laugh works the diaphragm,
fills the lungs with fresh oxygen and results in muscle relaxation. Stress hormones such as dopamine, epinephrine, and cortisol decrease when a person
laughs. Caretakers who add humor and laughter back into their lives will find
more pleasure and health as they decrease their stress.

Caregivers who nurture themselves will protect their health and increase
their enjoyment of life. By doing these things, caregivers can avoid feeling overwhelmed and crying, "It's too much."

Learning About Resources

A huge component of successful caregiving is utilizing resources. Caregivers
should learn about the disease process involving the ill family member. Online
information and resources about many diseases can be accessed. For example,
the Alzheimer's Association provides information at www.alz.org. Local support
groups give valuable information, assistance and comfort. Local hospitals/med-
ical centers often offer education and support groups. The ill family member's
doctor and office staff may offer sources of valuable information.

Getting family members involved may be impossible in some situations,
but if possible, all members will benefit. The ill family member will receive more
attention, the caregiver will get a respite (a break) and other family members
will feel good about helping. Some family members may be willing to help but
feel unsure how to start. Caregivers can call a family meeting at a neutral place
to discuss the need for others to help. An agenda of needed help should be
planned, a list of needed tasks made and all participants be allowed to volunteer for tasks. Participants should be heard and respected. Disagreements can
occur about the best way to approach caregiving. If so, listening to one another,
respecting each person's opinion and working to reach compromises improve
cooperation. One suggestion is having each person take responsibility for a
different area of caregiving. For example, one person could be responsible for
doctors' appointments and medications while another person can manage bill
paying and financial matters.

When caregivers receive offers to help from extended family and friends,
often they automatically respond, "No, I'm doing *ok*." The truth may be the opposite; the caregiver feels stressed and worn. Why do caregivers refuse the help
they desperately need? A caregiver may feel something bad will happen while
he/she is away or since he's the power of attorney, he should be there. Accepting

help may make the caregiver feel selfish or like a failure. The caregiver should consider the benefits of accepting help: the person offering help will feel good about doing a good deed, the aging, ill family member will benefit from the attention and the caregiver receives support and a break. These breaks from responsibility and caregiving "reduce burnout, help you to be more patient with loved ones and can even prevent premature placement in a nursing home."[20] The Family Caregiver Alliance recommends the caregiver make a list of chores that would be helpful and offer several choices to people offering to help. Suggested chores could include: help with yard work or running errands, sitting with a loved one so the caregiver can have a break. Some caregivers would enjoy a weekly phone call. Sometimes they need someone to listen to their complaints in a nonjudgmental way; other times they need a laugh or two.

Talking with the physician. "Over 40% of U.S. primary care physicians think they don't have enough time to spend with patients."[21] Caregivers who take family members to the doctor can maximize their time by doing a few simple things. Take a written medical history of the patient with you at every visit, which includes current medications (prescription, over the counter and herbal) and past treatments. A list of questions and concerns should be written down and taken to appointments so all pertinent concerns are discussed. The Family Caregiver Alliance also recommends that one "enlist the help of the nurse," as she can answer questions such as managing medications, preparing for tests or surgical procedures, and other day-to-day care issues. Most importantly, caregivers should "use assertive communication and 'I' messages. Enlist the medical care team as partners in care. Present what you need, what your concerns are, and how the doctor and/or nurse can help."[22]

Pharmacists provide another source of information about medications. Pharmacists do more than fill prescriptions; they provide information on the drugs and review a person's prescription list to avoid known problems, such as a person's allergic reactions. The elderly people who take multiple prescription medications and assorted over-the-counter drugs and herbal supplements can suffer "polypharmacy" or adverse side effects. "Most adverse drug events are the result of drug interactions; the more drugs a person takes, the higher the risk of interactions. The estimated incidence of drug interactions rises from 6% in patients taking two medications a day to as high as 50% in patients taking five a day."[23] A "brown bag" medication review at least once a year (more frequently if medications change often) can help avoid problems. A "brown bag" review entails packing up all the medications, whether prescription, over-the-counter or herbal in a brown sack and taking the bag of medications for the doctor/nurse practitioner and local pharmacist to review.* Information such as "how does

---

*Information about medications a caregiver should know can be accessed at: http://www.caregivers library.org/Default.aspx?tabid=405.

this medication work?" and "what are the possible side effects?" will help caregivers recognize side effect problems.[24]

Short-Term Caregiver Help for Joint Replacement Surgery

When people with arthritis reach the point of needing surgery, plans must be made for caregiver help. A spouse, child, sibling or other trusted family member or friend can fit this role. If the patient plans to return home when discharged from the hospital, around-the-clock help will probably be needed for a few days to a few weeks. At first, the caregiver needs to be with the patient to help with tasks of daily living such as getting up to go to the bathroom and getting dressed. Depending on the pre-operative health of the patient, he may move pretty slowly at first and help will be needed. As the person recovers, he becomes more independent. Chores like meal preparation and laundry may still be part of the caregiving tasks. Using a walker requires the use of both hands and makes it difficult to carry heavy items. Depending on the surgeon's instructions, hip, knee and ankle patients may not drive for several weeks. Errands such as grocery shopping, picking up medicines and transporting the patient to therapy and doctors' appointments may be necessary for four to eight weeks.[25] The patient and caregiver should receive information from the surgeon about anticipated time frames (when to drive, etc.) and instructions for post-operative recovery. If the patient goes to a skilled nursing facility rehabilitation center, staff will help with activities of daily living and provide many of the caregiver tasks. At many of these facilities, the patient receives intensive physical and occupational therapy for a few weeks post-operatively. Planning for post-operative rehabilitation is recommended for best results.

Persons wanting to help their family member by fulfilling the caregiver role need to plan on a multiple-week commitment. If the caregiver works full-time, he should talk to his supervisor about options for time off or leave of absence. The Family and Medical Leave Act (FMLA) of 1993 "provides eligible employees with up to 12 weeks of unpaid, job- and health benefits-protected leave each year." FMLA includes those who need to "care for an immediate family member (spouse, child, or parent) with a serious health condition."[26]*

Caregivers expecting to be away from home while fulfilling the caregiving role should prepare their home like they were going on an extended vacation.†

---

*Specific details about FMLA can be found at the U.S. Department of Labor website http://www.dol. gov/esa/whd/fmla/.
†A "before you leave home checklist" can be found at www.jointreplacement.com/DePuy/docs/Knee Replacement/Caregiver/caregiver_preparation.html.

Included in this checklist are safety tips such as telling a trusted neighbor you'll be away, activating timers for lights, arranging for mail and newspapers to be held or picked up by a neighbor, locking all windows and doors and turning on security alarms to help keep the home safe. The caregiver must make arrangements for pet care and plant care for the time away from home. The caregiver who takes the time and effort to clean the kitchen and bath, throw out trash, empty the dishwasher, adjust the thermostat, unplug small appliances and turn off the washing machine water valve will avoid potential problems upon return.[27]

Packing essentials include personal medications, comfortable clothes, socks and shoes, toiletries and underwear. Ask the hospital staff whether the caregiver can stay in the patient's room overnight. If so, should the caregiver bring a pillow and blanket? While the patient is sleeping and recuperating, the caregiver can utilize free time to read, write, pay bills or do craft hobbies such as knitting or crocheting. Check with hospital staff before using laptop computers and cell phones to ensure they don't interfere with the hospital's monitors. Thorough preparation will increase the caregiver's comfort while he cares for the person who has undergone surgery.[28]

Many individuals provide care for family members whether short-term or long-term. When the caregiving duties add extra work and demands to life, a person often finds his days too busy and feels stressed. Scientists believe "it's not the caregiver role per se but the amounts of stress people feel from it that determines how care giving affects their health."[29] Caregivers who care for themselves first will use the increased energy, knowledge and resources to provide quality care for their family member.

17

Researching Arthritis

Should one drink coffee in the morning or not? Will glucosamine-chondroitin decrease osteoarthritis pain? News reports often flash the latest research for the public to digest. Some news blips give contradictory information. What should a consumer believe? Many people throw up their hands in confusion. Wise consumers will not let news stories provide them with information that guides them in their pursuit of medical care. These news stories, an excellent source of information, should be the place to start finding medical information.

People should understand that researchers and doctors read the fine print of research studies to gauge whether the finding is accurate. They scrutinize studies to determine whether the studies were properly done and the results are valid and valuable. The gold standard (highest quality articles and studies) involves reputable scientific, medical and nursing magazines that publish only peer-reviewed articles and studies. When a study is peer-reviewed and impartial, knowledgeable scientists review the study details for accuracy and value.[1] "Submitting the entire study to an impartial, yet knowledgeable, set of peers helps identify flaws in the testing method, and further ensures that bias is eliminated."[2] When multiple studies show similar findings, the evidence points toward true answers.

People can read and interpret scientific studies better if they understand some basic facts about science. "A common misperception of science is that science defines 'truth.' Science does not define truth; rather, it defines a way of thought. It is a process in which experiments are used to answer questions. This process is called scientific method and involves steps."[3]

An example of scientific method involves Galileo's legendary experiment on gravity. Would a heavy object fall faster than a light object? People of the late 16th century believed the heavier object would fall faster. Galileo observed that objects of different weight fell at the same rate and made a hypothesis (or guess) that objects would fall at the same speed regardless of their size (provided we ignore wind resistance). Legend says that in 1590 Galileo tested his hypothesis when he climbed the Tower of Pisa and dropped several objects from the top. "Galileo's experiment proved his hypothesis correct; the acceleration of a falling object is independent of the object's mass."[4] Sir Isaac Newton later added to Galileo's theory when he proved that acceleration (speed of the fall) depends upon both force and mass. "While there is greater force acting on a larger object, this force is cancelled out by the object's greater mass. Thus two objects would fall [actually they are pulled] to the earth at exactly the same rate."[5]

The steps of scientific method are observation, hypothesis, prediction and testing.[6] The steps begin with observation. Someone sees an object or event and begins to consider it. For example, Galileo saw that objects of different size fell to the ground at the same time. Step two happens when the scientist makes a hypothesis or theory to explain the observation and an expected outcome (based on deductive reasoning). Galileo reasoned and predicted that a large heavy item should fall the same distance in the same time frame as a light item. The final step, testing, occurred when he dropped several objects from the top of the tower and observed the landings of those objects.

Testing for scientific studies is complex, but it involves "controlling the variables, restricting testing to one variable at a time; repeating the test at least several, if not many more times; gathering quantitative data that can be analyzed and compared statistically; and considering all data, including figures that fall outside the expected results."[7]

Medical or scientific journal articles cited (or quoted) in articles can often be accessed and read by consumers. If the journal article is listed at the end of the article, often the article can be obtained at a library or online.

Readers can understand a journal citation: "Hatch EE, Palmer JR, Titus-Ernstoff L, Noller KL, Kaufman RH, et al. Cancer risk in women exposed to diethylstilbestrol in utero. JAMA, 1998; 280(7): 630–4." Authors of the article are listed first. If there are multiple authors, the first few names will be listed and followed by "et al." The name of the article comes second, "Cancer risk in women exposed to diethylstilbesterol in utero." Third in order is the journal name. (JAMA stands for *Journal of the American Medical Association*.) The year the article is published comes next. The numbers at the end indicate the volume number (280), the issue number (7) and page numbers (630–4). These details make it possible for individuals to locate the article.[8]

While many reputable studies bring good news, sensational media releases cause confusion. The food and health industries deal with confusing, sensational news often. Easy-to-understand guidelines for evaluating medical research can be accessed at www.caregiver.org/caregiver/jsp/print_friendly.jsp?nodeid=402.

When evaluating medical research, the reader must evaluate the original research. Finding the research may be a challenge. The writer of a CBS News article made it easy for readers to read the research article. This writer linked the article, "Impotence Can Warn of Heart Disease"[9] to the *Journal of the American Medical Association* research article, "Erectile Dysfunction and Subsequent

Cardiovascular Disease" (*JAMA*, December 21, 2005). In this situation, only the abstract (short condensed version) of this study is available to non-subscribers to the *JAMA* journal. However, this abstract gives an attention-getting conclusion: "Erectile dysfunction is a harbinger of cardiovascular clinical events in some men. Erectile dysfunction should prompt investigation and intervention for cardiovascular risk factors."[10] This conclusion should send men with impotence problems to talk to their primary care doctors about risk factors such as smoking and family history of heart attack.

The Family Caregiver Alliance gives these suggestions to evaluate medical research.[11]

Does the study involve animals or people and where was it conducted? Research first involves lab work, animals second and people last in efforts to prevent harm to the people involved. This time frame of research involves years of work. Promising results of research done at the first stage, in the lab, requires years of work before a drug is recommended by doctors.

Was the research published in a peer-reviewed medical journal? A peer-reviewed journal means experts (other doctors with equal expertise and knowledge) read and judge the research for merit, proper procedure and ethics.

Who conducted and paid for the study? "Be particularly cautious about accepting claims about treatment effectiveness in articles by people who intend to sell the treatment." Any financial sponsorship should be disclosed. "There are many research partnerships among industry, university-based researchers, and institutes, so this can be a difficult issue to assess."[12]

How many people participated in the study? A study involving more people and for a longer time frame helps "ensure that any observed differences are not simply the result of chance."[13] For example, the study quoted above in "Impotence Can Warn of Heart Disease" involved 9,457 men over a period of nine years from 1994 to 2003. This size study (over 9,000 participants and a time frame of nine years) adds validity and accuracy to the results.[14]

What were the characteristics of study participants? "Studies of groups of people who differ from your age, gender, health status, and ethno-cultural background may or may not apply to you."[15]

Have other researchers found similar results to this study's question? Researchers believe similar outcomes verify the accuracy and validity of their results.

If the study involved testing a new drug, did side effects occur and if so, what were the side effects? Has the drug been FDA approved and available for sale?

A last bit of advice: patients should exercise common sense, look at the overall knowledge to see whether the news fits or contradicts current knowledge and use a healthy dose of skepticism for news that sounds too good. A conversation with a person's physician should help keep in perspective the most recent studies.

What You Should Know About Research Studies
(A Speak UP Initiative)

Courtesy of Joint Commission of Accreditation of Healthcare Organizations (JCAHO)

What you need to know about participating in a clinical research study

- At the time you sign up for the study, it will not be known if the experimental drug, medical device or treatment will help you more than the standard treatment.
- You may or may not receive a new drug, medical device or treatment. However, while the study may not help you personally, your participation can result in information that will help others in the future.
- Ask for a copy of the study protocol. Look for a description of potential side effects of the treatment.
- Some drugs, medical devices or treatments can have side effects that may be mild, severe or even life threatening.
- The costs of participating in a research study are not always covered or paid for by health insurance. Talk to the doctor conducting the research and your insurance provider to determine if there will be any extra expense to you.
- Clinical research studies involving drugs are usually conducted in several phases, beginning with a few volunteers to evaluate initial safety and dosage, and then progressing to larger groups that evaluate long-term safety and effectiveness. Make sure you understand what phase is being evaluated and how it will affect the treatment you receive.
- You will be asked to sign an informed consent form which explains the nature of the study, the risks involved, and what may happen to participants. Take the informed consent document home, read it thoroughly, and review it with your family.
- For help in understanding the informed consent or study protocol, seek out expert advice from a family physician, a patient advocate or a specialist who treats your disorder.
- Many clinical studies are reviewed by an Institutional Review Board (IRB). The IRB oversees the safety of the study and can halt a study at any time if there is a concern.

Questions to ask your doctor or the researcher conducting the research study

- Why is this experiment being conducted?
- Who is doing the study?
- Will I be able to continue to see my own doctor?
- Is there any cost to me or will I be paid to participate in this study?
- Does anyone receive money for my enrollment in the study?
- How long will this study last?
- What tests or treatments will be used in the study?
- What other options or choices do I have if I decide not to take part in this study?

(continued on next page)

(What You Should Know, *continued***)**

- Is it possible that I will receive a placebo?
- What could happen to me, good or bad, if I take part in the study? Have there been any ill effects reported to date? How serious were they?
- Could my condition get worse during the study? What will happen if it does? If my condition worsens, will I be notified? How?
- Can I stop participating in the study if I change my mind?
- Could there be any danger to me if I stop participating?
- Who pays for my care if I'm injured during the study?
- What will happen to me at the end of the study? Will I be told the results of the study?
- Whom do I contact for answers to questions and information about the study? Do you have any patient advocates, independent of your institution, I can talk to?
- Who stands to benefit financially from the results of this study? If there a conflict of interest with the researcher? If so, how is it being managed?
- Is the research program or reviewing IRB accredited?

For more information about clinical research, the following websites are offered:

www.circare.org
www.fda.gov/oc/gcp
www.hhs.gov/ohrp
www.research.va.gov/programs/pride/veterans/default.cfm
http://ciscrp.org

Clinical Trials

Doctors and researchers use clinical research to find new and improved ways to detect, control and treat illness. Clinical research turns into clinical trials when doctors and researchers study and test drugs or medical devices on people who volunteer to participate. Clinical trials involve years. "In the 1960s it took 8.1 years to develop a new drug—in the 1990s it took researchers 15.3 years, or nearly double the time."[16] After researchers in a lab setting develop a new drug or treatment, there are four phases of clinical trials involving humans and each phase involves a larger number of people.

Phase 1 concerns the safety of a drug or treatment and involves only a small number of healthy people, usually 20–80 people. For example, a new NSAID (non-steroidal anti-inflammatory) would be given to the small number of clinical trial volunteers. "The researchers look at how the drug is absorbed, used, and excreted by the body."[17] If Phase 1 shows promising results without major problems for study participants, the researchers move into Phase 2.

Phase 2 looks at a drug's effectiveness for a specific condition and involves a larger number of people (clinical trial volunteers) with that health condition, usually 100 to 300. The trial participants would receive either the new NSAID or a placebo (dummy or inactive pill). Researchers look for benefits and possible side effects of the NSAID drug.

Phase 3 trials enlarge the number of participants to between 1,000 and 3,000 and do additional study on the new NSAID drug, and its long-term benefits and side effects.

Phase 4 trials continue after the new drug has been approved and is available by prescription. These trials monitor long-term effectiveness and safety of the drug, as well as cost-effectiveness when compared to other treatments being used for this condition.[18]

All clinical studies are set up with protocols, "an action plan that describes what will be done in the study, how it will be conducted, and why each part of the study is necessary."[19] The protocol will also list who can participate, length of the study and scheduling of tests, medications and procedures.

The number of clinical trials continues to increase and the number of volunteers needed also continues to grow. "Only about 7% of people who respond to an ad for a clinical trial wind up participating in it, and some of those drop out. At these rates, roughly 19.8 million people will need to respond to clinical trial ads in 2005 to meet the projected need for volunteers."[20]

People participate in clinical trials for a variety of reasons, including the opportunity to learn more about their disease and gain access to specialty medical care, new treatments and tests before they're widely available. Persons who participate make a contribution to medical research. The risks of clinical trials include "the possibility of unpleasant, serious or even life-threatening side effects to experimental treatment."[21] Participants may find the experimental treatment ineffective. Participants should recognize that clinical trials may require extra time and effort, "including trips to the study site, more treatments, hospital stays or complex dosage requirements."[22]

Before a person volunteers to participate in a clinical trial, the person should learn as much as possible about the planned trial and what he will be expected to do. A list of questions entitled "An Introduction to Clinical Trials" can be found at www.clinicaltrials.gov/ct/info/whatis.[23] When individuals get answers to these questions, that person can make informed decisions about participating in clinical trials.

"What is the purpose of the study?

Who is going to be in the study?

Why do researchers believe the experimental treatment being tested may be effective? Has it been tested before?

What kinds of tests and experimental treatments are involved?

How do the possible risks, side effects, and benefits in the study compare with my current treatment?

How might this trial affect my daily life?

How long will the trial last?

Will hospitalization be required?

Who will pay for the experimental treatment?

Will I be reimbursed for other expenses?

What type of long-term follow-up care is part of this study?

How will I know that the experimental treatment is working? Will results of the trials be provided to me?

Who will be in charge of my care?"[24]

Before a person volunteers for clinical trials, he should discuss those plans with his healthcare provider. The person should print out information about the trial and take it to the office visit, along with any questions to ask his doctor.

A final bit of advice: Be your own best advocate.[25] Ask questions and learn about the research before you commit yourself to seeing the study through. "Otherwise, you're wasting the researchers' time and money, and you're being unfair to people who might benefit from the treatment down the road. This commitment isn't carved in stone, though. There are some perfectly legitimate reasons for quitting, such as side effects that are worse than expected."[26]

Research Involving Arthritis

In a November 2005 release, researchers at The University of Texas MD Anderson Cancer Center reported an exciting new discovery. They identified a type of "T helper" cell that they believe causes, or at least contributes to, chronic inflammatory autoimmune diseases such as asthma, arthritis and multiple sclerosis. By using the scientific process, these scientists observed, hypothesized, predicted and tested. They believe that this new T-helper cell (called THi) produces interleukin 17 (IL-17), a cytokine that causes a person's immune system to go awry. "These findings suggest that shutting down the activity of these THi cells might stop chronic diseases from developing in the first place," says the study's lead investigator, Che Dong, Ph.D., a Department of Immunology associate professor at University of Texas MD Anderson Cancer Center.[27] More research will be done to verify these results and build on future treatments to control the inflammation caused by THi and IL-17.

Rheumatoid arthritis is not infectious.[28] However, both virus and microbes (germs) can cause arthritis symptoms when infections occur within joints. Does infection trigger arthritis? Scientists believe infections "play a role in acute arthritis."[29] Speculations include that infection may be a trigger to develop arthritis when people have the genetic (inherited) makeup that's susceptible. While no definite answers can be given, there's no lack of research. A report on research being done was published in the July 2005 issue of *Current Opinion in Rheumatology*. Fifty studies by doctors around the world were included in this review. The oldest three studies were published in 1988, 1992 and 1994, with the remaining 47 studies published within the last 10 years.

Researchers in Massachusetts believe an "abnormal immune reaction to carbohydrates in joint cartilage" may be causing or contributing to the disease, but why the immune system reacts to them is unknown. These carbohydrates, known as GAGs (glycosaminoglycans), are found in joint cartilage and aren't believed to be affected by the carbohydrates people consume in their diet.[30]

Headlines read, "Doxycycline May Slow Progression of Knee Osteoarthritis." A study reported in the July 2005 *Arthritis and Rheumatism* magazine reports on a promising new treatment. Doxycycline or vibramycin is an antibiotic of the tetracycline family. Osteoarthritis isn't infectious, but researchers believe treatment with this drug may slow the progression of osteoarthritis of the knee. Prior in vitro (in a lab) studies had indicated that doxycycline slowed or stopped the breakdown of collagen found in articular cartilage and reduced some of the destructive enzyme actions that occur during osteoarthritis. Would it do the same in people? The "431 obese women aged 45 to 64" participating in the study had osteoarthritis in one knee. During the 30 months of the study, the women either took doxycycline 100 mg twice a day or placebo twice a day. The measure of results was "joint space narrowing" (JSN), which indicated increasing osteoarthritis damage at beginning of study, 16 months and 30 months. "Compared with the placebo group, mean loss of joint space width in the index knee in the doxycycline group was 40% less after 16 months of treatment and 33% less after 30 months."[31] The conclusion of the researchers was that "doxycycline slowed the rate of JSN in knees with established OA [osteoarthritis]. Its lack of effect on JSN in the contralateral [opposite knee] suggests that pathogenetic [cause of the disease] mechanisms in that joint were different from those in the index [studied] knee."[32] The researchers recommend more studies to verify their results.

Researchers look for biomarkers for arthritis. Biomarkers (in the form of blood tests) would help doctors diagnose a disease and gauge the success of treatments. Hyaluronic acid (HA) levels found in a person's blood may be considered a biomarker for osteoarthritis in the future. Researchers dealing with the Johnston County Osteoarthritis Project published their findings: "The concentration of HA was higher in patients with severe knee OA compared to those in the moderate stages of disease, higher in patients with two diseased knees compared to those with a single diseased knee, and higher in patients with hip OA in addition to knee OA compared to those with knee OA alone."[33]

Scientists continue searching for sources for stem cells. Researchers at UCLA and the University of Pittsburgh have grown "human tissue-bone, muscle, cartilage and fat using stem cells harvested from fat. The team obtained the fat using liposuction."[34] Another possible source is hair. Researchers at the Medical College of Wisconsin in Milwaukee reported that adult stem cells found in the bulge of hair follicles may provide an alternative to embryonic stem cells.[35] When implanted into mice with spinal cord injuries, the hair-follicle stem cells survived and became a part of the spinal cord. These researchers recognize the benefits of stem cell research without the moral and ethical dilemmas involved with embryonic (fetal) stem cells.

Doctors working on new techniques have a goal of helping patients heal the damaged articular cartilage in their joints. Normal healing of tissues in the body involves two mechanisms. "One is self repair by fully differentiated cells (healing), and the second is replacement with newly differentiated cells derived from stem cells."[36] According to the American Academy of Orthopaedic Surgeons, three techniques show promise osteochondral grafting, autologous chondrocytes implantation and mesenchymal stem cell regeneration.[37] Osteochondral grafting and autologous chondrocytes implantation techniques have been used to treat knee joint injuries. As successful results are obtained, doctors may look at utilizing some of these techniques to treat other joints.

Osteochondral (bone and cartilage) grafting involves a plug of bone and cartilage taken from a person's own body or a donor (allograft). The graft is placed surgically into the small area of cartilage to heal. Allograft must be a tissue match or treated to avoid rejection issues.

Autologous chondrocytes (person's own cartilage cells) implantation requires a two-step surgical procedure. During an arthroscopy procedure, the surgeon harvests cartilage cells from a non-weight-bearing area of the joint and packs them in a sterile container to be shipped to a company that grows (multiplies) those cells. When the multiplied cartilage cells are ready, the patient returns to the operating room where his own multiplied cartilage cells are placed in the damaged area of his cartilage. A thin piece of his body tissue called periosteum is used as a patch to hold those cells in place while healing. This implantation also is useful for small areas and it must be pre-approved by the patient's insurance carrier due to expense.[38]

A promising future treatment, mesenchymal stem cell regeneration, moved into the present with the December 2005 announcement that doctors at the University of Bristol, England grew a piece of cartilage using adult stem cells found in bone marrow in adults and periosteum (the outer layer of bones that aren't inside joints). These results demonstrate that "engineered cartilage tissue can grow and mature when implanted into patients with a knee injury."[39] Continued work and trials promise better ways to heal articular cartilage damage.

Coffee drinkers, enjoy your morning coffee in moderate amounts of one to two cups. A huge study of 83,000 participants followed for 18 years found no link between onset of rheumatoid arthritis and coffee or tea consumption.[40]

Data released in 2007 suggest that coffee contains healthy anti-oxidants and may "lower the risk of type-2 diabetes, gallstones, Parkinson's disease and Alzheimer's disease."[41] Before a person drowns his day in coffee consumption, that person should know about unanswered questions. Is there a link between caffeine and osteoporosis? Are older women who drink four or more cups of decaffeinated coffee at higher risk of developing RA as the research indicates? These questions are unanswered at present. For the present, researchers believe a one-to-two cup consumption of coffee is safe for most people. [42]

Current scientific studies involve many illnesses, including arthritis. Researching the causes and best treatments for illnesses keep scientists and doctors busy. Science, especially medical science, grows and new breakthroughs occur. Scientific studies help prove or disprove this knowledge through a step-by-step process. Individuals who learn the steps involved with scientific research can better judge the validity of research. A healthy dose of skepticism for news that sounds "too good" serves consumers well. These wise consumers can better judge the nightly medical headlines.

Glossary

A/P—Anterior-Posterior (anatomic terms)

AAOS—American Academy of Orthopaedic Surgeons

Abduct—To draw away from the midline

Abduction—The act of drawing away from the midline; opposite of adduction

Abscess—Localized collection of pus

Acetabulum—The cavity of the os coxae (hip) into which the head of the femur fits

Acromium—Bony part of the scapula that forms the point of the shoulder

Acute pain—Short-term pain suffered due to an injury. Short term pain goes away as the body heals from the injury

Adduct—To draw toward midline

Adduction—The act of drawing toward the midline; opposite of abduction

Adverse reaction (*see also* Side effects)—An unwanted effect caused by the administration of drugs. Onset may be sudden or develop over time

Alloy—A mix of metals designed to improve implant material properties for specific purposes

Allograft—A tissue transplanted to a different individual of the same species

All-poly—A component composed entirely of polyethylene, with no metal parts

Alternative medicines—Health practices not commonly used in conventional (western) medicine. When used instead of conventional medicine, these practices are called alternative. When used with conventional medicine, these practices are called complementary medicines

Anterior—Places in the front or forward part; opposite of posterior

Arthritis—Inflammation of a joint

Arthrodesis—Fusion of a joint, eliminating all motion

Arthroplasty—The surgical reconstruction of a joint

Arthrotomy—Cutting into a joint

Articular—Pertaining to a joint. Surfaces that "fit together"

Asepsis—A condition free from germs; free from infection

Aspirate—To remove by suction

Atrophy—A wasting away of tissue, usually through disuse

Autograph—A tissue transplanted from one part to another part of the same body

Beads, beaded, beading—A term used to describe implant coatings made of tiny spheres

Bilateral—Occurring on both sides of a midline point or pertaining to both sides of the body (e.g., bilateral knee replacement means having both knees replaced)

Biocompatibility—Materials that can coexist with living tissue without being harmful or toxic or being rejected by the host. The most common materials for joint replacement are polyethylene, metals and ceramics; each has specific biocompatible characteristics

Bone cement—Material usually made of polymethylmethacrylate (PMMA), which acts like a grout between an implant and the patient's bone

Broach, broaching—A broach is a tool or instrument used to enlarge the interior canal of bone and allow for insertion of implants. Broaching is the process of enlarging the canal

Calcaneus—The heel bone, also termed calcaneum

Calcar—A thickened plate of bone near the head of the femur

Cancellous bone—A type of bone characterized by a spongy or lattice-like structure. Also known as trabecular bone

Capsular—A ligament that surrounds a moveable joint

Catecholamine—Chemicals the body makes and releases in times of "fight and flight" response, and times of stress. These chemicals include epinephrine, norepinephrine and dopamine. These chemicals are also available for medical use

Cement, bone cement—Material usually made of polymethylmethacrylate (PMMA), which acts as grout between an implant and the patient's bone

Cemented—An implant that is secured in a patient's body with the aid of bone cement or the process of using cement to help fix an implant

Chondrocytes—Cells that make cartilage

Chondromalacia—Softening of the cartilage, usually considered early arthritis or pre-arthritis findings

Chromosome—"The gene-carrying component of cells that determines hereditary characteristics. Each cell contains 46 chromosomes. Each chromosome consists of a complex, compactly folded strand of DNA. The DNA is wound around a protein core. Half of the genetic material is derived from each parent. When a cell divides, its chromosomes split and reduplicate, with an equal amount of DNA going into each daughter cell"

Chronic pain—Pain that lasts past the time of healing, opposite of acute pain

Circadian clock—Body's biologic clock based on 24-hour day

Clavicle—Collar bone

Clinical pathway—Established methodologies and decision trees for use by health professionals and patients in planning and preparing for medical intervention

Clinical investigator—A medical researcher in charge of carrying out a clinical trial's protocol

Clinical trial—A clinical trial is a research study to answer specific questions about vaccines or new therapies or new ways of using known treatment. Clinical trials (also called medical research and research studies) are used to determine whether new drugs or treatments are both safe and effective

Coatings (*see also* Beads; Porous-coated)—Any number of different materials applied to the surface of an implant prosthesis to aid in fixation; porous coatings generally permit ingrowth into the implant

Cobalt-chrome (CoCr)—A metal alloy with excellent resistance to fatigue, cracking and stress used in orthopedic implants

Complementary and alternative therapy—Broad range of healing philosophies, approaches and therapies that Western (conventional) medicine does not commonly use to promote well-being or treat health conditions. Examples include acupuncture, herbs, etc

Component—A part of an implant system. For example, the patellar component that either replaces or enhances the original patella (knee cap)

Congenital—Present at birth, as in congenital dislocated hip

Contraindication—A specific circumstance when the use of certain treatments could be harmful

Cortisone—The first steroid medication produced in the 1940s and considered a miracle drug. Today a group of drugs called corticosteroids or "steroids" are utilized to suppress inflammation for a variety of diseases, including rheumatoid arthritis and osteoarthritis

Cruciate ligament—Any paired set of ligaments that cross over each other in an "×" formation, usually used to refer to the posterior cruciate ligament and the anterior cruciate ligament of the knee, which help stabilize the forward and backward motion of the knee

Cruciate-retaining—A knee system design that allows the surgeon to keep the patient's cruciate ligament

Cruciate-sacrificing (*see also* PS)—A knee system in which the design of the implant must serve to stabilize forward and back motion of the knee components because of an excised or deficient ligament

Custom—An implant manufactured to the demands of a surgeon based on the needs of one patient

Diagnosis—Recognition of disease from symptoms

Dislocation—The displacement of any part, especially the removal temporarily from its normal position in a joint

Distal—Remote, opposite of proximal

Double-blind study—A clinical trial design in which neither the participating individuals nor the study staff know which participants are receiving the experimental drug and which are receiving a placebo (or another therapy). Double-blind trials are thought to produce objective results, since the expectations of the doctor and the participant about the experimental drug do not affect the outcome, also called double-masked study

Experimental drug—A drug that is not FDA licensed for use in humans, or as a treatment for a particular condition

Etiology—The study of the causes of disease

Eversion—The act of turning outward, opposite of inversion

Evert—To turn out, to turn the sole of the foot outward; opposite of inversion

Extension—A movement at a joint bringing the two parts into or toward a straight line from a flexed position; opposite of flexion

External—On the surface or outer side; opposite of internal. Latin adjective *externus* or *externa*

FDA (Food and Drug Administration)—The U.S. Department of Health and Human Services agency responsible for ensuring the safety and effectiveness of all drugs, biologics, vaccines, and medical devices, including those used in the diagnosis, treatment and prevention of HIV infection, AIDS, and AIDS-related opportunistic infections. The FDA also works with the blood banking industry to safeguard the nation's blood supply. Internet address: http://www.fda.gov/

Femur—Thigh, bone of the thigh

Fixation—The act, process or operation of holding, suturing or fastening something into a fixed position. In orthopedics, often refers to the stability and immobilization of an implant into the patient's body

Flexion—Sagittal plane movement in which the anterior surfaces of two segments are brought closer to each other; opposite of extension; bending of the joint

Fracture—A break in the continuity of bone

Frontal cortex of brain—Area of brain involved with many functions, including thinking, judgment and impulse control, emotions, and learned motor skills

Gel phenomenon—Describes the osteoarthritis symptom of stiffness that people experience after periods of inactivity. This stiffness resolves quickly, within minutes

Genes—Those fragments of DNA that code for a specific chemical product (e.g., a protein) or human characteristic

Genetics—The study of genes, the inherited pattern of chromosomes and DNA that make individual plants, animals and humans

Glenoid—The socket of the shoulder joint

Hallux—The great toe, hallucis of the great toe

Harris Hip Score—A numerical rating scale used for evaluation of the hip. The Harris Hip Score evaluates pain, function, absence of deformity and range of motion. One hundred is the highest possible total

Hemiarthroplasty/hip prosthesis—Means half a total hip. Only the femoral portion is dealt with during this surgery. Often this procedure is performed when a hip fracture occurs. The femoral head (ball portion of the upper femur or thighbone) is removed. The inner canal of the femur is prepared and an implant stem is inserted. A large metal ball that fits the patient's hip socket is fit onto the stem

HSS Knee Scores—Hospital for Special Surgery Knee Scores, a numerical scale for rating knees

High tibial osteotomy—One type of surgery to straighten the lower leg, decrease abnormal stresses and prevent or treat arthritis in one portion of the knee (unicompartment)

Human Genome Project—During this project, scientists identified 3.2 million base pairs in the human genome. These findings are being used to develop new treatments for diseases

Humerus—Bone of the upper arm. The humerus is involved in the shoulder and elbow joints with a long straight shaft in between

Hydroxyapatite (or HA)—A bioactive calcium phosphate ceramic similar to normal bone; may be applied to implant surfaces

Implant (*see also* Stem; Prosthesis)—A device (or tissue or substance) that is transferred, grafted, or inserted into a living body

Immune system—The human body can recognize foreign products and mobilize its protective mechanisms. When a person receives a transplanted organ, the normal immune system will recognize the organ as foreign and try to reject it. In this situation, doctors use medications to avoid this response. In rheumatoid arthritis, an unknown trigger causes the body to attack itself and damage the articular cartilage as well as body organs. Many current treatments for RA involve controlling the immune response of the body

Index—Referring to the forefinger or "pointing" finger

Inferior—Situated or placed below; opposite of superior; *inferioris*, a Latin form of the adjective

Informed consent—The process of learning the key facts about a clinical trial before deciding whether to participate. It is also a continuing process throughout the study to provide information for participants. To help someone decide whether to participate, the doctors and nurses involved in the trial explain the details of the study

Ingrowth, bone or bony ingrowth—The process of living bone or tissue growing up to and into the surface of implant, very important for stabilization and long-term life of the implant

Instrument—A tool or implement used in surgery

Internal—Within or on the inside

Inversion—The act of turning inward; opposite of eversion

Invert—To turn in; to turn the sole of the foot inward, opposite of evert

Ischium—Bone of the hip, adjective is ischial or sciatic

Knee Society Scores—A numerical scale for evaluating knee function developed by the Knee Society

Lateral—Pertaining to the side; opposite of medial

Ligament—Fibrous connective tissue connecting the articular ends of bone serving to bind them together and to facilitate or limit motion

Limbic area of brain involves emotions and the control over emotional behavior

M/L—Medial/Lateral (anatomic term)

Medial—Pertaining to the center; opposite of lateral

Meniscectomy—Removal of the meniscus cartilage of the knee

Meniscus—A "C" shaped cartilage in the knee that provides a stabilization system for the knee and a measure of shock absorption

Metal-backed—Term used to describe implants that have a polyethylene liner set in a metal shell or on a metal base. The metal portion would rest in a prepared area in the bone and the polyethylene side would move against other non-metal components

Necrosis—Death of areas of tissue or bone surrounded by healthy tissue

Neurotransmitters—Chemicals secreted in the body to enable nerves to carry messages

Nociceptor—A free nerve ending that

helps the body respond to powerful, potentially harmful stimuli of several types, chemical, heat-related, and mechanical

Non-porous—An implant designed to be used with bone cement for stabilization that is not designed for nor coated with surfaces for ingrowth

Nonsteroidal anti-inflammatory drugs (NSAIDs)—A group of drugs, including aspirin, that decrease inflammation and pain. NSAIDs do not include steroid medications

NREM sleep—Stages 1 through 4 of sleep, with the higher numbers being a deeper, more restful sleep. NREM stands for nonREM (not rapid eye movement) sleep

Olecranon—From the Greek word for elbow. The prominence at the proximal (closer to shoulder) end of the elbow

Opposition—The act of opposing one part to another

Orthopedics—Branch of medical science that deals with treatment of disorders involving locomotor structures of the body, especially the skeleton, joints, muscle, fascia

Orthopedist—A physician specializing in orthopedics

Osteoarthritis—Also known as wear-and-tear arthritis or degenerative arthritis, the most common form of arthritis. Osteoarthritis occurs when the articular cartilage on the bones wears thin and causes pain

Osteophyte—An abnormal bony outgrowth. Also called bone spurs

Osteoporosis—Increased porosity of bone

Osteotomy—Cutting and repositioning bone to more functional position

Outcomes—The results of surgery in terms of patient satisfaction, reduction of pain, improved function, etc. Outcomes are tracked by hospitals and practices (physicians)

Pain management centers—A medical clinic that specializes in pain control, using multiple disciplines and strategies

Patella—The kneecap

Peer review—Review of a clinical trial by experts chosen by the study sponsor. These experts review the trials for scientific merit, participant safety, and ethical considerations

Periodic leg movement disorder (PLMD)—Leg movements and kicks that occur during sleep

Phalanges—Plural of phalanx, which refers to any bone of the finger or toe

Phase I trials—Initial studies to determine the metabolism and pharmacologic actions of drugs in humans, the side effects associated with increasing doses, and to gain early evidence of effectiveness, may include healthy participants and/or patients

Phase II trials—Controlled clinical studies conducted to evaluate the effectiveness of the drug for a particular indication or indications in patients with the disease or condition under study and to determine the common short-term side effects and risks

Phase III trials—Expanded controlled and uncontrolled trials after preliminary evidence suggesting effectiveness of the drug has been obtained, and are intended to gather additional information to evaluate the overall benefit-risk relationship of the drug and provide an adequate basis for physician labeling

Phase IV trials—Post-marketing studies to delineate additional information including the drug's risks, benefits, and optimal use

Placebo—A placebo is an inactive pill, liquid, or powder that has no treatment value. In clinical trials, experimental treatments are often compared with placebos to assess the treatment's effectiveness

Plastics—A common term that in orthopedic devices refers usually to polyethylene, more specifically to ultra-high molecular weight polyethylene (UHMWPE)

PMMA—Polymethylmethacrylate or bone cement

Polyethylene—A type of plastic formed by the polymerization of ethylene. Different properties come from differences in molecular weight, branching, cross linkage and crystallinity. The most common form used in orthopedic devices is ultra-high molecular weight polyethylene (UHMWPE)

Porous-coated—The design feature of a type of implant in which the metal has small openings into which bone or tissue is intended to grow for permanent stabilization

Polypharmacy (many drugs)—Refers to problems/side effects/interactions from taking many drugs, whether prescription, over the counter (OTC) or herbal and vitamin supplements

Posterior—Situated behind or toward the back; opposite of anterior

Press-fit (see also Uncemented)—Describes the fit at the interface of an implant with the surrounding bone, implant is implanted without cement and is tightly "pressed" or impacted into the patient's bone

Primary—Initial or first; in joint replacement, this term is used to indicate the first surgery to repair or replace a joint as opposed to a revision surgery which replaces or revises an implant

Prosthesis—Replacement of a missing part by an artificial substitute; an artificial organ or part

Proximal—Nearest; opposite of distal

PS (Posterior Stabilized)—A posterior stabilized knee is a type of semiconstrained total knee system that compensates for a deficient or absent posterior cruciate ligament through its surface geometry (its design minimizes forward and backward movement of the knees and substitutes for the function of the ligament

Radius—A bone of the forearm

Ream, reaming—A verb meaning to gouge out holes or enlarge holes already made. In orthopedic surgery, bones need to be reamed to allow for the implantation of a prosthesis

REM sleep—Stage 5 sleep in which the brain is active, eyes move quickly and dreams occur. REM sleep improves daytime performance and provides energy to brain and body

Restless legs syndrome (RLS)—Constant leg movements that disturb a person's rest. The person experiences sensations of crawling/tickling/aching deep inside the legs and a need to move the legs

Revision—In orthopedic surgery, this term indicates a subsequent surgery to alter, replace or remove an implant

Rheumatoid arthritis—An autoimmune disease in which the body begins to damage itself through uncontrolled inflammatory processes. RA occurs with resulting damage to articular cartilage and bone, but also to body organs

Roentgenogram—A photograph made by means of roentgen rays or x-rays. The x-rays are named in honor of their discoverer

ROM (range of motion)—The area through which a joint may be moved in all planes, measured in degrees. The greater the ROM, the more flexible the joint. One of the goals of joint replacement is to improve a patient's ROM in the joint that may have been lost to arthritis, trauma or deformity

Sensitization—Terms used to explain how the nerves become super-sensitive due to overstress. This explains why chronic-pain patients experience pain to a greater intensity and more frequently than would be expected

Septic—Infection due to presence of pathogenic organisms (germs)

Shell—The acetabular component, the part of a hip replacement system that serves for the hip socket

Side effects—Any undesired actions or effects of a drug or treatment. Negative or adverse effects may include headache, nausea, hair loss, skin irritation or other physical problems. Experimental drugs must be evaluated for both immediate and long-term side effects

Skeleton—The hard framework of the body; the bones of the body collectively

Somatosensory cortex of brain—Area of brain involved with physical sensations

Statistical significance—The probability that an event or difference occurred by chance alone. In clinical trials, the level of statistical significance depends on the number of participants studied and the observations made, as well as the magnitude of differences observed

Stem—A device (or tissue or substance) that is transferred, grafted, or inserted into a living body

Stem cell—Cells that scientists call building blocks of the body. Stem cells can mature into different cells, depending upon their environment (Arthritis-Support.com, "New Stem Cell Source Benefits Arthritis Treatment," http://www.arthritissupport.com/library/print.cfm?ID=253)

Subluxation—A partial or incomplete dislocation

Superior—Higher; opposite of inferior; *superioris*, a Latin form of the adjective

Surgical technique—A series of steps required to complete a surgical procedure (or operation)

Synovectomy—Removal of synovium (thin lining) tissue from a joint

Synovial membrane—A thin tissue that lines the capsule surrounding the joint

Talus—The ankle, a bone of the ankle; the tarsal bone articulating with the tibia and fibula

Tendon—Fibrous connective tissue serving for the attachments of muscles to bones and other parts

Thalamus—Area of the brain involved with sending and receiving messages from the body to physical, emotional and thinking areas of the brain and vice versa

Tibia—Latin name of shin bone; larger bone in the lower leg

Total hip replacement (arthroplasty)—A surgery in which the hip joint is resurfaced. The pelvic socket (acetabulum) is prepared by removing any rough surfaces and overgrowth of bone, then a new implant cup is put into place. The metal implant cup can be secured by screws or impacted into place. A high quality liner locks into the metal cup. The other half of the total hip involves the femur (thighbone). The inner canal is prepared, an implant metal stem is fit inside the canal and secured either by glue (methylmethacrylate) or by the porous outer edge of the stem itself and lastly, an implant ball attached to the implant stem

Total knee replacement (arthroplasty)—A surgery in which the knee joint is resurfaced. The walking surfaces of the femur (thighbone) and tibia (shin bone) are replaced with metal and polyethylene surfaces. The patella (kneecap) may be resurfaced also

Trochlear groove—The articular portion of the anterior surface of the distal femur (the front-facing notch at the lowest part of the femur where the femur joins the knee joint). This groove provides a shallow depression where the patella slides as the knee articulates

UHMWPE—Ultra-high molecular weight polyethylene, a type of polyethylene with superior wear properties, very commonly used in orthopedic devices

Ulna—The inner and larger bone of the forearm. In the correct anatomic position, palms forward, the inner and larger bone of the forearm, between the wrist and the elbow, on the side opposite the thumb

Uncemented—A prosthesis that is implanted without cement; press-fit implants

Unilateral—One-sided, affecting only one side. For example, a unilateral knee replacement would replace just one knee, not both

Valgus—A term denoting position meaning bent outward (knock-kneed) or twisted, applied especially to deformities in which a part is bent outward

Varus—Turned inward; bowlegged

Wear—The loss of material from solid surfaces due to mechanical abrasion

Appendix

American Academy of Orthopaedic
  Surgeons
1-800-824-BONES
www.aaos.org/ or www.orthoinfo.org/

American Apitherapy Society
  202 E. Main St.
  Suite 101
  Huntington, NY 11743
  631-470-9446
  www.apitherapy.org

American College of Rheumatology
Association of Rheumatology Health
  Professionals
  1800 Century Place, Suite 250
  Atlanta, GA 30345
  www.rheumatology.org

American Chronic Pain Foundation
  P.O. Box 850
  Rocklin, CA 95677
  Toll free 800-533-3231
  916-632-0922
  www.theacpa.org

American Dietetic Association (ADA)
  120 Riverside Plaza Suite 2000
  Chicago, IL 60606-6995
  www.eatright.org

American Pain Foundation
  201 N. Charles St.
  Suite 710
  Baltimore, MD 21201-4111
  www.painfoundation.org

Arthritis Foundation
  P.O. Box 7669
  Atlanta, GA 30357-0669
  www.arthritis.org

Association of Clinical Research
  Professionals (ACRP)
  500 Montgomery St.
  Suite 800
  Alexandria, VA 22314
  www.acrpnet.org/

Centers for Disease Control and
  Prevention (CDC)
Centers for Chronic Disease Prevention
  and Health Promotion
  1600 Clifton Rd.
  Atlanta, GA 30333
  800-311-3435
  www.cdc.gov/

Centerwatch
  www.centerwatch.com

Clinicaltrials.gov
  www.clinicaltrials.gov

Family Caregiver Alliance
National Center on Caregiving
  180 Montgomery Street, Suite 1100
  San Francisco, CA 94104
  www.caregiver.org

Federal Trade Commission (FTC)
  Toll free 1-877-FTC-HELP (1-877-382-
  4357)
  www.ftc.gov

Food and Drug Administration
Index to Drug-Specific Information site
www.fda.gov/cder/drug/DrugSafety/
DrugIndex.htm

MedicineNet
www.medicinenet.com/script/main/
ht.asp

Mind/Body Medical Institute
824 Boylston St.
Chestnut Hill, MA 02467
Toll free: 866-509-0732
MBMI@bidmc.harvard.edu

National Institute for Occupational
Safety and Health (a branch of Centers for Disease Control)
www.cdc.gov/niosh/topics/ergonomics/

National Osteoporosis Foundation
1232 22nd Street NW
Washington, D.C. 20037-1202
www.nof.org

National Institute of Arthritis and Musculoskeletal and Skin Diseases Information Clearinghouse
1 AMS Circle
Bethesda, MD 20892-3675
301-495-4484
1-877-22-NIAMS (toll free)
www.nih.gov/niams/

National Association to Advance Fat
Acceptance (NAAFA)
P.O. Box 22510
Oakland, CA 94609
www.naafa.org

National Center for Complementary
and Alternative Medicine
NCCAM Clearinghouse
P.O. Box 7923
Gaithersburg, MD 20892-7923
Toll free 1-888-644-6226
www.nccam.nih.gov

National Chronic Pain Outreach
   P.O. Box 274
   Millboro, VA 24460
   540-862-9437
   www.chronicpain.org/

National Family Caregivers Association
   10400 Connecticut Avenue, Suite 500
   Kensington, MD 20895-3944

Toll free:1-800-896-3650
301-942-6430
www.nfcadcares.org

National Library of Medicine (NLM)
   8600 Rockville Pike
   Bethesda, MO 20894
   Toll free 1-888-346-3656
   www.nlm.nih.gov

National Sleep Foundation
   1522 K St., NW, Suite 500
   Washington, DC 20005
   202-347-3471
   www.sleepfoundation.org

NIH Office of Dietary Supplements (ODS)
   6100 Executive Blvd.
   Bethesda, MD 20892-7517
   www.ods.od.nih.gov

National Women's Health Information Center
U.S. Department of Health & Human Services
   Toll free 800-994-9662
   www.4woman.gov/index.htm

On-Line Self-Management Program for Adults with Rheumatoid Arthritis
Missouri Arthritis Rehabilitation Research and Training Center (MAARTC)
University of Missouri-Columbia
     Arthritis Center
   Toll free 1-888-740-6626
   www.RAHelp.org

Trialscentral
www.trialscentral.org

U.S. Department of Health and
    Human Services
Administration of Aging
    Washington, DC 20201
    202 619-0724
    www.aoa.gov

Weight-Control Information Network
    1 WIN Way
    Bethesda, MD 20892-3665
    (202) 828-1025
    Toll free 1-877-946-4627
    Fax: 202-828-1028
    Email: win@info.niddk.nih.gov

    Several implant companies pro-
vide patient information regarding
arthritis and related treatments,
especially surgery.

Biomet, Inc. http://www.biomet.com/
    patients/
DePuy, Inc. http://www.depuyorthopae
    dics.com/bgdisplay.jhtml?itemname=
    patients
Smith & Nephew, Inc. http://ortho.
    smith-nephew.com/us/node.asp?
    NodeId=3206
Stryker http://www.aboutstryker.com/
Wright Medical Technologies http://
    www.wmt.com/Patients/default.asp
Zimmer, Inc. http://www.pacewithlife.
    com

Chapter Notes

Chapter 1

1. Arthritis Foundation, "Osteoarthritis," http://ww2.arthritis.org/conditions/disease center/OA/oa_who.asp

2. Maetzel A., Li LC, Pencharz J., et al., (2004), "The Economic Burden Associated with Osteoarthritis, Rheumatoid Arthritis, and Hypertension: A Comparative Study," *Annals of the Rheumatic Diseases*, 63(4), 395–401. Http://ard.bmj.com/cgi/content/ab stract/63/4/395?maxtoshow=&HITS=10&hits=10&RESU...

3. American Association of Orthopaedic Surgeons, "Osteoarthritis of the Hip," http://orthoinfo.aaos.org/topic.cfm?topic=A00213

4. J.H. Klippel, *Primer on the Rheumatic Diseases* (Atlanta: Arthritis Foundation, 2001), 289.

5. Ibid., 290.

6. National Institute of Arthritis and Musculoskeletal and Skin Diseases, "Handout on Health: Osteoarthritis," http://www.niams.nih.gov/Health_Info/Osteoarthritis/default.asp

7. Neame, R.L., Muir, K., Doherty, S., and Doherty, M. (2004), "Genetic Risk of Knee Osteoarthritis: A Sibling Study," *Annals of the Rheumatic Diseases*, 63, 1022–1027. Http://ard.bmj.com/cgi/content/ab stract/63/9/1022?maxtoshow=&HITS=10&hits=10&RES...

8. National Institute of Arthritis and Musculoskeletal and Skin Diseases, "Handout on Health: Osteoarthritis," http://www.niams.nih.gov/Health_Info/Osteoarthritis/default.asp

9. Ibid.

10. J.H. Klippel, *Primer on the Rheumatic Diseases*, 12th ed. (Atlanta: Arthritis Foundation, 2001), 285.

11. WebMD Health, "Meniscus Tear May Mean Arthritis," http://www.webmd.com/content/article/81/97031.htm

12. J.H. Klippel, *Primer on the Rheumatic Diseases*, 12th ed. (Atlanta: Arthritis Foundation, 2001), 285.

13. David Niven, *100 Simple Secrets of Healthy People: What Scientists Have Learned and How to Use It* (New York: Harper Collins, 2003), 146.

14. J.H. Klippel, *Primer on the Rheumatic Diseases*, 12th ed. (Atlanta: Arthritis Foundation, 2001), 285.

15. PersonalMD.com, "Estrogen Reduces Arthritis Risk," www.personalmd.com/news/a1996101503.shtml based on original study Nevitt, M.C,. Cummings, S.R., Lane, N.E., et al. (1996), Association of Estrogen Replacement Therapy with the Risk of Osteoarthritis of the Hip in Elderly White Women. Study of Osteoporotic Fractures Research Group, *Archives of Internal Medicine*, 156(18), 2073–2080. Http://archinte.ama-assn.org/cgi/content/abstract/156/18/2073

16. Heegh-Andersen, Pernille, Tanko, L.B., Andersen, T.L., Lundberg, C.V., Mo, J.A., Heegaard, A., Delaisse, J., and Christgau, S. (2004), "Ovariectomized Rats as a Model of Postmenopausal Osteoarthritis: Validation and Application," *Arthritis Research & Therapy*, http://www.arthritis-research.com/content/6/2/r169/abstract

17. Porth, C.M., *Pathophysiology* (Philadelphia: JB Lippincott Company, 1994), 1222.

18. National Institute of Arthritis and Musculoskeletal and Skin Diseases, "Handout on Health: Osteoarthritis," http://www.

niams.nih.gov/Health_Info/Osteoarthritis/default.asp

19. Arthritis Foundation, "Osteoarthritis," http://www.arthritis.org/conditions/DiseaseCenter/OA/oa_causes.asp

20. *Webster's New World Medical Dictionary*, 2nd ed. (New York: Wiley Publishing, Inc., 2003), 372.

21. H.M. Seidel, J.W. Ball, J.E. Dains, and G.W. Benedict, *Mosby's Guide to Physical Examination* (St. Louis: Mosby, 1995), 894.

22. J.H. Klippel, *Primer on the Rheumatic Diseases*, 12th ed. (Atlanta: Arthritis Foundation, 2001), 287.

23. National Institute of Arthritis and Musculoskeletal and Skin Diseases, "Handout on Health: Osteoarthritis," http://www.niams.nih.gov/Health_Info/Osteoarthritis/default.asp

24. Ibid.

25. K. Lorig, and J.F. Fries, *The Arthritis Helpbook*, 5th ed. (Cambridge: Perseus Books, 2000), 100.

26. National Institute of Arthritis and Musculoskeletal and Skin Diseases, "Handout on Health: Osteoarthritis," http://www.niams.nih.gov/Health_Info/Osteoarthritis/default.asp

27. Arthritis Foundation, "Cartilage Fragment a Biomarker for Osteoarthritis," http://www.arthritis.org/Resources/DisplayScreamingNews.asp?id=505

28. National Institute of Arthritis and Musculoskeletal and Skin Diseases, "Handout on Health: Osteoarthritis," http://www.niams.nih.gov/Health_Info/Osteoarthritis/default.asp

29. L.W. Andrews, "Beating the Blues," *Arthritis Self-Management*, 5(3), 14–19.

30. Ibid.

31. Arthritis Foundation, "The Facts About Arthritis," http://www.arthritis.org/facts.php

32. Centers for Disease Control (CDC), "Preventing Arthritis Pain and Disability," http://www.cdc.gov/nccdphp/publications/factsheets/Prevention/arthritis.htm

33. "Arthritis and Exercises," http://www.drfeely.com/PatientCare/articles_arthro_exercises.htm

34. "More Americans Than Ever Use CAM, Says CDC." *Nursing 2004*, 34(9), pg. 73.

35. American Academy of Orthopaedic Surgeons, "Joint Replacement," http://orthoinfo.org/menus/arthroplasty.cfm

36. Bone and Joint Decade Organization, "Bone and Joint Decade," http://www.usbjd.org/about/index.cfm

37. Arthritis Foundation, "Overcoming Arthritis," http://www.arthritis.org/research/ResearchUpdate/04_july_Aug/OA.asp

38. National Institute of Arthritis and Musculoskeletal and Skin Diseases (NIAMS), "Osteoarthritis Initiative (OAI): A Knee Health Study," http://www.clinicaltrials.gov/ct2/show/NCT00080171?term=osteoarthritis

39. National Institute of Arthritis and Musculoskeletal and Skin Diseases, "The Effect of Weight Loss and Exercise on Knee Osteoarthritis," http://www.clinicaltrials.gov/ct2/show/NCT00061490?term

40. National Institutes of Health, "Acupuncture Safety/Efficacy in Knee Osteoarthritis," http://www.clinicaltrials.gov/ct2/show/NCT00010946?term=safety

41. Jordan, J., Helmick, C.G., Renner, J.B., Luta, G., et al. (2007), "Prevalence of Knee Symptoms and Radiographic and Symptomatic Knee Osteoarthritis in African Americans and Caucasians: The Johnston County Osteoarthritis Project," *The Journal of Rheumatology*, 34, 172–180. Http://www.jrheum.com/abstracts/abstracts07/172.html

42. Ibid.

43. Arthritis Foundation, "Research Update," http://www.arthritis.org/research/ResearchUpdate/05Dec/year.asp

44. Ibid.

45. Ibid.

46. Ibid.

Chapter 2

1. All About Artists, "Pierre-Auguste Renoir," http://www.allaboutartists.com/bios/renoir.html

2. Booenen, Annelies, van de Rest, Jan, Dequeker, Jan, and van der Linden, Sjef (1997), "How Renoir Coped with Rheumatoid Arthritis," *British Medical Journal*, 1997 (315), 1704–1708. Http://www.bmj.com/cgi/content/full/315/7123/1704

3. Ibid.

4. Arthritis Foundation, *Practical Help from the Arthritis Foundation—Rheumatoid*

Arthritis (Atlanta: Arthritis Foundation, 2003), 2.

5. Peck, B. (2004), "About Arthritis: Rheumatoid Arthritis," *Arthritis Self-Management*, 5(5), 6–12.

6. Arthritis Foundation, *Practical Help from the Arthritis Foundation—Rheumatoid Arthritis* (Atlanta: Arthritis Foundation, 2003), 3.

7. National Institute of Arthritis and Musculoskeletal and Skin Diseases (NIAMS), Department of Health and Human Services, "Handout on Health: Rheumatoid Arthritis," http://www.niams.nih.gov/Health_Info/Rheumatic_Disease/default.asp

8. American College of Rheumatology, "Rheumatoid Arthritis," http://www.rheumatology.org/public/factsheets/ra_new.asp?aud=pat

9. West, Sterling, *Rheumatology Secrets*, 2nd ed. (Philadelphia: Hanley & Belfus, 2002) 119.

10. Ibid., 36.

11. National Institute of Arthritis and Musculoskeletal and Skin Diseases (NIAMS), Department of Health and Human Services, "Handout on Health: Rheumatoid Arthritis," http://www.niams.nih.gov/hi/topics/arthritis/rahandout.htm

12. Arthritis Foundation, *Practical Help from the Arthritis Foundation—Rheumatoid Arthritis* (Atlanta: Arthritis Foundation, 2003).

13. National Institute of Arthritis and Musculoskeletal and Skin Diseases (NIAMS), Department of Health and Human Services, "Handout on Health: Rheumatoid Arthritis," http://www.niams.nih.gov/hi/topics/arthritis/rahandout.htm

14. Ibid.

15. *Webster's New World Medical Dictionary*, 2nd ed. (New York: Wiley Publishing, Inc, 2003), 18.

16. J.H. Klippel, *Primer on the Rheumatic Diseases*, 12th ed. (Atlanta: Arthritis Foundation, 2001), 210.

17. West, Sterling, *Rheumatology Secrets*, 2nd ed. (Philadelphia: Hanley & Belfus, 2002) 117

18. C.M. Porth, *Pathophysiology* (Philadelphia: JB Lippincott Company, 1994), 259.

19. *Webster's New World Medical Dictionary*, 2nd ed. (New York: Wiley Publishing, Inc, 2003), 24.

20. West, Sterling, *Rheumatology Secrets*, 2nd ed. (Philadelphia: Hanley & Belfus, 2002), 17.

21. Arthritis Foundation, *Practical Help from the Arthritis Foundation—Rheumatoid Arthritis* (Atlanta: Arthritis Foundation, 2003), 3.

22. American College of Rheumatology, "Rheumatoid Arthritis," http://www.rheumatology.org/public/factsheets/ra_new.asp?aud=pat.

23. Peck, B. (2004), "About Arthritis: Rheumatoid Arthritis," *Arthritis Self-Management*, 5(5), 6–12.

24. Arthritis Foundation, "Top 10 Arthritis Advances of 2006," http://ww2.arthritis.org/resources/top_ten/2006/Summaries-06.asp?CampaignId=E07A1N1MYZZ020374642

25. Arthritis Foundation, "Rheumatoid Arthritis—How Is It Diagnosed?" http://www.arthritis.org/disease-center.php?disease_id=31&df=diagnosed

26. *Webster's New World Medical Dictionary*, 2nd ed. (New York: Wiley Publishing, Inc, 2003), 355.

27. Arthritis Foundation "Rheumatoid Arthritis—How Is It Diagnosed?" http://www.arthritis.org/disease-center.php?disease_id=31&df=diagnosed

28. West, Sterling, *Rheumatology Secrets*, 2nd ed. (Philadelphia: Hanley & Belfus, 2002), 68.

29. National Institute of Mental Health, National Institutes of Health, "Depression," http://www.nimh.nih.gov/publicat/depression.cfm#ptdep3

30. Foltz-Gray, D. (2003). "Stuck in the Dumps," *Arthritis Today*. http://www.arthritis.org/resources/arthritistoday/2003_archives/2003_11_12_stuck_dumps_1.asp

31. National Institute of Mental Health, National Institutes of Health, "Depression," http://www.nimh.nih.gov/publicat/depression.cfm#ptdep3

32. Ibid.

33. Ibid.

34. Ibid.

35. Karnes, Marie (2005), "When Stress Flares," *Arthritis Today*, June 2005. Http://www.arthritis.org/resources/arthritistoday/2005_archives/2005_05_06/2005_05_06_Stress_1.asp

36. Ibid.

37. Arthritis Foundation, *Practical Help*

from the Arthritis Foundation—Rheumatoid Arthritis (Atlanta: Arthritis Foundation, 2003), 7.

38. West, Sterling, *Rheumatology Secrets*, 2nd ed. (Philadelphia: Hanley & Belfus, 2002), 127.

39. Arthritis Foundation, "Understanding Heart Disease and Death in RA," Research Update-March/April 2005, http://www.arthritis.org/research/ResearchUpdate/05March_April/understanding.asp

40. Ibid.

41. Arthritis Foundation, "Treatment Options," http://www.arthritis.org/disease-center.php?disease_id=31&df=treatments

42. American College of Rheumatology, "Osteoporosis," http://www.rheumatology.org/public/factsheets/osteopor_new.asp?aud=pat

43. *Webster's New World Medical Dictionary*, 2nd ed. (New York: Wiley Publishing, Inc, 2003), 299.

44. American College of Rheumatology, "Osteoporosis," http://www.rheumatology.org/public/factsheets/osteopor_new.asp?aud=pat

45. National Institute of Arthritis and Musculoskeletal and Skin Diseases (NIAMS), Department of Health and Human Services, "Osteoporosis," http://www.niams.nih.gov/Health_Info/Bone/Osteoporosis/default.asp

46. American College of Rheumatology, "Osteoporosis," http://www.rheumatology.org/public/factsheets/osteopor_new.asp?aud=pat

47. National Osteoporosis Foundation, "Prevention—Calcium and Vitamin D Recommendations," http://www.nof.org/prevention/calcium.htm

48. Ibid.

49. Ibid.

50. Ibid.

51. National Osteoporosis Foundation, "Prevention—Exercise for Healthy Bones," http://www.nof.org/prevention/exercise.htm

52. Ibid.

53. National Institute of Arthritis and Musculoskeletal and Skin Diseases (NIAMS), Department of Health and Human Services, "Osteoporosis," http://www.niams.nih.gov/Health_Info/Bone/Osteoporosis/default.asp

54. Arthritis Foundation, "Coffee, Smoking and Risk of RA," Research Update, http://www.arthritis.org/research/ResearchUpdate/03Nov_Dec/coffee_smoking.asp?Camp.

55. Channing Laboratory, "Research Interests," http://www.channing.harvard.edu/wang_y.htm.

56. ArthritisSupport.com, "New Stem Cell Source Benefits Arthritis Treatment," http://www.arthritissupport.com/library/print.cfm?ID=253.

57. Arthritis Foundation, "Stem-Cell Transplants: A Cure for Arthritis?" http://www.arthritis.org/resources/news/news_stemupdate.asp

58. de Kleer, I. M., et al. (2004). "Autologous Stem Cell Transplantation for Refractory Juvenile Idiopathic Arthritis: Analysis of Clinical Effects, Mortality, and Transplant Related Morbidity," *Annals of the Rheumatic Diseases*, 63, 1318–1326. http://ard.bmj.com/cgi/content/abstract

59. Ibid.

60. Genetic Science Learning Center at the University of Utah, "Stem Cell Therapies Today," http://learn.genetics.utah.edu/units/stemcells/sctoday/

61. National Geographic News, "Umbilical Cord Blood the Future of Stem Cell Research?" http://news.nationalgeographic.com/news/2006/04/0406_060406_cord_blood_2.html

62. Ibid.

63. Arthritis Foundation, "Rheumatoid Arthritis: Treatment Options," http://www.arthritis.org/disease-center.php?disease_id=31&df=treatments

Chapter 3

1. Moskowitz, R.W., Howell, D.S. Goldberg, V.M., and Mankin, H.J. *Osteoarthritis—Diagnosis and Medical/Surgical Management* 2nd ed (Philadelphia: W.B. Saunders Co., 1992) 12.

2. Ibid., pg 12.

3. Ibid., pg. 12.

4. Ibid., pg. 13.

5. Ibid., pg. 13.

6. West, Sterling, *Rheumatology Secrets*, 2nd ed. (Philadelphia: Hanley & Belfus, 2002), 655.

7. James, Roderick (1994). "Art and Arthritis," *Arthritis News Magazine*, 12(3), http://www.arthritis.ca/programs%20and%20resources/news%20magazine/1994/art/default.asp?s=1

8. West, Sterling, *Rheumatology Secrets*, 2nd ed. (Philadelphia: Hanley & Belfus, 2002), 658.

9. Moore, J.E. *Orthopedic Surgery* (Philadelphia: W.B. Saunders, 1898), 215.

10. Ibid., 216.

11. Ibid., 26–27.

12. Funsten, Robert V., and Calderwood, Carmelita, *Orthopedic Nursing*, 2nd ed. (St. Louis: CV Mosby, 1949), 240.

13. Ibid., 243.

14. Ibid., 247.

15. *Webster's New World Dictionary*, 4th ed. (New York: Wiley, 2003), 221.

16. Ergoweb, "History of Ergonomics," http://www.ergoweb.com/resources/faq/history.cfm?print=on&

17. Ibid.

18. Ibid.

19. *Webster's New World Dictionary*, 4th ed. (New York: Wiley, 2003), 221.

20. Porth, Carol M., *Pathophysiology* (Philadelphia: JB Lippincott Co, 1994), 982.

21. St. Marie, Barbara, *Core Curriculum for Pain Management Nursing*, 1st ed. (Philadelphia: WB Saunders Company, 2002), 10.

22. Ibid., 10–13.

23. American Pain Society, "Decade of Pain Control and Research," http://www.ampainsoc.org/decadeofpain/

24. Whitney, E.N., and Rolfes, S.R., *Understanding Nutrition*, 7th ed. (Minneapolis/St. Paul: West Publishing Company, 1996), 375.

25. Fisher, Carol, *The American Cookbook: A History*, 1st ed. (Jefferson: McFarland & Co., Inc., 2006), 109.

26. Ibid., 110.

27. Davis, C., and Saltos, E. "Dietary Recommendations and How They Have Changed Over Time," US Department of Agriculture, Economic Research Service. http://www.ers.usda.gov/publications/aib750/aib750b.pdf

28. Ibid.

29. Jones, Val, "Thought for Food: 2400-Year-Old Advice for Today's Worldwide Weight Crisis," Medscape, http://www.medscape.com/viewarticle/510200

30. Robison, J.I. (1999). "Weight, Health and Culture: Shifting the Paradigm for Alternative Health Care," *Complementary Health Practice Review*, Vol. 5, No. 1, 45–69, http://chp.sagepub.com/cgi/content/abstract/5/1/45

31. "Barbie's Beginning," http://www.dolls4play.com/barbiehistory.html

32. Robison, J.I. (1999). "Weight, Health and Culture: Shifting the Paradigm for Alternative Health Care," *Complementary Health Practice Review*, Vol. 5, No. 1, 45–69, http://chp.sagepub.com/cgi/content/abstract/5/1/45

33. National Association to Advance Fat Acceptance (NAAFA), "A History of Obesity," http://www.naafa.org/press_room/history_obesity.html

34. Ibid.

35. Ibid.

36. Sneader, Walter (2000), "The Discovery of Aspirin: A Reappraisal," *British Medical Journal*, 321(1591–1594), http://www.bmj.com/cgi/content/full/321/7276/1591

37. "History of Tylenol," http://www.auburn.edu/~teagukl/tyhist.htm

38. "Mayo Clinic Celebrates the 50th Anniversary of the Discovery of Cortisone," http://www.mayoclinic.org/news2000-rst/707.html

39. Helms, Joseph (2006), "An Overview of Medical Acupuncture," American Academy of Medical Acupuncture, http://www.medicalacupuncture.org/acu_info/articles/helmsarticle.html

40. Acupuncture.com, "What Is Acupuncture and How Does It Work?" Http://www.acupuncture.com/education/tcmbasics/whatisacu.htm

41. American Acupuncture, "The History of Acupuncture," http://www.americanacupuncture.com/history.htm.

42. "Asepsis and Anti-sepsis, Scientific Anti-Vivisectionism," http://www.freewebs.com/scientific_anti_vivisectionism4/aspesisandantisepsis.htm

43. Ibid.

44. Ibid.

45. Ibid.

46. "Joseph Lister and Antiseptic Surgery," http://www.web.ukonline.co.uk/b.gardner/Lister.html

47. Ibid.

48. Ibid.

49. Phillips, R.S., ed., *Funk and Wagnalls*

New Encyclopedia (New York: Rand McNally & Co., 1983), volume 16, 154–155.

50. "Asepsis and Anti-sepsis, Scientific Anti-Vivisectionism," http://www.freewebs.com/scientific_anti_vivisectionism4/aspesisandantisepsis.htm

51. "Penicillin, the Wonder Drug." University of Hawaii Botany 135 syllabus. http://www.botany.hawaii.edu/faculty/wong/BOT135/Lect21b.htm

52. Lewis, Ricki, "The Rise of Antibiotic-Resistant Infections," http://www.fda.gov/fdac/features/795_antibio.html

53. Ibid.

54. Mary Washington College, "The History of the X-ray," http://www.umw.edu/hisa/resources/Student%20Projects/Amy%20Miller%20—%20X-Ray/students.mwc.edu/_amill4gn/XRAY/PAGES/immed.html

55. Ibid.

56. Ibid.

57. *Webster's New World Medical Dictionary*, 2nd ed. (New York: Wiley Publishing, 2003), 19.

58. Barash, Paul G., Cullen, Bruce, Stoelting, and Robert K., *Clinical Anesthesia* (Philadelphia: J.B. Lippincott Co., 1989), 3.

59. Ibid., 6.

60. Ibid., 9.

61. Ibid., 27.

62. Ibid., 6.

63. Ibid., 13.

64. WorldOrtho: "History of Orthopaedics," pg. 2, http://www.worldortho.com/index.php?option=com_content&task=view&id=149&Itemid=146

65. Wikipedia, "Orthopaedic Surgery," http://www.wikipedia.org/wiki/Orthopaedic_surgery

66. Ibid.

67. "History of Total Joint Replacement," http://www.utahhipandknee.com/history.htm

68. Ibid.

69. "History of Total Hip Replacement," http://www.thehipdoc.com/history.htm

70. "History of Total Joint Replacement," http://www.utahhipandknee.com/history.htm

71. Palmer, Simon H., "Total Knee Arthroplasty." eMedicine online. http://www.emedicine.com/orthoped/topic347.htm

72. National Institutes of Health (NIH), "Consensus Development Conference on Total Knee Replacement," http://consensus.nih.gov/2003/2003TotalKneeReplacement117html.htm

Chapter 4

1. UW Student Counseling Center, "Healthy Grieving," http://depts.washington.edu/counsels/resources/4students/grieving/grieving.html

2. Baptist Hospital East, "Grief and Loss: The Healing Process," http://www.baptisteast.com/healthinfo/disorders/gre001.cfm

3. J.W. Worden, *Grief Counseling and Grief Therapy: A Handbook for the Mental Health Practitioner*, 2nd ed. (New York: Springer, 1997), 12.

4. Ibid., 14.

5. Baptist Hospital East, "Grief and Loss: The Healing Process," http://www.baptisteast.com/healthinfo/disorders/gre001.cfm

6. J.W. Worden, *Grief Counseling and Grief Therapy: A Handbook for the Mental Health Practitioner*, 2nd ed. (New York: Springer, 1997), 15–16.

7. Ibid., 17–18.

8. Baptist Hospital East, "Grief and Loss: The Healing Process," http://www.baptisteast.com/healthinfo/disorders/gre001.cfm

9. J.R. White, *Grieving: Our Path Back to Peace* (Minneapolis: Bethany House Publishers, 1997), 84.

10. Ibid.

11. M.C. Townsend, *Psychiatric Mental Health Nursing*, 4th ed. (Philadelphia: F.A. David Co., 2003), 45.

12. National Institute of Arthritis and Musculoskeletal and Skin Diseases, "Handout on Health: Osteoarthritis," http://www.niams.nih.gov/hi/topics/arthritis/oahandout.htm.

13. Arthritis Foundation, *Managing Your Health Care* (Atlanta: Arthritis Foundation, 1997), 3.

14. J.H. Klippel, ed., *Primer on the Rheumatic Diseases*, 12th ed. (Atlanta: Arthritis Foundation, 2001), 294.

15. R. Sutherland, "The Big Five-O," *Arthritis News Magazine*, http://www.arthritis.ca/programs%20and%20resources/news%20magazine/1998/the%20big%20fifty/default.asp?s=1

16. David Niven, *100 Simple Secrets of Healthy People What Scientists Have Learned and How You Can Use It*, 1st ed. (New York: HarperCollins Publishers, Inc., 2003), 84.

17. R. Sutherland, "The Big Five-O," *Arthritis News Magazine*, http://www.arthritis.ca/programs%20and%20resources/news%20magazine/1998/the%20big%20fifty/default.asp?s=1

18. National Institute of Arthritis and Musculoskeletal and Skin Diseases, "Handout on Health: Osteoarthritis," http://www.niams.nih.gov/hi/topics/arthritis/oahandout.htm.

19. J.A. Maville, and C.G. Huerta, *Health Promotion in Nursing* (Albany: Delmar of Thomson Learning, Inc., 2002), 335

20. K. Lorig, and J.F. Fries, *The Arthritis Helpbook*, 5th ed. (Cambridge: Perseus, 2000), 125–6.

21. United States Department of Health and Human Services, "The Facts About Overweight and Obesity," http://www.surgeongeneral.gov/topics/obesity/calltoaction/fact_glance.htm

22. David Niven, *100 Simple Secrets of Healthy People What Scientists Have Learned and How You Can Use It*, 1st ed. (New York: HarperCollins Publishers, Inc., 2003), 64.

23. Ibid., 126.

24. J.A. Maville, C G Huerta, *Health Promotion in Nursing* (Albany: Delmar of Thomson Learning, Inc., 2002), 358.

25. Ibid., 359.

26. HealthCaring, "Growing Hope" http://www.religionandhealth.org/newsletters/newsletteraprmay07.pdf

27. Gallup, "Religion Poll 2007," http://www.gallup.com/poll/1690/Religion.aspx.

28. Learnwell.org, "Health and Spirituality: Help or Harm." Http://www.learnwell.org/spirituality.htm

29. P.E. Becker, and Dhingra, P. (2001), "Religious Involvement and Volunteering Implications for Civil Society," *Sociology of Religion*, http://findarticles.com/p/articles/mi_m0SOR/is_3_62/ai_79353382/pg_11

30. K. Lorig, and J.F. Fries, *The Arthritis Helpbook*, 5th ed. (Cambridge: Perseus, 2000), 270.

31. Arthritis Society, "Develop Effective Communication Skills," http://www.arthritis.ca/tips%20for%20living/communicating%20your%20needs/develop%20skills/default.asp?s=1

32. Arthritis Foundation, "52 Ways to Bite Back," http://www.arthritis.org/resources/arthritistoday/2003_archives/2003_09_10_52_Ways_Intro.asp

33. Office of Special Education and Rehabilitative Services (OSERS), "Welcome to RSA," http://www.ed.gov/about/offices/list/osers/rsa/index.html

34. Apples for Health.com, "Medicaid Funds Going Directly to People," http://www.applesforhealth.com/HealthyFeatures/medfungoidp4.html

35. Ibid.

36. Centers for Disease Control, "Targeting Arthritis: Improving Quality of Life for Over 46 Million Americans," http://www.cdc.gov/nccdphp/publications/AAG/arthritis.htm

37. Missouri Arthritis Rehabilitation Research and Training (MARRTC), "Mission Statement," (2004). http://marrtc.missouri.edu/about/mission.html

38. Missouri Arthritis Rehabilitation Research and Training (MARRTC), "Farmers Project Highlighted in National Magazine," http://marrtc.missouri.edu/media/releases/farm-7-31-02.html

39. Arthritis Foundation's *Guide to Good Living with Rheumatoid Arthritis*, 2nd ed. (Atlanta: Arthritis Foundation, 2004), 5.

Chapter 5

1. Karnes, Marie (2005), "When Stress Flares," *Arthritis Today*, http://www.arthritis.org/resources/arthritistoday/2005_archives/2005_05_06/2005_05_06_Stress_1.asp

2. Lewis, Carol, "Arthritis: Timely Treatments for an Ageless Disease," http://www.fda.gov/fdac/features/2000/300_arth.html

3. *Webster's New World Dictionary* (New York: Pocket Books, 2003), 221.

4. Ergoweb, "Blackberry Thumb—A Painful but Avoidable Musculoskeletal Disorder," http://www.ergoweb.com/news/detail.cfm?print=on&id=1210.

5. American Academy of Orthopaedic Surgeons (AAOS), "Tips to Prevent Baseball Injuries," http://orthoinfo.aaos.org/fact/thr_report.cfm?Thread_ID=192&topcategory=Injury%20Prevention

6. Missouri Arthritis Rehabilitation Research and Training Center (MARRTC), "Kids Warm Up to Prevent Arthritis," http://www.marrtc.org/warmup/

7. Roos, Ewa M., "Joint Injury Causes Knee Osteoarthritis in Young Adults," Medscape, http://www.medscape.com/viewarticle/500181_print.

8. National Center on Physical Activity and Disability (NCPAD), "Seated Strengthening Exercises," http://www.ncpad.org/videos/fact_sheet.php?sheet=1

9. Arthritis Foundation, "10 Ways You Can Protect Your Joints," http://www.arthritis.org/conditions/tips_jointprotection.asp

10. Ibid.

11. Niven, David, *100 Secrets of Healthy People* (San Francisco: Harper Collins, 2003), 145–6.

12. Kerrigan, D. Casey, "High Heels—Wide vs. Narrow Heeled Shoes and Knee Osteoarthritis," http://www.healthsystem.virginia.edu/internet/pmr/Highheels.cfm?printfriendly=1&

13. Ibid.

14. Foltz-Gray, Dorothy, "Get Square with Your Feet," *Arthritis Today*, http://www.arthritis.org/conditions/feet/feet_intro.asp

15. Foltz-Gray, Dorothy, "Get Square with Your Feet," *Arthritis Today*, http://www.arthritis.org/conditions/feet/feet_prevention.asp

16. American Academy of Orthopaedic Surgeons (AAOS), "What's Crushing Your Feet?" http://www6.aaos.org/news/Pemr/press_release.cfm?PRNumber=304

17. Foltz-Gray, Dorothy, "Get Square with Your Feet," *Arthritis Today*, http://www.arthritis.org/conditions/feet/feet_boot camp.asp

18. Zhang, Yuqing, et al. (2004). "Association of Squatting with Increased Prevalence of Radiographic Tibiofemoral Knee Osteoarthritis: The Beijing Osteoarthritis Study," Arthritis & Rheumatism, 50(4), 1187–1192. Http://www3.interscience.wiley.com/cgi-bin/abstract/107642825/ABSTRACT

19. Ibid.

20. Arthritis Foundation, "Safe or Sorry: A Parent's Guide to Sports Injury Prevention," http://www.arthritis.org/resources/sip/intro.asp

21. Ibid.

22. Ibid.

23. Ibid.

24. Ibid.

25. Ibid.

26. American Academy of Orthopaedic Surgeons (AAOS), "Tips to Prevent Baseball Injuries," http://orthoinfo.aaos.org/fact/thr_report.cfm?Thread_ID=192&topcategory=Injury%20Prevention

27. Ibid.

28. Parents.com (2005), "Play It Safe," http://parents.com/parents/story.jhtml?storyid=/templatedata/parents/story/data/2147.xml

29. American Academy of Orthopaedic Surgeons (AAOS), "Tips to Prevent Basketball Injuries," http://orthoinfo.aaos.org/fact/thr_report.cfm?Thread_ID=146&topcategory=Injury%20Prevention

30. Parents.com (2005), "Play It Safe," http://parents.com/parents/story.jhtml?storyid=/templatedata/parents/story/data/2147.xml

31. AAOS News Release, "Preventing Severe Head and Neck Injuries in High School and Collegiate Athletes: Orthopaedic Research Reveals Benefits of Enhanced Protective Gear, Preventive Strategies, Rule Revisions," http://www6.aaos.org/news/Pemr/press_release.cfm?PRNumber=408

32. Ibid.

33. American Academy of Orthopaedic Surgeons (AAOS), "Football" http://orthoinfo.aaos.org/fact/thr_report.cfm?Thread_ID=50&topcategory=Injury%20Prevention

34. Parents.com (2005), "Play It Safe," http://parents.com/parents/story.jhtml?storyid=/templatedata/parents/story/data/2147.xml

35. AAOS News Release, "Preventing Severe Head and Neck Injuries in High School and Collegiate Athletes: Orthopaedic Research Reveals Benefits of Enhanced Protective Gear, Preventive Strategies, Rule Revisions," http://www6.aaos.org/news/Pemr/press_release.cfm?PRNumber=408

36. American Academy of Orthopaedic Surgeons (AAOS), "Tips to Prevent Soccer Injuries," http://orthoinfo.aaos.org/fact/thr_report.cfm?Thread_ID=195&topcategory=Injury%20Prevention

37. Roos, Ewa M., "Joint Injury Causes Knee Osteoarthritis in Young Adults," Medscape, http://www.medscape.com/viewarticle/500181

38. American Academy of Orthopaedic

Surgeons (AAOS), "Tips to Prevent Soccer Injuries," http://orthoinfo.aaos.org/fact/thr_report.cfm?Thread_ID=195&topcategory=Injury%20Prevention

39. Ibid.

40. American Academy of Orthopaedic Surgeons (AAOS), "Tips to Prevent Volleyball Injuries," http://orthoinfo.aaos.org/fact/thr_report.cfm?Thread_ID=187&topcategory=Injury%20Prevention

41. Ibid.

42. Ibid.

43. Arthritis Foundation (2005), "Gardening and Arthritis," http://www.arthritis.org/resources/Home_Life/gardening.asp

44. Arthritis Foundation, "10 Tips for Easier Gardening," http://www.arthritis.org/resources/Home_Life/tips.asp

45. American Academy of Orthopaedic Surgeons (AAOS), "Prevent Golf Injuries," http://orthoinfo.aaos.org/fact/thr_report.cfm?Thread_ID=107&topcategory=Injury%20Prevention

46. Ibid.

Chapter 6

1. Mersky, H., ed. (1986), "Classification of Chronic Pain: Descriptions of Chronic pain Syndromes and Definitions of Pain Terms," Pain (Suppl. 3, Pt II), S215–221.

2. Carol Mattson Porth, Pathophysiology, (Philadelphia: JB Lippincott Co, 1994), 982.

3. Mayo Clinic, "How You Feel Pain," Mayo Foundation for Medical Education and Research, http://www.mayoclinic.com/health/pain/PN00017

4. National Chronic Pain Outreach Association homepage. http://www.chronicpain.org/

5. Carol Mattson Porth, Pathophysiology (Philadelphia: JB Lippincott Co, 1994), 982.

6. Mayo Clinic, "How You Feel Pain," Mayo Foundation for Medical Education and Research, http://www.mayoclinic.com/health/pain/PN00017

7. Carol Mattson Porth, Pathophysiology (Philadelphia: JB Lippincott Co, 1994), 984.

8. Weber, S.E. (1996), Cultural Aspects of Pain in Childbearing Women. Journal of Obstetric, Gynecologic and Neonatal Nursing, 25, 67–72.

9. Webster's New World Dictionary, 4th ed. (New York: Wiley Publishing, 2003), 28.

10. Horstman, Judith, The Arthritis Foundation's Guide to Alternative THERAPIES (Atlanta: Arthritis Foundation, 1999), 57.

11. Mayo Clinic, "How You Feel Pain," Mayo Foundation for Medical Education and Research, http://www.mayoclinic.com/health/pain/PN00017

12. St. Marie, Barbara, Core Curriculum for Pain Management Nursing, 1st ed. (Philadelphia: WB Saunders Company, 2002), 159.

13. National Sleep Foundation, "Pain and Sleep," http://www.sleepfoundation.org/nsfalert/index.php?id=9&secid=30

14. "Pain and Insomnia: What Every Clinician Should Know," Medscape Neurology and Neurosurgery 6(2), 2004, http://www.medscape.com/viewarticle/494872

15. Broderick, Joan E., "Pain and the Power of Your Mind," Arthritis Self-Management, 5(4), 28–33.

16. The National Sleep Foundation, "Sleep & Aging," http://www.sleepfoundation.org/sleeplibrary/index.php?secid=&id=64

17. Ibid.

18. Ibid.

19. Gott, Peter, Live Longer, Live Better (Sanger, California: Quill Driver Books/Word Dancer Press, Inc. 2004), 295.

20. The National Sleep Foundation, "Sleep & Aging," http://www.sleepfoundation.org/sleeplibrary/index.php?secid=&id=64

21. Ibid.

22. National Sleep Foundation, "Healthy Tips for Better Sleep," http://www.sleepfoundation.org/quiz/index.php

23. Horstman, Judith, The Arthritis Foundation's Guide to Alternative THERAPIES (Atlanta: Arthritis Foundation, 1999), 118.

24. Field, T., Schanberg, S.M., Scafidi, F., Bauer, C.R., Vega-Lahr, N., Garcia, R., Nystrom, J., and Kuhn, C.M. (1986), "Tactile/Kinesthetic Stimulation Effects on Preterm Neonates," Pediatrics, 77, 654–658.

25. Touch Research Institute, "Welcome to the Touch Research Institute." http://www6.miami.edu/touch-research/

26. Field, T., Hernandez-Reif, M., Seligman, S., Krasnegor, J., Sunshine, W., Rivas-Chacon, R., Schanberg, S., and Kuhn, C. (1997), "Juvenile Rheumatoid Arthritis:

Benefits from Massage Therapy," *Journal of Pediatric Psychology*, 22, 607–617.

27. Field, T., Hernandez-Reif, M., Quentino, O., Schanberg, S. and Kuhn, C. (1998), "Elderly Retired Volunteers Benefit from Giving Massage Therapy to Infants," *Journal of Applied Gerontology*, 17, 229–239.

28. Porth, Carol Mattson, *Pathophysiology* (Philadelphia: JB Lippincott Co, 1994), 983.

29. Horstman, Judith, *The Arthritis Foundation's Guide to Alternative THERAPIES* (Atlanta: Arthritis Foundation, 1999), 127.

30. Ibid.

31. *Funk & Wagnalls Standard Desk Dictionary* (New York: Lippincott & Crowell, 1980), 399.

32. Mendoza, N.F., "The A to Z Guide to Massages," *Women's Health and Fitness* (April 2005), 82–83.

33. Intelihealth Complimentary and Alternative Therapy, "Massage," http://www.intelihealth.com/IH/ihtIH/WSIHW000/8513/34968/365286.html?d=dmtContent

34. Horstman, Judith, *The Arthritis Foundation's Guide to Alternative THERAPIES* (Atlanta: Arthritis Foundation, 1999), 119–132.

35. Ibid.

36. Intelihealth Home Page, "Reflexology, Complimentary and Alternative Therapies," http://www.intelihealth.com/IH/ihtIH/WSIHW000/8513/34968/360060.html?d=dmtContent

37. American Reflexology Certification Board, "The Differences Between Reflexology and Massage," http://www.reflexology-usa.org/articles/differences.html

38. Ibid.

39. Intelihealth Home Page, "Reflexology, Complimentary and Alternative Therapies," http://www.intelihealth.com/IH/ihtIH/WSIHW000/8513/34968/360060.html?d=dmtContent

40. Intelihealth Complimentary and Alternative Therapy, "Meditation," http://www.intelihealth.com/IH/ihtIH/WSIHW000/8513/34968/362173.html?d=dmtContent

41. Ibid.

42. Mind/Body Medical Institute, "Mindfulness," http://www.mbmi.org/basics/mstress_M.asp

43. Kabat-Zinn, J., Lipworth, L. and Burney, R. (1985), "The Clinical Use of Mindfulness Meditation in the Self-Regulation of Chronic Pain." *Journal of Behavioral Medicine*, 8:163–190.

44. Mind/Body Medical Institute, "Clinical Findings," http://www.mbmi.org/programs/clinical_findings.asp

45. American College of Rheumatology (2005), "Still the Mind, Calm the Rheumatoid Arthritis," http://www.rheumatology.oirg/press/2005/pradhan.asp

46. American Music Therapy Association, "Frequently Asked Questions About Music Therapy," http://www.musictherapy.org/faqs.html

47. American Music Therapy Association homepage, http://www.musictherapy.org/

48. Arthritis Foundation, "Music Therapy Reduces Pain," http://www.arthritis.org/Resources/DisplayScreamingnews.asp?id=444

49. Ikonomidou, E., Rehnstrom, A., and Naesh, O. (2004), "Effect of Music on Vital Signs and Postoperative Pain," *AORN Journal*, 80(2), 269–278.

50. National Chronic Pain Outreach Association homepage, http://www.chronicpain.org

Chapter 7

1. Brainy Quote, "Hippocrates Quotes," http://www.brainyquote.com/quotes/quotes/h/hippocrate153531.html

2. Bruce, B. (2005), "Arthritis and Food: Are There Links?" *Arthritis Self-Management*, 6(3), 11.

3. Hill, S. "Alphabet Soup: An A-to-Z Guide to Favorite Foods," *Arthritis Today*, http://www.arthritis.org/resources/nutrition/undiet.asp

4. Ibid.

5. USDA Agricultural Research Service, "Nutritional Implications for Rheumatoid Arthritis," http://www.ars.usda.gov/is/AR/archive/jul04/nutr0704.htm

6. Ibid.

7. Whitney, E.N., and Rolfes, S.R., *Understanding Nutrition*, 7th ed. (Minneapolis: West Publishing Company, 1993), 4.

8. Ibid., 4.

9. Ibid., 154.

10. Ibid., 345.

11. Ibid., 430.

12. Lorig, K., and Fries, J.F., *The Arthritis Helpbook*, 5th ed. (Cambridge: Perseus Books, 2000), 198.

13. United States Department of Agriculture (USDA), "My Pyramid.gov," http://www.mypyramid.gov/

14. United States Department of Agriculture (USDA), "Why Is It Important to Eat Grains, Especially Whole Grains?" http://www.mypyramid.gov/pyramid/grains_why_print.html

15. United States Department of Agriculture (USDA), "Why Is It Important to Eat Vegetables?" http://www.mypyramid.gov/pyramid/vegetables_why_print.html

16. United States Department of Agriculture (USDA), "Why Is It Important to Eat Fruits?" http://www.mypyramid.gov/pyramid/fruits_why.html

17. United States Department of Agriculture (USDA), "What Are 'Oils'?" http://www.mypyramid.gov/pyramid/oils_why.html

18. United States Department of Agriculture (USDA), "Health Benefits and Nutrients of Milk," http://www.mypyramid.gov/pyramid/milk_why.html

19. United States Department of Agriculture (USDA), "Why Is it Important to Make Lean or Low-Fat Choices from the Meat and Beans Group?" http://www.mypyramid.gov/pyramid/meat_why.html

20. USDA Center for National Policy and Promotion (2002), "Report Card of the Quality of Americans' Diets," http://www.cnpp.usda.gov/Publications/NutritionInsights/Insight28.pdf

21. *Webster's New World Dictionary*, 4th ed. (New York: Wiley, 2003), 184.

22. Weight-Control Information Network (WIN), "Understanding Adult Obesity," http://win.niddk.nih.gov/publications/understanding.htm

23. Weight-Control Information Network (WIN), "Weight and Waist Measurement: Tools for Adults," http://www.win.niddk.nih.gov/publications/tools.htm

24. National Heart, Lunch and Blood Institute (NHLBI), "Calculate Your BMI," http://www.nhlbisupport.com/bmi/bmicalc.htm

25. Flegal, Katherine, et al. "Excess Deaths Associate with Underweight, Overweight, and Obesity," *Journal of the American Medical Association*, 293 (15), http://www.jama.ama-assn.org/cgi/content/abstract/293/15/1861

26. National Institutes of Arthritis and Musculoskeletal and Skin Diseases (NIAMS), Department of Health and Human Services, "Osteoporosis," http://www.niams.nih.gov/Health_Info/Bone/Osteoporosis/default.asp

27. Maine, Margo (2005), "Eating Disorders and Body Image Distress in Women in Midlife," Medscape, http://www.medscape.com/viewprogram/4302

28. Ibid.

29. National Alliance on Mental Illness (NAMI), "Anorexia Nervosa," http://www.nami.org/Content/ContentGroups/Helpline1/Anorexia_Nervosa.htm

30. National Alliance on Mental Illness (NAMI) "Bulimia Nervosa," http://www.nami.org/Content/ContentGroups/Helpline1/Bulimia.htm

31. Doctors for Adults, "What Is Your Body Mass Index (BMI)?" Http://www.doctorsforadults.com/topics/dfa_obes.htm

32. Henderson, Carol J., "Dietary Outcomes in Osteoarthritis Disease Management," *Bulletin on the Rheumatic Diseases*, http://www.arthritis.org/research/Bulletin/Vol52No12/Introduction.asp

33. Medical News Today, "Non-Dieters More Successful at Boosting Health Than Dieters, Study Finds," 31 May 2005 Http://www.medicalnewstoday.com/printerfriendlynews.php?newsid=25384

34. Robison, Jon, "Health at Every Size: Toward a New Paradigm of Weight and Health," Medscape, http://www.medscape.com/viewarticle/506299

35. Medical News Today, "Non-Dieters More Successful at Boosting Health Than Dieters," Study Finds, 31 May 2005 Http://www.medicalnewstoday.com/printerfriendlynews.php?newsid=25384

36. Ibid.

37. Robison, J.I. (1999), "Weight, Health and Culture: Shifting the Paradigm for Alternative Health Care," *Complementary Health Practice Review*, Vol. 5, No. 1, 45–69, http://chp.sagepub.com/cgi/content/abstract/5/1/45

38. Personal interview with Dr. Jon Robinson.

39. Dinsmoor, R.S. (2005), "Taking Up

Walking One Step at a Time," *Arthritis Self-Management*, 6 (5), 17–23.

40. Barclay, L. (2004), "Getting Sufficient Sleep May Help Reduce Weight Gain," Medscape Medical News, http://www.medscape.com/viewarticle/495410

41. Liu, S., et al. (2003), "Relation Between Changes in Intakes of Dietary Fiber and Grain Products and Changes in Weight and Development of Obesity Among Middle-Aged Women," *American Journal of Clinical Nutrition*, 78 (5), 920–7. http://www.ncbi.nlm.nih.gov/pubmed/14594777?ordinalpos=5&itool=EntrezSystem2.PEntrez.Pubmed.Pubmed_ResultsPanel.Pubmed_RVDocSum

42. USDA Center for National Policy and Promotion, "More Than One in Three Older Americans May Not Drink Enough," http://www.cnpp.usda.gov/Publications/Nutrition Insights/Insight27.pdf

43. Harvard Medical School, "Water," http://www.intelihealth.com/IH/ihtIH?d=dmtContent&c=34048&p=~br,IHWx~st,24479x~r,WSIHW000x~b,*x

44. Valtin, Heinz (2002), "Drink at Least Eight Glasses of Water a Day. Really? Is There Scientific Evidence for '8 × 8'?" *American Journal of Physiology-Regulatory, Integrative and Comparative Physiology*, 283(5), 993–1004. Http://ajpregu.physiology.org/cgi/content/abstract/283/5/R993

45. Harvard Medical School, "Water," http://www.intelihealth.com/IH/ihtIH?d=dmtContent&c=34048&p=~br,IHWx~st,24479x~r,WSIHW000x~b,*x

46. MayoClinic.com, "Water: How Much Should You Drink Every Day?" http://www.mayoclinic.com/health/water/NU00283

47. Harvard Medical School, "Water," http://www.intelihealth.com/IH/ihtIH?d=dmtContent&c=34048&p=~br,IHWx~st,24479x~r,WSIHW000x~b,*x

48. Hill, S., "Alphabet Soup: An A-to-Z Guide to Favorite Foods," *Arthritis Today*, http://www.arthritis.org/resources/nutrition/TtoW.asp

49. Block, G. (2004), "Foods Contributing to Energy Intake in the US: Data from NHANES III and NHANES 1999–2000," http://www.sciencedirect.com

50. National Heart, Lungs, and Blood Institute, "Portion Distortion? Do You Know How Food Portions Have Changed in 20 Years? http://hp2010.nhlbihin.net/portion/

51. *Arthritis Today*, "2005 Vitamin and Mineral Guide," http://ww2.arthritis.org/resources/arthritistoday/2005_archives/2005_09_10/Vitamin_Mineral_Guide/MultiVitamins.asp

52. Ibid.

53. Ibid.

Chapter 8

1. "Arthritis and Exercises," http://www.drfeely.com/PatientCare/articles_arthro_exercises.htm

2. Lorig, Kate, and Fries, James, *The Arthritis Helpbook*, 5th ed. (Cambridge: Perseus Books, 2000.), 122.

3. Arthritis Foundation, "Exercise and Arthritis," http://www.arthritis.org/conditions/exercise/default.asp

4. Dunkin, Mary Ann, "This Is Medicine," *Arthritis Today*, http://www.arthritis.org/resources/arthritistoday/2005_archives/2005_01_02/2005_01_02_Medicine_2.asp

5. Ibid.

6. Weil, Richard M., "Exercises to Improve Your Balance," *Arthritis Self-Management*, 6(1), 15–26.

7. Centers for Disease Control (CDC), "Falls Among Older Adults: An Overview," http://www.cdc.gov/ncipc/factsheets/adult falls.htm

8. Weil, Richard M., "Exercises to Improve Your Balance," *Arthritis Self-Management*, 6(1), 15–26.

9. Ibid.

10. Ibid.

11. Lorig, Kate, and Fries, James, *The Arthritis Helpbook*, 5th ed. (Cambridge: Perseus Books, 2000), 135.

12. The Cleveland Clinic, "How Occupational and Physical Therapy Can Help You," http://www.clevelandclinic.org/health/health-info/docs/0500/0561.asp?index=4266

13. Ibid.

14. Arthritis Foundation, "Exercise and Arthritis," http://www.arthritis.org/conditions/exercise/default.asp

15. Arthritis Foundation booklet, *Practical Help from the Arthritis Foundation: Exercise and Your Arthritis*, Arthritis Foundation, 2003.

16. Arthritis Foundation, "Top Three Types of Exercises," http://www.arthritis.org/types-exercise.php
17. Ibid.
18. Ibid.
19. Ibid.
20. Dinsmoor, Robert S., "Taking Up Walking One Step at a Time," *Arthritis Self-Management*, 6(5), pg17–23.
21. Ibid.
22. Lorig, Kate, and Fries, James, *The Arthritis Helpbook*, 5th ed. (Cambridge: Perseus Books, 2000), 190.
23. Ibid., 191.
24. Ibid., 191.
25. Brainy Quote, "Hippocrates Quotes," http://www.brainyquote.com/quotes/authors/h/hippocrates.html
26. *Arthritis Today Walking Guide*, "The Perfect Fit," 7.
27. Ibid.
28. *Arthritis Self-Management*, "Those Winter Walks," 6(1), 43.
29. Dinsmoor, Robert S., "Taking Up Walking One Step at a Time," *Arthritis Self-Management*, 6(5), pg17–23.
30. Ibid.
31. Ibid.
32. Horstman, J., "Tai Chi," *Arthritis Today*, http://www.arthritis.org/resources/arthritistoday/2000_archives/2000_07_08_taichi.asp
33. Arthritis Foundation, "Tai Chi Program," http://www.arthritis.org/events/get involved/ProgramsServices/TaiChi.asp
34. Horstman, J., "Tai Chi," *Arthritis Today*, http://www.arthritis.org/resources/arthritistoday/2000_archives/2000_07_08_taichi.asp
35. National Institute on Aging, "Tai Chi for Older People Reduces Falls, May Help Maintain Strength," http://www.nia.nih.gov/NewsAndEvents/PressReleases/PR19960502TaiChi.htm
36. Horstman, J., "Tai Chi," *Arthritis Today*, http://www.arthritis.org/resources/arthritistoday/2000_archives/2000_07_08_taichi.asp
37. Lorig, Kate, and Fries, James, *The Arthritis Helpbook*, 5th ed. (Cambridge: Perseus Books, 2000), 188.
38. Arthritis Foundation," Let's Do Yoga," http://www.arthritis.org/conditions/exercise/Yoga/default.asp

39. American Academy of Orthopaedic Surgeons, "Patterns and Trends in Physical Activity," http://orthoinfo.aaos.org/fact/thr_report.cfm?Thread_ID=69&topcategory=Sports%20%2F%20Exercise
40. Arthritis Foundation, "10 Tips for Easier Gardening," http://www.arthritis.org/resources/Home_Life/tips.asp
41. Arthritis Foundation, "Golf and Arthritis," http://www.arthritis.org/conditions/exercise/golf.asp
42. Ibid.
43. Ibid.
44. Ibid.

Chapter 9

1. Centers for Disease Control (CDC) Press Release, "Almost Half of Americans Use at Least One Prescription Drug, Annual Report on Nation's Health Shows." Http://www.cdc.gov/od/oc/media/pressrel/r041202.htm
2. Family Caregiver Alliance, Fact Sheet: "Caregiver's Guide to Medications and Aging," http://www.caregiver.org/caregiver/jsp/content_node.jsp?nodeid=1104
3. Family Caregiver Alliance, Fact Sheet: "Caregiver's Guide to Medications and Aging," http://www.caregiver.org/caregiver/jsp/content_node.jsp?nodeid=1104
4. Arthritis Foundation, 2006 *Arthritis Today Drug Guide* booklet.
5. Larson, Anne M., et al. (2005), "Acetaminophen-Induced Acute Liver Failure: Results of a United States Multicenter, Prospective Study," *Hepatology*, 42(6), 1364–1372.
6. Ibid.
7. National Pain Foundation, "Arthritis Pain Medications," http://www.painconnection.org/MyTreatment/articles/Arthritis_TO_Medications.asp
8. Forman, J.P., Rimm, E.B., and Curhan, G.C. (2007), "Frequency of Analgesic Use and Risk of Hypertension Among Men," Archives of Internal Medicine, 167(4), http://archinte.ama-assn.org/cgi/content/abstract/167/4/394
9. Arthritis Foundation, "Common Pain Relievers Associated with High Blood Pressure," http://www.arthritis.org/research/summaries/pain-relievers-bp.asp?CampaignId=E07C2X1...

10. Brigham and Women's Hospital, "Low-dose Aspirin Proven to Offer Healthy Adults Inflammation Protection," http://www.brighamandwomens.org/publicaffairs/Newsreleases/low_dose_aspirin_10_11_03.aspx

11. Green, G.A. (2001), "Understanding NSAIDs: From Aspirin to COX-2," *Clinical Cornerstone*, 3(5), 50–60, http://www.ncbi.nlm.nih.gov/entrez/query.fcgi?db=pubmed&cmd=Retrieve&dopt=AbstractPlus&list_uids=11464731&query_hl=16&itool=pubmed_docsum

12. Mann, Denise, and Donna Siegfired (2004), "Life After Vioxx," *Arthritis Today*, http://www.arthritis.org/resources/arthritistoday/2005_archives/2005_01_02/2005_01_02_Vioxx.asp

13. Ruddy, Shaun (2005), "Life After Rofecoxib," Medscape, http://www.medscape.com/viewarticle/499393

14. Arthritis Foundation, "Many Patients Take More Pain Relievers Than Recommended," http://www.arthritis.org/Resources/DisplayScreamingNews.asp?id=489

15. West, Sterling, *Rheumatology Secrets*, 2nd ed. (Philadelphia: Hanley & Belfus, 2002), 564.

16. Arthritis Foundation, *Arthritis Today's Drug Guide Supplement* 2005, "Spare Your Stomach," 7.

17. American Heart Association Journal Report, "American Heart Association Addresses Use of Pain Medication," 03/22, 2005, http://www.americanheart.org/presenter.jhtml?identifier=3029683#pain

18. Henderson, Diedtra, "Scientists Plan Huge Painkiller Risk Study," *Boston Globe* Press Release, http://www.boston.com/business/globe/articles/2005/12/14/scientists_plan_huge_painkiller_risk_study/

19. Arthritis Foundation, "Straight Talk About Selective Cox-2 Inhibitors and NSAIDS," http://www.arthritis.org/conditions/nsaids/straight_talk_faq.asp

20. Arthritis Foundation, *Arthritis Today's Drug Guide Supplement* 2006, 9.

21. Ibid.

22. Lorig, Kate, and James F. Fries, *The Arthritis Helpbook*, 5th ed. (Cambridge, MA: Perseus Books, 2000),319

23. Ibid., 322.

24. *Webster's New World Medical Dictionary*, 2nd ed. (New York: Wiley Publishing, Inc., 2003), 299.

25. Arthritis Foundation, "Osteoporosis Meds Reduce Risks of Jaw Degradation" January 2008, http://www.arthritis.org/osteoporosis-meds-jaw.php

26. American College of Rheumatology press release, "Aggressive Treatment Reduces Long-Term Costs of Rheumatoid Arthritis," November 2005, http://www.rheumatology.org/press/2005/tanaka.asp

27. Breedveld, Ferdinand C., Michael H. Weisman, Arthur F. Kavanaugh, Stanley B. Cohen, Karel Pavelka, Ronald van Vollenhoven, John Sharp, John L. Perez, and George T. Spencer-Green, The PREMIER Study: A Multicenter, Randomized, Double-Blind Clinical Trial of Combination Therapy with Adalimumab Plus Methotrexate Versus Methotrexate Alone or Adalimumab Alone in Patients with Early, Aggressive Rheumatoid Arthritis Who Had Not Had Previous Methotrexate Treatment, *Arthritis & Rheumatism* 54(1), 26–37. Http://www3.interscience.wiley.com/cgi-bin/abstract/112223450/ABSTRACT

28. Arthritis Foundation, "Top 10 Arthritis Advances of 2005," http://ww2.arthritis.org/resources/Top_Ten/2005/Summaries.asp

29. Evans, R,. Setter, SM (2006), "FAQ: Biologic Response Modifiers," *Arthritis Self-Management*, 7(5), 4–7.

30. Dunkin, M.A., "The New Drugs: Six Doctors' Opinions," *Arthritis Today*, http://www.arthritis.org/resources/arthritistoday/2000_archives/2000_01_02_new_drugs.asp

31. Academy of Orthopaedic Surgeons (AAOS), "Viscosupplementation Treatment for Arthritis," http://orthoinfo.aaos.org/fact/thr_report.cfm?Thread_ID=245&top category=Knee

32. Blakely, Judith A., and Violeta E.S. Ribeiro (2004), "Glucosamine and Osteoarthritis," *American Journal of Nursing*, 104 (2), pg. 54–59.

33. American College of Rheumatology Press Release November 13, 2005, "GUIDE Results Tap Glucosamine Sulfate as Preferred Med for the Pain of Knee Osteoarthritis," http://www.rheumatology.org/press/2005/herrero-beaumont.asp

34. American College of Rheumatology press release November 13, 2005, "Glucosamine and Chondroitin Sulfate May Be Useful for Patients with Moderate to Severe

Pain from Knee Osteoarthritis," http://www.
rheumatology.org/press/2005/clegg.asp

35. Reichenbach, S., Sterchi, R., Scherer, M., Trelle, S., Burgi, E., Burgi, U., Dieppe, P.A., and Juni, P., "Meta-analysis: Chondroitin for Osteoarthritis of the Knee or Hip," *Annals of Internal Medicine*, 2007, 146(8):580–590.

36. Felson, D.T., "Chondroitin for Pain in Osteoarthritis," *Annals of Internal Medicine*, 2007, 146(8):611–612.

37. Arthritis Foundation, *Glucosamine and Chondroitin Sulfate* brochure.

38. Ibid.

39. Horstman, Judith, "Glucosamine: The Truth About the Talk." *Arthritis Today* brochure, Arthritis Foundation, 2000.

40. Arthritis Foundation, *Arthritis Today's Buyer's Guide Supplement 2005*, "Get Some Relief," 16.

41. Kraemer, William J., et al. "Effect of a Cetylated Fatty Acid Topical Cream on Functional Mobility and Quality of Life of Patients with Osteoarthritis," *The Journal of Rheumatology*, 2004, 32, 767–74. Http://www.jrheum.com/abstracts/abstracts04/767.html

42. Haak, L.B., Melcher, Rick, and Romaine, Deborah. *Smart Buys Drug Wise—How to Save a Fortune on Prescription and Over-the-Counter Drugs*, 1st ed. (Gig Harbor: Harbor Press, 2003), 69.

43. Ibid., 4.

44. Ibid., 69.

45. Ibid., 79.

46. Ibid., 34–35.

47. U.S. Food and Drug Administration (FDA) "Buying Medicines and Medical Products Online." http://www.fda.gov/oc/buy online/default.htm

48. Ibid.

49. Haak, L.B., Melcher, Rick, and Romaine, Deborah. *Smart Buys Drug Wise—How to Save a Fortune on Prescription and Over-the-Counter Drugs*, 1st ed. (Gig Harbor: Harbor Press, 2003), 51.

50. Ibid., 42.

51. Ibid., 42.

52. Ibid., 50.

53. Arthritis Foundation, "Straight Talk About Selective Cox-2 Inhibitors and NSAIDS," http://www.arthritis.org/condi tions/nsaids/straight_talk_faq.asp

Chapter 10

1. American Medical Association, 1998, "Alternative Choices," *Journal of American Medical Association*, 280 (18), http://jama. ama-assn.org/cgi/reprint/280/18/1640

2. National Institutes of Health News Advisory, "More Than One-Third of U.S. Adults Use Complementary and Alternative Medicine, According to New Government Survey," National Center for Complementary and Alternative Medicine, National Institutes of Health, http://nccam.nih.gov/news/2004/052704.htm

3. Ibid.

4. Ibid.

5. National Center for Complementary and Alternative Medicine, "Are You Considering Using Complementary and Alternative Medicine (CAM)?" Http://nccam.nih.gov/health/decisions/index.htm

6. Ibid.

7. American Medical Association, 1998, "Alternative Choices," *Journal of American Medical Association*, 280 (18), http://jama. ama-assn.org/cgi/reprint/280/18/1640

8. Ibid.

9. Horstman, Judith, *The Arthritis Foundation's Guide to Alternative THERAPIES* (Atlanta: Arthritis Foundation, 1999), 136.

10. Sierpina, V.S., and Frenkel, Moshe A. (2005), "Acupuncture: A Clinical Review," Medscape, http://www.medscape.com/view article/501973_print.

11. Ibid.

12. Porth, Carol Mattson, *Pathophysiology—Concepts of Altered Health States*, 4th ed. (Philadelphia: J.B. Lippincott Co, 1994), 970.

13. Bristol University News (2006), "Acupuncture Deactivates 'Pain Area' in Brain," http://www.bris.ac.uk/news/2006/889.html

14. Ibid.

15. Foltz-Gray, Dorothy, *Alternative Treatments for Arthritis* (Atlanta: Arthritis Foundation, 2005), 41–42.

16. NIH News Advisory, "Acupuncture Relieves Pain and Improves Function in Knee Osteoarthritis," National Center for Complementary and Alternative Medicine (NCCAM), National Institutes of Health, http://nccam.nih.gov/news/2004/acu-osteo/pressrelease.htm

17. Ibid.

18. Soloway, Bruce (2005), "Acupuncture Reduces Osteoarthritis Symptoms, But for How Long?" Medscape Journal Watch, www.medscape.com/viewarticle/512486

19. Foltz-Gray, Dorothy, Alternative Treatments for Arthritis (Atlanta: Arthritis Foundation, 2005), 41–42.

20. Ibid., 39–40.

21. Horstman, Judith, The Arthritis Foundation's Guide to Alternative THERAPIES (Atlanta: Arthritis Foundation, 1999), 150.

22. Foltz-Gray, Dorothy, Alternative Treatments for Arthritis (Atlanta: Arthritis Foundation, 2005), 54–56.

23. Ibid., 76.

24. Horstman, Judith, The Arthritis Foundation's Guide to Alternative THERAPIES (Atlanta: Arthritis Foundation), 43–46.

25. Associated Press, "Unsafe Imports Slip Through Regulatory Net," USA Today, March 19, 2006, http://www.usatoday.com/news/health/2006-03-19-unsafe-imports_x.htm

26. Arthritis Foundation, "Tips for Selecting and Using Supplements," http://www.arthritis.org/conditions/tips_supplements.asp

27. NCCAM, "Questions and Answers About Using Magnets to Treat Pain," http://www.nccam.nih.gov/health/magnet/magnet.htm

28. Foltz-Gray, Dorothy, Alternative Treatments for Arthritis (Atlanta: Arthritis Foundation, 2005), 156–158.

29. National Center for Complementary and Alternative Medicine (NCCAM), "Mind-Body Medicine: An Overview," http://nccam.nih.gov/health/backgrounds/mindbody.htm

30. Davis, Jeanie Lerche, "Biofeedback: Trains Mind, Body to Make Changes," http://www.webmd.com/content/article/99/105313.htm?printing=true

31. Academy of Orthopaedic Surgeons (AAOS), "Complementary Therapies: Biofeedback," http://orthoinfo.aaos.org/fact/thr_report.cfm?Thread_ID=272&topcategory=General%20Information

32. Davis, Jeanie Lerche (2006), "Hypnosis: Focusing Subconscious on Change," WebMD, http://www.webmd.com/content/article/99/105337.htm?printing=true

33. American Psychological Association, "Hypnosis for the Relief and Control of Pain," http://www.psychologymatters.org/hypnosis_pain.html

34. Ibid.

35. Davis, Jeanie Lerche (2006), "Hypnosis: Focusing Subconscious on Change," WebMD, http://www.webmd.com/content/article/99/105337.htm?printing=true

36. Foltz-Gray, Alternative Treatments A to Z, 140–142.

37. Ibid., 203

38. Health Journeys, "What Is Guided Imagery?" http://www.healthjourneys.com/what_is_guided_imagery.asp#3principles

39. Ibid.

40. Ibid.

41. Baird, Carol L., and Sands, Laura (2006), "A Pilot Study of the Effectiveness of Guided Imagery with Progressive Muscle Relaxation to Reduce Chronic Pain and Mobility Difficulties of Osteoarthritis, Pain Management Nursing, 5(3), 97–104. http://www.painmanagementnursing.org/article/PIIS1524904204000049/abstract

Chapter 11

1. Gabriel, Peggy, Hip Replacement or Hip Resurfacing (Bloomington, IN: 1st Books Library, 2003), 4.

2. American Academy of Orthopaedic Surgeons (AAOS), "New Techniques to Restore Articular Cartilage," http://orthoinfo.aaos.org/fact/thr_report.cfm?Thread_ID=242&topcategory=Arthritis

3. Moseley, J.B., O'Malley, K, et al. (2002), "A Controlled Trial of Arthroscopic Surgery for Osteoarthritis of the Knee," The New England Journal of Medicine, 347 (81–88), http://content.nejm.org/cgi/content/abstract/347/2/81

4. Arthritis Foundation, All You Need to Know About Joint Surgery (Atlanta: Arthritis Foundation, 2002), 78.

5. Medline Plus, Medical Encyclopedia: "Knee Arthroscopy," http://www.nlm.nih.gov/medlineplus/print/ency/article/002972.htm

6. Arthritis Foundation, All You Need to Know About Joint Surgery (Atlanta: Arthritis Foundation, 2002), 79.

7. Arthritis Foundation, "Benefits and Risks of Joint Replacement Surgery," http://

www.arthritis.org/conditions/SurgeryCen ter/benefits.asp

8. American Academy of Orthopaedic Surgeons, "Joint Replacement," http://ortho info.org/menus/arthroplasty.cfm

9. Arthritis Foundation. "How Do You Know It's Time for Surgery?" http://www. arthritis.org/conditions/SurgeryCenter/ when_surgery.asp

10. Kanegan, Gail Van, and Boyette, Michael, *How to Survive Your Hospital Stay* (New York: Fireside Books, 2003), 9.

11. Ibid., 10–12.

12. American Board of Medical Specialties, "Frequently Asked Questions: How Do I Find Out If My Doctor Is Board Certified?" http://www.abms.org/login.asp

13. Sherer, David, and Karinch, Maryann, *Dr. David Sherer's HOSPITAL Survival Guide 100+ Ways to Make Your Hospital Stay Safe and Comfortable* (Washington D.C.: Claren Books, 2003), 10.

14. Healthgrades, Inc. Home Page, http://www.healthgrades.com

15. Kanegan, Gail Van, and Boyette, Michael, *How to Survive Your Hospital Stay* (New York: Fireside Books, 2003), 64–5.

16. The American Health Quality Association, "Making Surgery Safer," http://www. ahqa.org/pub/uploads/FS_SCIP_Burness_ 2C.pdf

17. Joint Commission International Center for Patient Safety, "2007 National Patient Safety Goals," http://www.jointcommission. org/PatientSafety/NationalPatientSafety Goals/07_hap_cah_npsgs.htm

18. Dudley, R.A., Johansen, Kirsten L., Brand, Richard, Rennie, Deborah J., and Milstein, Arnold. "Selective Referral to High-Volume Hospitals," *Journal of American Medical Association,* http://www.jama.ama-assn.org/cgi/content/abstract/283/9/ 1159?maxtoshow=&HITS=10&hits=10.

19. Ibid.

20. 2007 Gallup Poll, "Nurses Top List of Most Honest and Ethical Professions," http://www.gallup.com/poll/1654/Hon esty-Ethics-Professions.aspx

21. Kanegan, Gail Van, and Boyette, Michael, *How to Survive Your Hospital Stay* (New York: Fireside Books, 2003), 40.

22. Ibid., 40.

23. Sherer, David, and Karinch, Maryann, *Dr. David Sherer's HOSPITAL Survival Guide*

100+ Ways to Make Your Hospital Stay Safe and Comfortable (Washington D.C.: Claren Books, 2003), 223.

24. Hohler, S.E. (2004), "Minimally Invasive Total Hip Arthroplasty," *AORN Journal,* 79(6), 1243–1261.

25. Ibid.

26. Kanegan, Gail Van, and Boyette, Michael, *How to Survive Your Hospital Stay* (New York: Fireside Books, 2003), 61.

27. AAOS Online Service, "2005 Annual Meeting Podium Presentations. Internet Provides Public with Misleading Information on Hip Replacement Surgery," http://www6. aaos.org/news/Pemr/press_release_archive. cfm?prnumber=312

28. American Association of Hip and Knee Surgeons (AAHKS) "Information for Patients—Office Visit Tips," http://www. aahks.org/index.asp/fuseaction/patients.tips

29. Ibid.

30. American Academy of Orthopaedic Surgeons (2004), "Travelers with Implants face Increased Scrutiny from Airport Security," AAOS News Release, http://www6. aaos.org/news/Pemr/press_release_archive. cfm?PRNumber=233

31. Ibid.

32. Biomet—Advanced Science for Real Living. "A Caregiver's Guide for the Joint Replacement Patient at Home," http://www. biomet.com/patients/caregiver/index.cfm

33. AAOS, "Total Joint Replacement," http://orthoinfo.aaos.org/fact/thr_report. cfm?Thread_ID=274&topcategory=Joint% 20Replacement

34. Ibid.

35. AAOS, "Preparing for Joint Replacement Surgery," http://orthoinfo.aaos.org/ fact/thr_report.cfm?Thread_ID=269&top category=Joint%20Replacement

36. AAOS, "Activities After Hip Replacement," http://orthoinfo.aaos.org/topic.cfm? topic=A00356&return_link=0

37. Biomet—Advanced Science for Real Living. "A Caregiver's Guide for the Joint Replacement Patient at Home," http://www. biomet.com/patients/caregiver/index.cfm

Chapter 12

1. Fisher, John C., personal interview with author, 06/12/05.

2. Ibid.

3. Ibid.

4. American Academy of Orthopaedic Surgeons (AAOS), "Total Hip Replacement." http://orthoinfo.aaos.org/fact/thr_report.cfm?Thread_ID=504&topcategory=Joint%20Replacement

5. Arthritis Foundation, "Osteoarthritis, What Is It?" http://www.arthritis.org/disease-center.php?disease_id=32

6. Arthritis Foundation, "Rheumatoid Arthritis, What Is It?" http://www.arthritis.org/disease-center.php?disease_id=31

7. Drake, C., Ace, Marcia, and Maale, Gerhard (2002), "Revision Total Hip Arthroplasty," AORN Journal, 76(3), 414–428.

8. Arthritis Foundation. "Symptoms," http://www.arthritis.org/conditions/DiseaseCenter/OA/oa_symptoms.asp

9. American Academy of Orthopaedic Surgeons (AAOS), "Osteoarthritis of the Hip," http://orthoinfo.aaos.org/fact/thr_report.cfm?Thread_ID=208&topcategory=Arthritis

10. American Academy of Orthopaedic Surgeons (AAOS), "Hip Implants," http://www.orthoinfo.org/fact/thr_report.cfm?Thread_ID=271&topcategory=Hip

11. Archibeck, M.J., Berger, R.A., Jacobs, J.J. Quigley, L.R., Gitelis, S., Rosenberg, A.G., and Galante, J.O. (2001), "Second-Generation Cementless Total Hip Arthroplasty," The Journal of Bone and Joint Surgery (83:1666–1673), http://www.ejbjs.org/cgi/content/abstract/83/11/1666

12. Gabriel, Peggy, Hip Replacement or Hip Resurfacing (Bloomington, IN: 1st Books Library, 2003), 9.

13. Gabriel, Peggy, Personal interview with author, June 15, 2005.

14. Ibid.

15. Amstutz, Harlan C., Beaule, Paul E., Dorey, Frederick, J. Dorey, LeDuff, Michel J., Campbell, Pat A., and Gruen, Thomas A. (2004). "Metal-on-Metal Hybrid Surface Arthroplasty: Two to Six-Year Follow-Up Study," The Journal of Bone and Joint Surgery (86: 28–39). Http://www.ejbjs.org/cgi/content/abstract/86/1/28.

16. Drake, C., Ace, Marcia, and Maale, Gerhard (2002), "Revision Total Hip Arthroplasty," AORN Journal, 76(3), 414–428.

17. Berry, D.J., Harmsen, W.S., Cabanela, M.E., and Morrey, B.F. (2002) "Twenty-Five-Year Survivorship of Two Thousand Consecutive Primary Charnley Total Hip Replacements," The Journal of Bone and Joint Surgery, 84:171–177.

18. Sherer, David, and Karinch, Maryann, Dr. David Sherer's HOSPITAL Survival Guide (Washington, D.C.: Claren Books, 2003), 17.

19. Highlights of the American Academy of Orthopaedic Surgeons 2005 Annual Meeting, Paper Number 147, "Minimally Invasive Total Hip Arthroplasty: Comparison Between One-Incision and Two-Incision Technique," http://www.medscape.com/viewarticle/504931

20. Highlights of the American Academy of Orthopaedic Surgeons 2005 Annual Meeting, Paper Number 139, "A Prospective Randomized Patient-Blinded Comparison of Mini vs. Standard Incision THA," http://www.medscape.com/viewarticle/504931

21. Highlights of the American Academy of Orthopaedic Surgeons 2005 Annual Meeting, Paper Number 137, "Total Hip Arthroplasty: Does Incision Length Matter?" http://www.medscape.com/viewarticle/504931

22. Fisher, John C., personal interview with author, 06/12/05.

Chapter 13

1. American Academy of Orthopaedic Surgeons (AAOS), "Frequently Asked Questions About Osteoarthritis of the Knee," http://orthoinfo.aaos.org/topic.cfm?topic=A00228

2. American Academy of Orthopaedic Surgeons (AAOS), "Total Knee Replacement," http://orthoinfo.aaos.org/fact/thr_report.cfm?Thread_ID=513&topcategory=Joint%20Replacement

3. Ibid.

4. American Academy of Othopaedic Surgeons, "Your Orthopaedic Connection: Arthritis of the Knee," http://orthoinfo.aaos.org/fact/thr_report.cfm?Thread_ID=177&topcategory=Arthritis

5. American Academy of Orthopaedic Surgeons, "Minimally Invasive Total Knee Replacement," http://orthoinfo.aaos.org/fact/thr_report.cfm?Thread_ID=472&topcategory=Joint%20Replacement

6. Lorig, Kate, and Fries, James F., The

Arthritis Helpbook, 5th ed. (Cambridge: Perseus Books) 121.

7. Lyman, S., Sherman, S., Dunn, WR, and Marx, Robert G., "Advancements in the Surgical and Alternative Treatment of Arthritis," Medscape, http://www.medscape.com/viewarticle/500179

8. Day, R., et al. (2004), "A Double Blind, Randomized, Multicenter, Parallel Group Study of the Effectiveness and Tolerance of Intraarticular Hyaluronan in Osteoarthritis of the Knee," *The Journal of Rheumatology*, 31, 775–782, http://www.jrheum.com/abstracts/abstracts04/775.html

9. Arthritis Foundation (2004), "Arthritis Foundation Statement on Hyaluronic Acid in Treatment for Osteoarthritis of the Knee," http://www.arthritis.org/resources/news/hyaluronic_statement.asp

10. Ibid.

11. Ibid.

12. American Academy of Orthopaedic Surgeons (AAOS), "Knee Implants," http://orthoinfo.aaos.org/fact/thr_report.cfm?Thread_ID=279&topcategory=Joint%20Replacement

13. Ibid.

14. Ibid.

15. Ibid.

16. Ibid.

17. Rush University Medical Center, "Am I a Candidate for Minimally Invasive Total Knee Replacement Surgery?" http://www.rush.edu/rumc/print-page-1099918807949.html

18. Lonner, Jess H. (2005), "What's New in Total Knee Replacement," *Outpatient Surgery Magazine*, 6(7), 26–29.

19.. American Academy of Orthopaedic Surgeons, "Minimally Invasive Total Knee Replacement," http://orthoinfo.aaos.org/fact/thr_report.cfm?Thread_ID=472&topcategory=Joint%20Replacement

20. Lonner, Jess H. (2005), "What's New in Total Knee Replacement," *Outpatient Surgery Magazine*, 6(7), 26–29.

21. Dunbar, C. (2006), "1955 Knee Procedure Gets New Life," *AORN Connections*, 4(4), 19.

22. Ibid.

23. Ritter, M.A., Harty L.D., Davis, K.E., et al. (2003), Simultaneous Bilateral, Staged Bilateral and Unilateral Total Knee Arthroplasty. A Survival Analysis, *Journal of Bone and Joint Surgery*, 85-A(8), 1532–7. Http://www.ncbi.nlm.nih.gov/entrez/query.fcgi?itool=abstractplus&db=pubmed&cmd=Retrieve&dopt=abstractplus&list_uids=1292 5634

Chapter 14

1. American Academy of Orthopaedic Surgeons (AAOS), "Total Knee Replacement," http://orthoinfo.aaos.org/fact/thr_report.cfm?Thread_ID=513&topcategory=Joint%20Replacement

2. Callinan, Nancy, "Surgery of the Hand and Wrist," *Arthritis Self-Management*, 6(6), 11–16.

3. National Institute of Arthritis and Musculoskeletal and Skin Diseases, "Questions and Answers About Shoulder Problems," http://www.niams.nih.gov/hi/topics/shoulderprobs/shoulderqa.htm

4. American Sports Medicine Institute, "Anatomy—The Elbow," http://www.asmi.org/sportsmed/anatomy/anatomy_elbow.html

5. American Academy of Orthopaedic Surgeons, "Osteoarthritis of the Elbow," http://orthoinfo.aaos.org/fact/thr_report.cfm?Thread_ID=239&topcategory=Arm

6. Seidel, Henri, Ball, Jane, Dains, Joyce, and Benedict, G. William, *Mosby's Guide to Physical Examination*, 3rd ed. (St. Louis: Mosby, 2002) 655.

7. American Academy of Orthopaedic Surgeons, "Arthritis of the Wrist," http://orthoinfo.aaos.org/fact/thr_report.cfm?Thread_ID=261&topcategory=Hand

8. Wilson, Frank R., *The Hand: How Its Use Shapes the Brain, Language, and Human Culture*, 1st ed. (New York: Pantheon, 1998), 3.

9. Callinan, Nancy, "Surgery of the Hand and Wrist," *Arthritis Self-Management*, 6,(6), 11–16.

10. Wilson, Frank R., *The Hand: How Its Use Shapes the Brain, Language, and Human Culture*, 1st ed. (New York: Pantheon, 1998), 128.

11. American Academy of Orthopaedic Surgeons, "The Foot and Ankle," http://orthoinfo.aaos.org/fact/thr_report.cfm?Thread_ID=100&topcategory=Foot

12. American College of Foot and Ankle

Surgeons, "Osteoarthritis of the Foot and Ankle," http://www.footphysicians.com/footankleinfo/osteoarthritis.htm

13. Nugent, "What's the Best Fix for an Ankle?" *Arthritis Today*, http://www.arthritis.org/resources/arthritistoday/2003_archives/2003_11_12_OnCall_p1.asp

14. American Academy of Orthopaedic Surgeons, "The Foot and Ankle," http://orthoinfo.aaos.org/fact/thr_report.cfm?Thread_ID=100&topcategory=Foot

15. Meadows, Michelle, "Taking Care of Your Feet," U.S. Food and Drug Administration, http://www.fda.gov/fdac/features/2006/206_feet.html

16. David Niven, *100 Simple Secrets of Healthy People: What Scientists Have Learned and How to Use It* (New York: Harper Collins, 2003), 146.

17. Meadows, Michelle, "Taking Care of Your Feet," U.S. Food and Drug Administration, http://www.fda.gov/fdac/features/2006/206_feet.html

18. Answers.com, "Postoperative Care," http://www.answers.com/topic/postoperative-care?cat=health

19. Cheng, C.J., Smith, I., and Watson B.J., "A Multicenter Telephone Survey of Compliance with Postoperative Instructions," *Anaesthesia* 57:805, 2002. http://www.ncbi.nlm.nih.gov/pubmed/12133095?dopt=AbstractPlus

Chapter 15

1. Lorig, Kate, and Fries, James F., "The Arthritis Helpbook." 5th ed. (Cambridge: Perseus Books) 9.

2. American Heart Association, "Heart Attack, Stroke & Cardiac Arrest Warning Signs," http://www.americanheart.org/presenter.jhtml?identifier=3053

3. Ibid.

4. US Department of Health and Human Services Public Health Service, AHRQ Fact Sheet Pub Co. 04-P003, "Research on Cardiovascular Disease in Women," http://www.ahrq.gov/research/womheart.htm

5. American Heart Association, "Heart Attack, Stroke & Cardiac Arrest Warning Signs," http://www.americanheart.org/presenter.jhtml?identifier=3053

6. American Academy of Orthopaedic Surgeons (AAOS), "Total Hip Replacement," http://orthoinfo.aaos.org/fact/thr_report.cfm?Thread_ID=504&topcategory=Joint%20Replacement

7. Ibid.

8. Kanegan, Gail Van, and Boyette, Michael. How to Survive Your Hospital Stay (New York: Fireside Books, 2003), 126.

9. Centers for Disease Control (CDC) Media Relations: Press Release, "Hand Hygiene Guidelines Fact Sheet," http://www.cdc.gov/od/oc/media/pressrel/fs021025.htm

10. American Academy of Orthopaedic Surgeons (AAOS), "Dental Work After a Joint Replacement," http://orthoinfo.aaos.org/fact/thr_report.cfm?Thread_ID=364&topcategory=Joint%20Replacement

11. "A Caregiver's Guide for the Joint Replacement Patient at Home," Biomet http://www.biomet.com/patients/caregiver/index.cfm

12. Medline Plus, Medical Encyclopedia: "Gingivitis," http://www.nlm.nih.gov/medlineplus/ency/article/001056.htm

13. AAOS, "Preparing for Joint Replacement Surgery," http://orthoinfo.aaos.org/fact/thr_report.cfm?Thread_ID=269&topcategory=Joint%20Replacement

14. American Academy of Orthopaedic Surgeons (2004), "Joint Replacement Outcomes Affected by Mood Disorders—New Study Shows That Depression May Adversely Affect Outcomes of Primary Joint Replacements," AAOS News Release. http://www6.aaos.org/news/Pemr/press_release_archive.cfm?PRNumber=214

15. Medline Plus, Medical Encyclopedia: "CBC count," http://www.nlm.nih.gov/medlineplus/ency/article/003642.htm

16. Medline Plus, Medical Encyclopedia: "Platelets," http://www.nlm.nih.gov/medlineplus/ency/article/003647.htm

17. Medline Plus, Medical Encyclopedia: "Chem-7," http://www.nlm.nih.gov/medlineplus/ency/article/003462.htm

18. Medline Plus, Medical encyclopedia: "Prothrombin Time (PT)," http://www.nlm.nih.gov/medlineplus/ency/article/003652.htm

19. Medline Plus, Medical encyclopedia: "Partial thromboplastic time (PTT)," http://www.nlm.nih.gov/medlineplus/ency/article/003653.htm

20. Sherer, David, and Karinch, Maryann, *Dr. David Sherer's HOSPITAL Survival Guide* (Washington, D.C.: Claren Books, 2003), 71.

21. Ibid., 77.

22. Ibid., 77.

23. Ibid., 77.

24. Sherer, David, and Karinch, Maryann, *Dr. David Sherer's HOSPITAL Survival Guide* (Washington, D.C.: Claren Books, 2003), 73.

25. AAOS, "Preparing for Joint Replacement Surgery," http://orthoinfo.aaos.org/fact/thr_report.cfm?Thread_ID=269&topcategory=Joint%20Replacement

26. Joint Commission International Center for Patient Safety, "Facts About Patient Safety," http://www.jointcommission.org/PatientSafety/UniversalProtocol/

27. Association of Perioperative Nurses, "Role of the Perioperative Nurse," http://www.aorn.org/CareerCenter/CareerDevelopment/RoleOfThePerioperativeNurse/

28. Ibid.

29. Grelsamer, Ronald P., *What Your Doctor May Not Tell You About Hip and Knee Replacement Surgery* (New York: Warner Books, 2004), 137.

30. Ibid., 136.

31. American Academy of Orthopaedic Surgeons (AAOS), "Activities After a Hip Replacement," http://orthoinfo.aaos.org/fact/thr_report.cfm?Thread_ID=274&topcategory=Joint%20Replacement

32. American Academy of Orthopaedic Surgeons, "Total Knee Replacement," http://orthoinfo.aaos.org/fact/thr_report.cfm?Thread_ID=513&topcategory=Joint%20Replacement

33. American Academy of Orthopaedic Surgeons (AAOS), "Knee Replacement Exercise Guide," http://orthoinfo.aaos.org/booklet/view_report.cfm?Thread_ID=16&topcategory=Joint%20Replacement

34. American Academy of Orthopaedic Surgeons, "Total Knee Replacement," http://orthoinfo.aaos.org/fact/thr_report.cfm?Thread_ID=513&topcategory=Joint%20Replacement

35. Grelsamer, Ronald P., *What Your Doctor May Not Tell You About Hip and Knee Replacement Surgery* (New York: Warner Books, 2004), 202.

36. Medline Plus, Medical Encyclopedia: "Hip Joint Replacement-series: Aftercare," http://www.nlm.nih.gov/medlineplus/ency/presentations/100006_5.htm

37. American Academy of Orthopaedic Surgeons (AAOS), "Total Knee Replacement," http://orthoinfo.aaos.org/fact/thr_report.cfm?Thread_ID=513&topcategory=Joint%20Replacement

38. American Occupational Therapy Association, Inc. (AOTA), "Daily Activities After Hip Replacement Surgery," http://www.aota.org/Consumers/Tips/Adults/Hip/35162.aspx

39. American Academy of Orthopaedic Surgeons (AAOS), "Dental Work After a Joint Replacement," http://orthoinfo.aaos.org/fact/thr_report.cfm?Thread_ID=364&topcategory=Joint%20Replacement

Chapter 16

1. National Family Caregivers Association, "Caregiving Statistics," http://www.thefamilycaregiver.org/who_are_family_caregivers/care_giving_statstics.cfm

2. Ibid.

3. Ibid.

4. Ibid.

5. *Webster's New World Dictionary*, 4th ed. (New York: Simon & Schuster, Inc., 2003), 638.

6. American Heart Association, "How Can I Manage Stress?" http://www.americanheart.org/presenter.jhtml?identifier=3007448

7. Ibid.

8. Wein, Harrison, "Stress and Disease: New Perspectives," National Institutes of Health (NIH) October 2000, http://www.nih.gov/news/WordonHealth/oct2000/story01.htm

9. Ibid.

10. U.S. Department of Health and Human Service, Administration of Aging, "Taking Care of You," http://www.aoa.gov/prof/aoaprog/caregiver/carefam/taking_care_of_you/taking_care_of_you.asp

11. Schulz, Richard, Beach, S.R. (1999), "Caregiving as a Risk Factor for Mortality," *Journal of the American Medical Association*, 282(23). Http://jama.ama-assn.org/cgi/content/abstract/282/23/2215

12. Familydoctor.org, "Stress: How to Cope Better with Life's Challenges," http://www.familydoctor.org/167.xml?printxml

13. Wein, Harrison, "Stress and Disease: New Perspectives," National Institutes of Health (NIH) October 2000, http://www.nih.gov/news/WordonHealth/oct2000/story01.htm

14. Family Caregiver Alliance, Fact Sheet: "Taking Care of YOU: Self-Care for Family Caregivers," http://www.caregiver.org/caregiver/jsp/print_friendly.jsp?nodeid=847

15. Familydoctor.org, "Stress: How to Cope Better with Life's Challenges," http://www.familydoctor.org/167.xml?printxml

16. U.S. Department of Health and Human Services Administration on Aging, "Working Caregivers: Finding a Balance," http://www.aoa.gov/press/nfc_month/2004/fact_sheets/Fact%20Sheet%20-%20Employed%20Caregivers%20in%20Template%20with%20pic%202.pdf

17. American Heart Association, "How Can I Manage Stress?" Http://www.americanheart.org/presenter.jhtml?identifier=3007448

18. Ibid.

19. Holistic online.com, "Therapeutic Benefits of Laughter," http://www.holisticonline.com/Humor_Therapy/humor_therapy.htm

20. Family Caregiver Alliance, "Saying 'Yes' to Offers of Help," http://caregiver.org/caregiver/jsp/content_node.jsp?nodeid=1385

21. National Family Caregivers Association, "Caregiving Statistics," http://www.thefamilycaregiver.org/who_are_family_caregivers/care_giving_statstics.cfm

22. Family Caregiver Alliance, Fact Sheet: "Taking Care of YOU: Self-Care for Family Caregivers," http://www.caregiver.org/caregiver/jsp/print_friendly.jsp?nodeid=847

23. Wooten, James, Galavis, J. (2005), "Polypharmacy Keeping the Elderly Safe," RN, 68(8), 44–51.

24. Family Care America, "Knowing Medications," http://www.caregiverslibrary.org/Default.aspx?tabid=405

25. American Academy of Orthopaedic Surgeons (AAOS), "Activities After a Hip Replacement," http://orthoinfo.aaos.org/fact/thr_report.cfm?Thread_ID=274&topcategory=Joint%20Replacement

26. Family Care America, "Caregiver's Rights," http://www.caregiverslibrary.org/Default.aspx?tabid=155

27. Joint Replacement.com, "Packing for the Hospital Visit," http://www.jointreplacement.com/DePuy/docs/Knee/Replacement/Caregiver/caregiver_preparation.html?searchCriteria=Caregiver

28. Ibid.

29. Andrews, Linda (2005), "Caring for Someone with Arthritis," Arthritis Self-Management, 6(4), 19–21.

Chapter 17

1. Centers for Disease Control (CDC), "Understanding Scientific Research," http://www.cdc.gov/DES/consumers/research/understanding_scientific.html

2. Food Product Design, "Good Studies, Bad Studies," http://www.foodproductdesign.com/articles/464/464_1299pr.html

3. Visionlearning. "The Scientific Method," http://www.visionlearning.com/library/module_viewer.php?mid=45 Accessed 05/2007.

4. Ibid.

5. Ibid.

6. Food Product Design, "Good Studies, Bad Studies," http://www.foodproductdesign.com/articles/464/464_1299pr.html

7. Ibid.

8. Center for Disease Control (CDC), "Understanding Scientific Research," http://www.cdc.gov/DES/consumers/research/understanding_scientific.html

9. CBS News, "Impotence Problems May Warn of Heart Disease," http://www.cbc.ca/health/story/2005/12/20/heart-impotence051220.html

10. Thompson, I.M., Tangen, Catherine M., Goodman, Phyllis, et al. "Erectile Dysfunction and Subsequent Cardiovascular Disease," Journal of the American Medical Association, 294(23), http://jama.ama-assn.org/cgi/content/abstract/294/23/2996

11. Family Caregiver Alliance, Fact Sheet: "Evaluating Medical Research Findings and Clinical Trials," http://www.caregiver.org/caregiver/jsp/print_friendly.jsp?nodeid=402

12. Ibid.

13. Ibid.

14. Thompson, I.M., Tangen, Catherine M., Goodman, Phyllis, et al. "Erectile Dysfunction and Subsequent Cardiovascular Disease," Journal of the American Medical Asso-

ciation, 294(23). http://jama.ama-assn.org/cgi/content/abstract/294/23/2996

15. Family Caregiver Alliance, Fact Sheet: "Evaluating Medical Research Findings and Clinical Trials," http://www.caregiver.org/caregiver/jsp/print_friendly.jsp?nodeid=402

16. Center for Information and Study in Clinical Research Participation, http://www.ciscrp.org/information/facts.asp

17. Andrews, Linda Wasmer, "Clinical Trials: Should You Volunteer?" *Arthritis Self-Management*, 6(1), 4–9.

18. National Human Genome Research Institute, "Frequently Asked Questions about Clinical Research," http://www.genome.gov/10000771

19. Family Caregiver Alliance, Fact Sheet: "Evaluating Medical Research Findings and Clinical Trials," http://www.caregiver.org/caregiver/jsp/print_friendly.jsp?nodeid=402

20. Andrews, Linda Wasmer, "Clinical Trials: Should You Volunteer?" *Arthritis Self-Management*, 6(1), 4–9.

21. U.S. National Institutes of Health, "An Introduction to Clinical Trials and Human Research Studies," http://www.clinicaltrials.gov/ct/info/whatis

22. Ibid.

23. Ibid.

24. Ibid.

25. Andrews, Linda Wasmer, "Clinical Trials: Should You Volunteer?" *Arthritis Self-Management*, 6(1), 4–9.

26. Ibid.

27. Arthritis Foundation, "Autoimmune Disease: Researchers Discover Molecular Roots of Inflammatory and Autoimmune Diseases," http://www.arthritis.org/resources/news/aidisease_root_discovered.asp

28. Arthritis Foundation, *Rheumatoid Arthritis* booklet, pg. 4.

29. Leirisalo-Repo, Marjatta (2005), "Early Arthritis and Infection," *Current Opinion in Rheumatology*, 17(4), 433–439. Http://www.medscape.com/viewarticle/507250

30. Arthritis Foundation, "Arthritis Foundation Statement on Glycosaminoglycans (GAGs) Class of Carbohydrates," http://www.arthritis.org/resources/news/RAandGAGs_statement.asp

31. Barclay, Laurie (2005) "Doxycycline May Slow Progression of Knee Osteoarthritis," Medscape Medical News, July 1, 2005, http://www.medscape.com/viewarticle/507629

32. Brandt, Kenneth D., et al. (2005), "Effects of Doxycycline on Progression of Osteoarthritis: Results of a Randomized, Placebo-Controlled, Double-Blind Trial." *Arthritis & Rheumatism*, 52(7), 2015–2025. Http://www3.interscience.wiley.com/cgi-bin/abstract/110549612/ABSTRACT

33. Arthritis Foundation, "High Levels of Hyaluronic Acid Predict Severe Osteoarthritis," http://www.arthritis.org/Resources/DisplayScreamingNews.asp?id=590

34. ArthritisSupport.com, "New Stem Cell Source Benefits Arthritis Treatment," http://www.arthritissupport.com/library/print.cfm?ID=253.

35. Penn Medicine, "New Source of Multipotent Adult Stem Cells Found in Human Hair Follicles," http://www.uphs.upenn.edu/news/News_Releases/jul06/stemfoll.htm

36. Jorgensen, C., et al. (2001), "Stem Cells for Repair of Cartilage and Bone: The Next Challenge in Osteoarthritis and Rheumatoid Arthritis," *Annals of the Rheumatic Diseases*, 2001(60), 305–309.

37. American Academy of Orthopaedic Surgeons, Fact Sheet: "New Techniques to Restore Articular Cartilage," http://orthoinfo.aaos.org/topic.cfm?topic=A00422

38. Ibid.

39. Future Pundit, "Cell Therapy Repairs Knee Osteoarthritis Damage," 07/06/2006, http://www.futurepundit.com/archives/cat_biotech_tissue_engineering.html

40. Arthritis Foundation, "Coffee, Smoking and Risk of RA," http://www.arthritis.org/research/researchupdate/03nov_dec/coffee_smoking.asp

41. Arthritis Today, "New Research Shows Coffee's Benefits," http://www.arthritis.org/the-latest-on-coffees-benefits.php

42. Ibid.

Bibliography

Books and Articles

Andrews, Linda Wasmer. "Clinical Trials: Should You Volunteer?" *Arthritis Self-Management* 6, no. 1 (2005): 4–9.

Barash, Paul G., Cullen, Bruce, and Stoelting, Robert K. *Clinical Anesthesia.* Philadelphia: J.B. Lippincott, 1989.

Callinan, Nancy. "Surgery of the Hand and Wrist." *Arthritis Self-Management* 6, no. 6 (2005):11–16.

Fisher, Carol. *The American Cookbook: A History*, lst ed. Jefferson, NC: McFarland, 2006.

Foltz-Gray, Dorothy. *Alternative Treatments for Arthritis.* Atlanta: Arthritis Foundation, 2005.

Gabriel, Peggy. *Hip Replacement or Hip Resurfacing.* Bloomington, IN: lst Books Library, 2003.

Grelsamer, Ronald. *What Your Doctor May NOT Tell You about Hip and Knee Replacement Surgery.* New York: Warner Books, 2004.

Haak, Lee B., Melcher, Rich, and Romaine, Deborah. *Smart Buys Drug Wise.* Gig Harbor: Harbor Press, 2003.

Horstman, Judith. *The Arthritis Foundation's Guide to Alternative Therapies.* Atlanta: Arthritis Foundation, 1999.

Kanegan, Gail Van, and Boyette, Michael. *How to Survive Your Hospital Stay.* New York: Fireside, 2003.

Klippel, John H., ed. *Primer on the Rheumatic Diseases.* Atlanta: Arthritis Foundation, 2001.

Lorig, Kate, and Fries, James F. *The Arthritis Helpbook.* Cambridge: Perseus Books, 2000.

Moskowitz, Roland W., Howell, David S., Goldberg, Victor M., and Mankin, Henry J. *Osteoarthritis—Diagnosis and Medical/Surgical Management*, 2nd ed. Philadelphia: W.B. Saunders, 1992.

Niven, David. *The 100 Simple Secrets of Healthy People.* New York: Harper Collins, 2003.

Peck, Brian. "About Arthritis: Rheumatoid Arthritis." *Arthritis Self-Management* September/October (2004):6–12.

Porth, Carol M. *Pathophysiology: Concepts of Altered Health States*, Philadelphia: JB Lippincott, 1994.

Sherer, David, and Karinch, Maryann. *Dr. David Sherer's Hospital Survival Guide.* Washington: Claren Books, 2003.

Whitney, Eleanor N, and Rolfes, Sharon R. *Understanding Nutrition.* Minneapolis: West Publishing, 1996.

West, Sterling. *Rheumatology Secrets*, 2nd ed. Philadelphia: Hanley & Belfus, 2002.

Wilson, Frank R. *The Hand.* New York: Vintage Books, 1998.

Booklets

Arthritis Foundation. *All You Need to Know about Joint Surgery.* Atlanta: Arthritis Foundation, 2002.

Arthritis Foundation. *The Arthritis Foundation's Guide to Good Living with Rheumatoid Arthritis.* Atlanta: Arthritis Foundation, 2004.

Arthritis Foundation. *Arthritis Today's Drug Guide Supplement.* Atlanta: Arthritis Foundation, 2006.

Internet Resources and References

American Academy of Orthopaedic Surgeons (AAOS). "Activities after a Hip Replacement." http://orthoinfo.aaos.org/fact/thr_report.cfm?Thread_ID=274&topcategory=Joint%20Replacement

American Academy of Orthopaedic Surgeons (AAOS). "Arthritis of the Knee." http://orthoinfo.aaos.org/fact/thr_report.cfm?Thread_ID=177&topcategory=Arthritis

American Academy of Orthopaedic Surgeons (AAOS). "Arthritis of the Wrist." http://orthoinfo.aaos.org/fact/thr_report.cfm?Thread_ID=261&topcategory=Hand

American Academy of Orthopaedic Surgeons (AAOS). "Dental Work after a Joint Replacement." http://orthoinfo.aaos.org/fact/thr_report.cfm?Thread_ID=364&topcategory=Joint%20Replacement

American Academy of Orthopaedic Surgeons (AAOS). "Hip Implants." http://www.orthoinfo.org/fact/thr_report.cfm?Thread_ID=271&topcategory=Hip

American Academy of Orthopaedic Surgeons (AAOS). "Knee Implants." http://orthoinfo.aaos.org/fact/thr_report.cfm?Thread_ID=279&topcategory=Joint%20Replacement

American Academy of Orthopaedic Surgeons (AAOS). "New Techniques to Restore Articular Cartilage." http://orthoinfo.aaos.org/fact/thr_report.cfm?Thread_ID=242&topcategory=Arthritis

American Academy of Orthopaedic Surgeons (AAOS). "Osteoarthritis of the Elbow." http://orthoinfo.aaos.org/fact/thr_report.cfm?Thread_ID=239&topcategory=Arm

American Academy of Orthopaedic Surgeons (AAOS). "Osteoarthritis of the Hip." http://orthoinfo.aaos.org/fact/thr_report.cfm?Thread_ID=208&topcategory=Arthritis

American Academy of Orthopaedic Surgeons (AAOS). "Preparing for Joint Replacement Surgery." http://orthoinfo.aaos.org/fact/thr_report.cfm?Thread_ID=269&topcategory=Joint%20Replacement

American Academy of Orthopaedic Surgeons (AAOS). "Total Hip Replacement." http://orthoinfo.aaos.org/fact/thr_report.cfm?Thread_ID=504&topcategory=Joint%20Replacement

American Academy of Orthopaedic Surgeons (AAOS). "Total Joint Replacement." http://orthoinfo.aaos.org/fact/thr_report.cfm?Thread_ID=274&topcategory=Joint%20Replacement

American Academy of Orthopaedic Surgeons (AAOS). "Total Knee Replacement." http://orthoinfo.aaos.org/fact/thr_report.cfm?Thread_ID=513&topcategory=Joint%20Replacement

American Academy of Orthopaedic Surgeons (AAOS). "Your Orthopaedic Connections." American Academy of Orthopaedic Surgeons. December 2006. http://orthoinfo.aaos.org/

American Association of Hip and Knee Surgeons (AAHKS). "Information for Patients—Office Visit Tips." http://www.aahks.org/index.asp/fuseaction/patients.tips

American College of Foot and Ankle Surgeons. "Osteoarthritis of the Foot and Ankle." http://www.footphysicians.com/footankleinfo/osteoarthritis.htm

American College of Rheumatology. "Patient Information." http://www.rheumatology.org/public/factsheets/index.asp

American College of Rheumatology. "Still the Mind, Calm the Rheumatoid Arthritis." http://www.rheumatology.org/press/2005/pradhan.asp

American Heart Association. "How Can I Manage Stress?" http://www.americanheart.org/presenter.jhtml?identifier=3007448

American Psychological Association. "Hypnosis for the Relief and Control of Pain." http://www.psychologymatters.org/hypnosis_pain.html

Arthritis Foundation. "Disease Center." http://www.arthritis.org/conditions/diseasecenter/default.asp

Arthritis Foundation. "Drug Guide." http://www.arthritis.org/arthritistoday/DrugGuide/drug_index.asp

Arthritis Foundation. "Exercise and Arthritis." http://www.arthritis.org/conditions/exercise/default.asp

Arthritis Foundation. "Music Therapy Reduces Pain." http://www.arthritis.org/Re sources/DisplayScreamingnews.asp?id= 444

Arthritis Foundation. "Nutrition." http:// www.arthritis.org/arthritistoday/nutri tion/default.asp

Arthritis Foundation. "Safe or Sorry: A Parent's Guide to Sports Injury Prevention." http://www.arthritis.org/resources/sip/ intro.asp

Arthritis Foundation. "Arthritis Foundation Statement on Hyaluronic Acid in Treatment for Osteoarthritis of the Knee." http://www.arthritis.org/resources/news /hyaluronic_statement.asp

Arthritis Foundation. "Straight Talk about Selective Cox-2 Inhibitors and NSAIDS." http://www.arthritis.org/conditions/ nsaids/straight_talk_faq.asp

Arthritis Foundation. "Top 10 Arthritis Advances of 2006." http://www.arthri tis.org/resources/top_ten/2006/Sum maries-06.asp?CampaignId= E07A1N1MYZZO20374642

Arthritis Foundation. "Ten Ways You Can Protect Your Joints." http://www.arthri tis.org/conditions/tips_jointprotection.as p

Arthritis Foundation. "3 Types of Exercises You Need to Do." http://www.arthri tis.org/conditions/Exercise/three_you_ need.asp

Arthritis Foundation. "What Is Hip and Knee Replacement Surgery?" http://www. arthritis.org/AFStore/StartRead.asp?id Product=3603

Centers for Disease Control (CDC). "Falls Among Older Adults: An Overview." http://www.cdc.gov/ncipc/factsheets/ adultfalls.htm

Centers for Disease Control (CDC) Media Relations Press Release. "Hand Hygiene Guidelines Fact Sheet." http://www.cdc. gov/od/oc/media/pressrel/fs021025.htm

Centers for Disease Control (CDC). "Understanding Scientific Research." http:// www.cdc.gov/DES/consumers/research/ understanding_scientific.html

Davis, Jeanie Lerche. "Biofeedback: Trains Mind, Body to Make Changes." http:// www.webmd.com/content/article/ 99/105313.htm?printing=true

Family Caregiver Alliance. "Fact Sheet: Caregivers' Guide to Medications and Aging."

http://www.caregiver.org/caregiver/jsp/ content_node.jsp?nodeid=1104

Family Caregiver Alliance. "Fact Sheet: Evaluating Medical Research Findings and Clinical Trials." http://www.caregiver.org/ caregiver/jsp/print_friendly.jsp?nodeid= 402

Family Caregiver Alliance. "Fact Sheet: Taking Care of YOU: Self-Care for Family Caregivers." http://www.caregiver.org/ caregiver/jsp/print_friendly.jsp?nodeid= 847

Foltz-Gray, Dorothy. "Get Square with Your Feet," Arthritis Today, http://www.arthri tis.org/conditions/feet/feet_intro.asp

Joint Replacement.com. "Caregiver Packing: Getting Ready for Your Loved One's Joint Replacement Surgery." http://www.joint replacement.com/xq/ASP.default/pg.con tent/content_id.34/mn./joint_id./joint_ nm./local_id.0/nav.caregiver/qx/default. htm

Karnes, Marie. "When Stress Flares." Arthritis Today, June 2005. http://www.arthritis. org/arthritistoday/yourlife/articles/ 2007_archives/when-stress-flares.asp

Meadows, Michelle. "Taking Care of Your Feet." U.S. Food and Drug Administration. http://www.fda.gov/fdac/features/ 2006/206_feet.html

Mind/Body Medical Institute. "Clinical Findings." http://www.mbmi.org/pro grams/clinical_findings.asp

National Chronic Pain Outreach Association. National Chronic Pain Outreach Association homepage. http://www.chronic pain.org

National Sleep Foundation. "National Sleep Foundation Homepage." http://www. sleepfoundation.org/

National Institute of Arthritis and Musculoskeletal and Skin Diseases (NIAMS). "Health Information." April 5, 2007. http://www.niams.nih.gov/hi/index.htm.

National Institute of Arthritis and Musculoskeletal and Skin Diseases (NIAMS). "Depression." April 5, 2007. http://www. nimh.nih.gov/healthinformation/depres sionmenu.cfm

National Institute of Health News Advisory. "Acupuncture Relieves Pain and Improves Function in Knee Osteoarthritis." National Center for Complementary and Alternative Medicine (NCCAM), National

Institutes of Health. http://nccam.nih.gov/news/2004/acu-osteo/pressrelease.htm

National Institute of Health. "An Introduction to Clinical Trials and Human Research Studies." http://www.clinicaltrials.gov/ct/info/whatis

National Institute of Health News Advisory. "More than One-Third of U.S. Adults Use Complementary and Alternative Medicine, According to New Government Survey."

National Center for Complementary and Alternative Medicine, National Institutes of Health. http://nccam.nih.gov/news/2004/052704.htm

National Institute of Health. Osteoporosis and Related Bone Diseases—National Resource Center Fact Sheets: "What People with Rheumatoid Arthritis Need to Know about Osteoporosis." http://www.niams.nih.gov/bone/hi/osteoporosis_arthritis.htm

National Osteoporosis Foundation. National Osteoporosis Foundation Home Page. February 23, 2007. http://www.nof.org/

Robison, Jon I. "Weight, Health and Culture: Shifting the Paradigm for Alternative Health Care." *Alternative Health Practitioner 5, no. 10.* http://www.jonrobison.net/AHParticle.html

United States Department of Agriculture (USDA). "My Pyramid.gov." http://www.mypyramid.gov/

U.S. Food and Drug Administration (FDA). "Buying Medicines and Medical Products Online." http://www.fda.gov/oc/buyonline/default.htm

U.S. Department of Health and Human Services, Administration of Aging. "Taking Care of You." http://www.aoa.gov/prof/aoaprog/caregiver/carefam/taking_care_of_you/taking_care_of_you.asp

Visionlearning, "The Scientific Method." http://www.visionlearning.com/library/module_viewer.php?mid=45

Wein, Harrison. "Stress and Disease: New Perspectives." National Institutes of Health (NIH). http://www.nih.gov/news/WordonHealth/oct2000/story01.htm

Index